ESSENTIALS OF REAL ESTATE ECONOMICS

Third Edition

Dennis J. McKenzie
MBA, MA Economics, and Realtor®
McKenzie Real Estate Seminars

Richard M. Betts
MAI, SRA, ASA (Real Estate)
Property Analyst

 Prentice Hall, Englewood Cliffs, New Jersey 07632

Library of Congress Cataloging-in-Publication Data
McKenzie, Dennis J.
    Essentials of real estate economics / Dennis J. McKenzie, Richard
M. Betts.—3rd ed.
        p.   cm.—(Prentice Hall series in California real estate)
    Includes bibliographical references and index.
    ISBN 0-13-287723-6
    1. Real estate business.   2. Real estate investment.   I. Betts,
Richard M.   II. Title.   III. Series.
HD1375.M37   1992
333.33—dc20
                                                    91-7700
                                                    CIP

Editorial/production supervision and
    interior design: **Janet M. DiBlasi**
Cover design: **Mike Fender**
Manufacturing buyer: **Ed O'Dougherty**
Prepress buyer: **Ilene Levy**
Acquisition editor: **Jim Boyd**
Marketing Manager: **Robert B. Kern**
Copy editor: **Eleanor Walter**
Editorial assistant: **Irene Hess**

© 1992 by Prentice-Hall, Inc.
A Simon & Schuster Company
Englewood Cliffs, New Jersey 07632

Printed in the United States of America

10   9   8   7   6   5   4   3   2   1

ISBN 0-13-287723-6

Prentice-Hall International (UK) Limited, *London*
Prentice-Hall of Australia Pty. Limited, *Sydney*
Prentice-Hall Canada Inc., *Toronto*
Prentice-Hall Hispanoamericana, S.A., *Mexico*
Prentice-Hall of India Private Limited, *New Delhi*
Prentice-Hall of Japan, Inc., *Tokyo*
Simon & Schuster Asia Pte. Ltd., *Singapore*
Editora Prentice-Hall do Brasil, Ltda., *Rio de Janeiro*

Prentice Hall Series in California Real Estate

Dennis J. McKenzie, Editor

California Real Estate Finance, 5th Edition
Robert J. Bond, Alfred Gavello, Dennis J. McKenzie, and Carden Young

California Real Estate Principles, 4th Edition
Dennis J. McKenzie, Lowell Anderson, Frank Battino, and Cecilia Hopkins

Essentials of Real Estate Economics, 3rd Edition
Dennis J. McKenzie and Richard M. Betts

Basic Real Estate Appraisal, 2nd Edition
Richard M. Betts and Silas Ely

Legal Aspects of California Real Estate, 2nd Edition
Louis B. Hansotte

Contents

Chapter 4
MONEY, CREDIT, AND REAL ESTATE 49

Chapter 5
IMPORTANT ECONOMIC FEATURES OF REAL ESTATE 69

Part 2   Understanding Real Estate Markets

Chapter 6
REGIONAL AND COMMUNITY ANALYSIS 79

Chapter 7
COMMUNITY GROWTH PATTERNS 97

Part 3   Influences on Real Estate Development

Part 4   Real Estate Investment: The Economics of the Parcel

Preface

This third edition is a complete update of the second edition. The format of the book has been retained, but new topics have been added. For example, this edition contains new material on international trade, foreign ownership of U.S. businesses and real estate, the economic impact of the savings and loan crisis and deregulation of money markets. The sections on cash flow analysis and federal income tax rules for real estate investments have been completely updated. All other material has been reviewed and revised where needed. In short, this new edition presents the current information needed for a successful course in real estate economics.

As noted in the earlier edition, this book is an outgrowth of years of teaching real estate economics at California community colleges and private schools. The material is structured in convenient blocks to allow all instructors to adapt the book to various formats. The textbook follows the *Instructor's Guide and Student Study Guide for Real Estate Economics*. The guides were written by Dennis J. McKenzie, a co-author of this textbook. The guides are published by the California Community College Real Estate Education Center, Yosemite Community College District, P.O. Box 4065, Modesto, California 95352. The Instructor's Guide contains lecture outlines, overhead transparencies, and examination questions. Instructors wishing copies should contact the center for information.

This book emphasizes the factors that cause real estate value to change. To present this complex subject in a practical manner, we have heeded Thoreau's plea to "simplify." The text is intended for real estate students who have little or no background in formal economics. Thus the approach is direct and practical.

It is not possible to acknowledge all the assistance we have received from our students, colleagues, and friends. We hope we have successfully communicated the insights that they have given. In addition, we dedicate this third edition to our mentors and role models: Dr. Russell Connett, Professor Emeritus of Real Estate, Humboldt

State University, Dr. John Grobey, Professor of Economics, Humboldt State University and Dr. Paul Wendt, Professor Emeritus of Real Estate, University of California, Berkeley.

Dennis J. McKenzie
Richard M. Betts

Chapter   1

Introduction to Real Estate Economics

As you begin reading this textbook, you probably have certain questions in mind: What is *real estate economics*? Why should you study real estate economics? What topics are covered in this book? How is the material organized? This introductory chapter answers these questions so you will know what to expect from this textbook.

WHAT IS REAL ESTATE ECONOMICS?

Real estate economics is about people and how their actions affect real estate values. A formal definition would be: *Real estate economics is a study that uses economic principles to analyze the impact that national, regional, community, and neighborhood trends have on real estate values.*

In our society, our desire for goods and services frequently exceeds the supply available. This scarcity gives rise to the idea of economic value. Real estate economics focuses on the economic principles that affect real estate values.

WHAT REAL ESTATE ECONOMICS IS NOT

Real estate economics is neither the study of general economics nor a course in the practice of real estate. Rather, real estate economics is the link between general economic theory and applied real estate practice. A course in general economics concentrates on how society attempts to use limited resources to satisfy the wants of its people. However, such a course does not examine how this affects local real estate markets. On the other hand, a course in real estate practice concentrates on the specific techniques needed to complete a real estate transaction but spends little time discussing the economic influences that determine whether an investment will be profitable over the years.

Real estate economics draws principles from both general economics and real estate practice and then combines them in order to study changes in real estate activity. The main thrust of real estate economics is to help real estate students become aware of future trends and what impact these trends will have on local real estate values.

Figure 1.1 illustrates the relationship between general economics, real estate economics, and real estate practice.

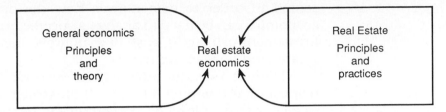

FIGURE 1.1   The field of real estate economics draws principles from general economics and real estate practice.

WHY STUDY REAL ESTATE ECONOMICS?

Real estate economics helps people to understand what causes fluctuations in real estate activity and how these changes can affect local real estate markets. Investors and licensed agents make real estate decisions that influence the shape, form, and value of property in a given community. Real estate decisions made today will be reflected in real estate values within the cities and neighborhoods of tomorrow; a course in real estate economics aids people in understanding what impact today's real estate actions will have on future real estate values. In California, for instance, real estate economics is considered so important that state law requires that a course in real estate economics, or its equivalent, be completed before a person can become a licensed real estate broker.

A GENERAL OVERVIEW

We suggest that you study this brief introduction to the text as well as the Contents in order to keep in mind the relation of each chapter to the overall thrust of this book.

Our study is divided into four parts, starting with general economic principles and moving on to applied real estate economics. Part I, "Basic Economic Background for Real Estate Analysis," contains five chapters that review the major principles of economics and discusses why these principles are important to real estate students. After establishing the basic economic principles of our mixed capitalist economy, we explore the role of the government and foreign interests in the economy, study the money supply, and discuss the economic characteristics of real estate markets.

In Part II, "Understanding Real Estate Markets," we devote six chapters to regional, community, and neighborhood real estate analysis. Our objective is to discuss why local and regional economies change and how these changes are reflected in the real estate market.

Part III, "Major Influences on New Real Estate Development," presents one chapter on each of four topics: real property taxation, land-use controls, real estate development procedures, and required government reports. These subjects are controversial issues in the field of real estate.

In Part IV, "Real Estate Investment: The Economics of the Parcel," four chapters bring together all the material previously presented in order to demonstrate how the principles of real estate economics can be used to analyze a specific property. Topics include: investment principles, cash flow analysis, income tax aspects of real estate, and forecasting trends.

There is a steadily building process underlying the application of real estate economics. Figure 1.2 illustrates how this textbook advances from one level of understanding to the next. The steps outlined therein form the basis for sound real estate decision making.

CHAPTER OUTLINES

Each chapter in this textbook begins with a short preview of the material and a list of objectives that you should be able to achieve upon completion of the chapter. After each section within a chapter, there is a series of brief questions that will help you check your understanding of the material in that section. You should work methodically through each chapter, taking the time to review each section for any points you have not understood.

At the end of each chapter, there is a brief summary and a list of the important terms and concepts found in that chapter, plus ten multiple choice questions. Answers are given at the back of the book. Once again, you can test your understanding of what you have read by studying the chapter summary and reviewing your understanding of the terms and concepts and answering the multiple choice questions. This material is a valuable aid in preparing for examinations.

A number of figures and other special interest inserts have been included to clarify some of our analyses and provide variety to your reading.

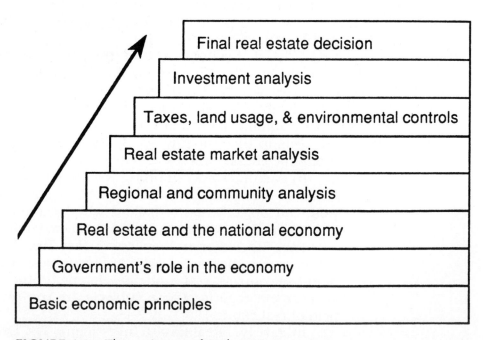

FIGURE 1.2   The stairway of real estate economics.

A FINAL WORD

The study of real estate economics can be approached from the mathematical view, called *econometrics*, or from the nonmathematical perspective, called *descriptive economics*. Econometrics combines economics, mathematics, and statistics in order to express economic relationships in terms of mathematical equations. The descriptive approach uses words rather than equations to describe economic relationships.

We use the descriptive approach, and we have emphasized a streamlined and summarized approach to economic concepts wherever possible. Students who wish to pursue economic principles in more detail are encouraged to contact their local college and obtain information about course offerings in economics.

Chapter 2

Review of the Economic Principles of Capitalism

Preview

This chapter reviews the basic economic principles of capitalism. Section 2.1 examines the purpose of an economic system and the characteristics of a pure capitalist economy. Section 2.2 describes the factors needed to produce goods and services and includes a model showing the flow of goods, services, and income in a capitalistic economy. Section 2.3 deals with the importance of a market and how prices and output are established in a competitive market. When you have completed this chapter you will be able to:

1. Describe why every society must have an economic system.
2. List the basic characteristics of pure capitalism.
3. List the factors of production that enable our economy to produce goods and services.
4. Describe how prices are established in a competitive market.

2.1   BASIC ECONOMIC CONCEPTS

WHAT IS ECONOMICS?

Economics is defined as *a social science that studies the production, distribution, and consumption of goods and services.* A social science is concerned with human behavior. Economics studies how people allocate scarce resources in order to satisfy their needs for food, clothing, housing, and recreation.

The desire for material goods and services usually exceeds the supply available, and economics attempts to determine how scarce goods and services can be distributed efficiently. For example, imagine how many families would like to live on a 10- to 15-acre ranch within a fifteen-mile drive to their jobs in a large city. When such a mini-ranch becomes available, who gets it? Who decides which family gets the land and the opportunity to enjoy a rural setting, and which families must continue to live in the congested city? Should names be drawn out of a hat? Should it go to the highest bidder? Should the land be subdivided? Should the government make it into a park? As you can see, this is a problem involving scarcity. There is simply not enough land to satisfy all of the families who wish to live on mini-ranches. It is the role of the economist to examine alternate solutions to scarcity problems, pointing out the advantages and disadvantages of each solution and indicating a preference for the best solution.

ECONOMICS IS AN INEXACT SCIENCE

As a social science, economics is concerned with human behavior, not mere physical objects. A chemist can predict with great accuracy what will occur when certain chemicals are mixed. But an economist cannot always predict with absolute accuracy what will occur when certain economic ingredients are mixed. For example, if a country is in a recession, reducing income taxes should stimulate the economy because people will have extra dollars to spend. But a tax cut will not immediately stimulate the economy if people decide to save rather than spend their newfound dollars. The key point is that people can change their behavioral patterns, and these changes add uncertainty to economic predictions. However, by constantly studying human behavior and by upgrading their analytical tools, economists continually attempt to improve the accuracy of their forecasts.

ECONOMIC SOLUTIONS MAY CONTAIN VALUE JUDGMENTS

Frequently, economists can agree on the nature of an economic problem, but because of data interpretation and their own personal beliefs, economists can differ as to the best solutions. For example, if a nation is suffering rapid inflation caused by too much spending driving up prices faster than businesses can increase supply, most economists would agree that inflation should be reduced. But what actions should be taken to stop inflation? Should the government increase taxes to cut consumer spending? If so, whose taxes should be increased? Or should the government cut back on its own spending? If so, which government programs—welfare, defense, highways, low-income housing—need to be cut?

Students should not become bewildered by disagreements among economists. Disagreements among experts exist in most fields of study. How can two equally qualified real estate brokers arrive at different conclusions as to the ideal use for the same parcel of land? Is there not just one ideal land use? Or does the interpretation of an ideal land use depend on the circumstances, interests, and experiences of the person giving the solution?

As trained social scientists, economists attempt to minimize the amount of personal value judgments that enter into their analyses, but students should recognize that some bias can exist. When disagreements arise among experts, students should carefully listen to all sides and then form their own opinions.

DIFFERENT ECONOMIC SYSTEMS

What will be produced? How will it be produced? For whom will it be produced? These are the economic questions that every society must answer, and economists have agreed that there are three general types of answers to these questions. If the society chooses to continue doing things as they have been done before, we call its system a *traditional economy.* Child follows parent's trade, farmer uses age-old methods, social stratification remains fixed— these are the hallmarks of a traditional economy like that of medieval Europe and found today in some underdeveloped countries. If the great majority of decisions about production and distribution are made by private individuals in competitive markets, the system is called a *market economy,* or *capitalism.* If it is the government that makes most of the economic decisions in society, the system is

THEORIES AND THEORETICIANS
Famous Capitalist

The Bettmann Archive

Adam Smith (1723–1790)

In 1776, in addition to the American Revolution, another event took place that would have a profound effect on the world: Adam Smith, professor at the University of Glasgow in Scotland, wrote *The Wealth of Nations*. This book described an economic system based on the concept of private ownership and free competitive markets without government interference. Smith used the term *laissez-faire* (hands off) to describe the government's role.

Smith stressed that an economy free of government, where individuals were motivated by profit and self-interest, would unknowingly provide for the efficient allocation of resources.

Modern-day capitalistic theories spring from the ideas set forth by Adam Smith in 1776.

---

a *command economy*, more commonly known as *socialism* or *communism*.

Although some of the underdeveloped world still has a traditional economy, our concern will be with the market and command solutions to the basic questions of production and distribution. The major distinction between these two systems is the role of the government. In a "pure" market—or capitalist—society, the government provides only defense needs and a judicial system that will protect the rights of individuals and foster competitive markets. Private individuals own the property and resources of the society. They produce goods and services and distribute them according to supply and demand using a competitive market system. It is the ability to pay, not the need to have, that determines who gets what in this system. In a "pure" command—or socialist—society, the government owns major resources as a trustee for the people. The government produces and distributes goods and services according to its interpretation of its citizen's needs.

In the real world, there is no such thing as pure capitalism or pure socialism. All large economies are a mixture of the two. Some countries are much more socialistic, while others tend toward capitalism. The United States is primarily a capitalistic system, but its economy has many features of the command system: just look at the uses the government makes of our tax dollars. Whether we like it or not, we build missiles, support families on welfare, build roads, and give food to developing nations. On the other hand, countries with socialist economies allow their farmers to have private plots of land, follow public buying patterns to determine what consumer goods to produce, and create profit incentives for some categories of workers.

BASIC PRINCIPLES OF PURE CAPITALISM

The present economic system of the United States has its roots in the principles and theories of pure capitalism. Therefore, it is important to understand certain key elements known as the principles of capitalism.

1. Private Property: the right of the individual to own, control, and dispose of property.

2. Private Enterprise: the major resources and businesses are owned and controlled by private citizens, with the freedom of choice in the use of these resources.

THEORIES AND THEORETICIANS

Famous Socialist

New York Public Library Picture Collection

Karl Marx (1818–1883)

In 1867, another important book was published which would also have a profound effect on the world. Karl Marx, an impoverished philosopher living in England, wrote a book entitled *Das Kapital* (Capital).

In his book, Marx predicted that capitalism was doomed to fail because capitalists motivated by profits would force workers to take less money, thus lowering wages to the "subsistence" level. In time, a few rich capitalists would have all the wealth, while the workers would be living in misery. Workers would then arise, overthrow the capitalists, and seize the wealth on behalf of the workers.

Marx believed that this revolution would lead to a new, classless society. All would willingly work according to their abilities and receive goods according to their needs.

Some modern-day socialism and much of today's communism stem from the ideas of Karl Marx.

---

3. Competitive Markets: markets where numerous buyers and sellers are pitted against one another as they bargain for the exchange of goods and services. No one buyer or seller has enough power to manipulate prices. Ultimately, the bargaining process results in goods being allocated at the lowest possible price.

4. Profit Motive: the desire for personal gain that motivates individuals to take risks and form businesses to produce the goods and services demanded by society. Failure to produce what society wants at the correct price will cause personal bankruptcy, while success will generate profit and personal wealth.

5. Laissez-Faire (hands off): the government should not interfere in the economic affairs of the country.

HOW PURE CAPITALISM ANSWERS THE QUESTIONS "WHAT?," "HOW?," AND "FOR WHOM?"

In a pure capitalistic economy, how do we answer the critical questions of what to produce, how, and for whom to produce? The answers are determined by the interaction of supply and demand . . . what Adam Smith, the famous capitalist, called the "invisible hand." "What to produce" is determined by businesses that produce goods and services demanded by buyers. Do you remember the Pontiac Fiero car? General Motors built it, but there was insufficient demand and the Fiero went out of production. On the other hand, illegal drugs continue to be produced and distributed in spite of government efforts to prevent the flow of these harmful substances. Why? Because demand drives up prices and high prices in turn stimulate the supply, even if the supplier runs the risk of imprisonment.

The question of "how to produce?" is answered by the lowest possible production cost. To remain competitive, a manufacturer must constantly seek ways of producing at lower costs. According to pure capitalistic theory, these lower costs should ultimately result in lower consumer prices.

For whom shall the items be produced? Who gets the goods and services and who must do without? According to the theory of capitalism, goods and services will go to those who have something of value to exchange. Usually the medium of exchange is money. In short, goods and services go to those who can pay for them.

MODERN MIXED CAPITALISM IN THE UNITED STATES

It should be clear from your understanding of American economic society that the United States does not have a pure form of

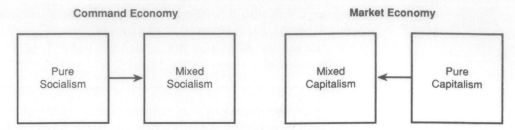

FIGURE 2.1   Span of Economic Systems

capitalism. Economists refer to the American economy as a *mixed capitalistic system*. Although most goods and services are produced by private enterprise, the government plays an important role either directly or indirectly in controlling the economy.

The government in a mixed capitalistic system attempts to correct what it and the majority of its citizens consider to be the major faults of pure capitalism. Especially since the Great Depression, the government has played a major role in attempting to maintain full employment, general economic stability, and a reasonable level of economic growth. Other governmental interventions in the economy involve regulation of business, income redistribution, and welfare.

As befits a democratic society, we hear voices of gloom on the right and doom on the left preaching, respectively, the adoption of a less or more active governmental role to preserve the fundamental essence of the American system. See Figure 2.1 for a spectrum of economic systems. In the field of real estate you might hear voices asking for less regulation over land use, then a few minutes later the same voices are demanding that the government do something to lower interest rates to make housing more affordable! Today there are many spokespersons for the present system of economic compromise. This mixed capitalistic system has evolved over many decades, and the voters have made it abundantly clear that neither pure capitalism nor pure socialism is acceptable.

Before taking a closer look at the American economy to see how goods are produced, how income is generated, and the importance of land, review the questions below.

REVIEWING YOUR UNDERSTANDING

Basic Economic Concepts

1. What does an economic system attempt to do?

2. What is government's role under capitalism? Under socialism?

3. Explain the following: private property, private enterprise, competitive markets, profit motive, and laissez-faire.

2.2 ECONOMIC PRINCIPLES IN ACTION

This section provides a simplified model of our economy that illustrates how goods, services, and income flow through our economic system.

FACTORS OF PRODUCTION

According to economists, there are four essential resources—called *factors of production*—that are needed to produce goods and services: land, labor, capital, and entrepreneurship.

1. *Land* refers to all natural resources—trees, minerals, and water—as well as the surface of the earth. The land provides the raw materials needed to manufacture goods, to grow food, and to provide shelter.

2. *Labor* is the human effort needed to transform raw materials into finished products or to perform services.

3. *Capital* is any manufactured instrument used to increase production, such as machinery, tools, and buildings. Although *money capital* is needed to purchase *capital equipment*, money itself cannot extract resources or produce goods and services. The role of money capital in the real estate market is discussed later.

4. *Entrepreneurship* is the assembling of the other factors of production in a systematic manner to produce goods or services. This activity is performed by the owner, or entrepreneur, and is commonly known as "going into business."

These four elements come together to produce and distribute goods and services in the U.S. economy.

RENT, WAGES, INTEREST, PROFIT, AND INCOME

In a capitalistic economy, private individuals own the factors of production, and they insist upon payment for the use of their "property." Owners of land receive *rent* for the use of their land. Workers sell their labor for *wages*. Lenders of money receive *interest* from borrowers who want to purchase capital equipment. And successful entrepreneurs earn *profits* from the operation of their businesses. (Unsuccessful entrepreneurs, of course, incur losses—or go out of business.)

Rents, wages, interest, and profits constitute *income*. If you are like most people, you spend a major portion of your income buying goods and services. Thus *our economy has a circular flow*. Business

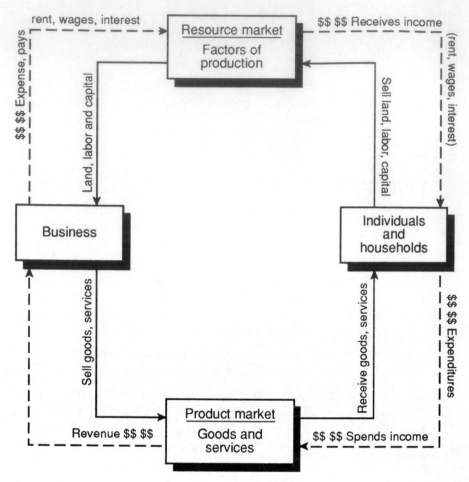

FIGURE 2.2   The circular flow of the economy, simplified model, excluding government's role

buys land, labor, and capital from individuals, and individuals use this income to buy goods and services from business.

THE CIRCULAR FLOW OF THE ECONOMY

Figure 2.2 illustrates the circular flow of our economy. The role played by the government will be discussed in the next chapter. For now, we will assume that the government does not participate in the economy.

The solid inner lines in Figure 2.2 show the flow of resources and goods. The outer dotted lines show the flow of income. As you see, the individual is both buyer and seller. He or she sells land, labor, or capital in the resource market and buys goods and services in the product market. Businesses buy land, labor, and capital in the resource market and sell goods and services in the product market. Check your understanding of this circular flow by answering the following questions.

REVIEWING YOUR UNDERSTANDING

Economic Principles in Action

What will happen to this circular flow if the following occurs:

1. Business experiences a decline in sales and decides to cut back on production. Will the economy expand or contract? Will employment rise or decline? Will household income increase or decrease?

2. What will happen to this flow if the reverse takes place and high profits motivate business to expand its output? You should be able to trace the changes through each section of Figure 2.2.

2.3 MARKETS AND PRICES

This section defines the term *market* and describes how prices and output are established in competitive markets. Special emphasis is placed on the factors that cause prices to change.

WHAT DETERMINES PRICES AND OUTPUT?

What determines the rent charged for land? The interest rate charged for capital? The wage level charged by labor? The price of goods and services? The amount of goods produced? In our economy, most of these questions are answered in the marketplace. A *market* is defined as a *place where buyers and sellers meet to bargain and exchange items of value at negotiated prices.*

The characteristics of a market can influence the level of output and the prices paid for goods and services. Let us compare conditions of *perfect competition* with those of *imperfect competition.* When conditions of perfect competition prevail in the market, there are many buyers and sellers bidding against each other for available goods and services. No one buyer or seller can exert influence over the market or control prices. The goods or services being offered are similar enough so that the buyer will select the lowest-priced offering, and it is bargaining between buyers and sellers that establishes the prices.

If either the buyer or the seller exercises some control over the market, then conditions of imperfect competition prevail. If there are several sellers and one buyer, a lower price will result. If there are several buyers and one seller, a higher price will result. Consider the example of the mini-ranch in the suburbs: if there is one property for sale, the many prospective suburbanites will drive the price up by bidding against each other. But if 500 mini-ranches came on the market, the price would obviously fall.

DEMAND AND SUPPLY—THE CLASSICAL ANSWER TO PRICE DETERMINATION

Our economy has become so complex that it is difficult to find examples of perfect competition, but people tend to understand the market forces that influence prices more clearly by viewing them under conditions of perfect competition. Therefore the following discussion assumes a perfectly competitive market. Later, the principles discussed below will be modified in order to analyze prices in the imperfect real estate market.

Prices in a market economy are determined by the interaction of buyers and sellers as they compete against one another for goods and services in the marketplace. *The total quantity that buyers are willing to buy at a given time at certain prices is called demand. The total quantity that sellers are willing to sell at a given time at certain prices is called supply.*

DEMAND

People must be careful not to confuse desire or need with demand. Demand is desire or need coupled with the ability and the willingness to spend. For example, Family A wants a $400,000 home, but they cannot afford it. Family B wants the same home and can afford it, but Mr. and Mrs. B do not want to make the necessary high monthly payments. Family C wants the house, can afford it, and will make high monthly payments. Only Family C exercises real demand for this house. Families A and B are lookers, not buyers. Some economists use the term *demand* for desire or need, and when ability to pay is joined to desire or need, they use the term *effective demand*. Regardless of which terms we use, it is effective demand, not wishful desire or need, that is the key to understanding demand in the marketplace.

The Law of Demand

We said earlier that economists do tend to agree on some things. One of these common points is the existence of a few economic laws. An important law is the *law of demand*, which states: *The lower the price, the more consumers will buy. The higher the price, the less they will buy.*

At lower prices, consumers will buy more goods because they can afford more and because a lower price may entice them to buy more after their initial purchase. For example, you may buy one can of Brand A for $1.00, but to entice you to buy more, the grocer may lower the price to two cans for $1.75. At higher prices, consumers will buy fewer goods because they cannot afford as much, and because each additional unit purchased will give less satisfaction than the original unit.

Changes in Demand

Changing circumstances may change demand by causing an increase or decrease in the number of available buyers. Some of the causes of change in demand are listed below:

1. An increase or decrease in population—*Demand rises or falls with population: as the number of people increases, demand increases; as the number of people declines, demand declines.*

2. An increase or decrease in per capita income—*Demand also rises and falls with the level of per capita income: the higher the level of income, the greater the demand; the lower the level of income, the less the demand.*

3. Changes in consumer taste and substitute products—*If consumers favor smaller cars over large sedans, demand for the former grows and demand for the latter slackens. The same is true in housing: if city-dwellers create a trend to move to the suburbs, then the demand for city apartments will decline and demand for suburban homes will grow.*

4. The amount of credit available—*Easy credit tends to increase demand, while tight credit tends to slacken it. Of course, you must pay back later what you borrow now, and this will affect future demand.*

5. The effect of advertising—*The well-written newspaper ad or the catchy TV commercial can create desires that eventually lead to purchases—and increased demand.*

SUPPLY

Demand represents the buyer's side of the market. Now let us look at the seller's side. *The total quantity that sellers are willing to sell at a particular time and at a certain price is called supply.*

The Law of Supply

The *law of supply* states: *Producers will offer more products for sale as prices increase and less as prices decrease.* Higher prices may mean higher profits, so businesses increase output. As prices decline, profits usually decline, and businesses cut back on output.

Changes in Supply

Supply, like demand, reflects changing circumstances. Some of the causes of changes in supply follow.

1. Changes in the cost of the factors of production—*If land, labor, or capital gets more expensive, some producers will be unable to make a profit and may have to drop out of business, thereby reducing the supply. If the factors of production become cheaper perhaps due to better technology, some producers might seek a profit by moving into that particular business, thereby increasing supply.*

2. A change in demand for one product can cause a change in supply of another product—*For example, if people decide to live in tents instead of houses, you could expect to see a cutback in the supply of homes and an increase in the supply of tents.*

3. Business anticipation of future prices and profits can change the amount of goods supplied—*Sellers will increase output if they think that future prices and profits will increase; they will decrease output, or even get out of business, if they think that future prices and profits will decrease.*

SUPPLY AND DEMAND TOGETHER DETERMINE OUTPUT AND PRICE LEVELS

If all the sellers and buyers of goods and services come together, there will eventually be an auction-type agreement between them, which will determine the selling (buying) price of the goods and services. If sellers insist on prices that are too high, some buyers will refuse to purchase. Not wanting excess goods on hand, sellers would then lower prices until they have sold the merchandise. If prices are too low, sellers will not be able to make a profit. They will stop production, and the buyers, not wanting to do without the products, will gradually increase their bids until sellers are enticed back into production.

After much movement back and forth, prices settle at the point where the quantity that buyers are willing to purchase equals the quantity that sellers are willing to sell. This is called the *equilibrium point*; here buyers and sellers are matched and the goods and services for sale in the market are sold. Rents, wages, interest rates, and prices of goods and services in a perfectly competitive market are established by this interaction of supply and demand.

But in a dynamic economy, things never stay the same for very long. The changes that have been discussed cause both supply and demand to alter, and these alterations change the equilibrium point. If supply remains the same while demand increases, for example, would you expect prices to increase or decrease? Would supply remain at the same point or would it change in response to the increase in demand? Prices would of course increase: more buyers are after fewer goods. Suppliers would then increase production—and the quantity supplied—to take advantage of the higher prices.

And what would happen if demand remained constant while supply increased? Prices would go down as sellers try to liquidate their stocks, but this trend might force some sellers out of business.

Soon the supply would decrease to reach a new equilibrium point with demand.

THE FLOW OF THE ECONOMY—REVISITED

Figure 2.3 shows the flow of the economy again, but this time we have included supply and demand. You can see that the individuals and households in the resource market represent supply—they are the sellers of land, labor, and capital. How much business must pay, and how much individuals and households receive as income, depend on the price and quantity as established by supply and demand. In the product market, the roles are reversed. Business is now the supplier, selling goods and services to individuals and households.

IMPACT OF INTERNATIONAL TRADE

Up to this point in our overview of a pure capitalistic economy we have been illustrating a closed economy, one ignoring the impact of foreign imports and exports. In reality most economies are somewhat "open," allowing some imports and exports. This flow of

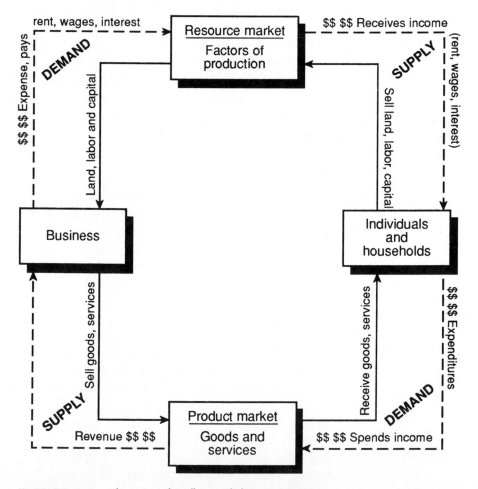

FIGURE 2.3   The circular flow of the economy

imports and exports can directly affect domestic incomes and prices.

INTERNATIONAL TRADE CONCEPTS

1. Free Trade: Restrictions, quotas, and tariffs are removed and all goods and services can flow between countries without restriction, in an open competitive market.

2. Principle of Comparative Advantage: This principle states that the entire world's standard of living will be increased if each nation specializes in producing those goods and services for which it has the lowest unit cost.

3. Balance of Payments: A record of all transactions between the citizens of one nation and another or all other countries.

4. Balance of Trade: A record of the merchandise (goods, not services) between one nation and another or all other nations. An unfavorable balance of trade means that imports exceed exports. A favorable balance of trade means exports exceed imports.

5. Rate of Exchange: The rate or price at which the currency of one nation can be converted into the currency of another. Example: dollars for pounds, marks, or yen. A "strong dollar" means that a dollar buys more foreign currency. A "weak dollar" means that a dollar buys less foreign currency. A weakness in one currency means an automatic strength in another currency. If the dollar is down, the yen is up, and so on.

6. Foreign Impact on Gross National Product (GNP): "Net exports," the amount that our imports and exports exceed one another, usually only runs about 3-5% of the gross national product.

INTERNATIONAL TRADE—IS SELF-SUFFICIENCY BETTER?

International trade between countries has an important impact on domestic economies. The flow of imports and exports can directly affect domestic incomes and prices.

Many people think that a nation is better off economically if it can become self-sufficient by producing all of its own goods and services. Economic theory has proven that a nation that attempts to become self-sufficient will do so at a higher cost to its citizens than if the nation had entered into free trade agreements with other nations. Example: The climate of Costa Rica is ideal for growing coffee, while the United States has the resources and capacity to produce computers. If the U.S. wishes to become self-sufficient and grow its own coffee, it can do so only by creating massive hothouses at tremendous costs. This in turn will drive up the price of coffee for U.S. citizens. In the process, resources will be drawn away from the production of computers, reducing output and raising the price of computers. Therefore it makes more sense for Costa Rica to concentrate on coffee and the U.S. to concentrate on computers and for each to trade. The result will be higher quality coffee and computers at lower prices for both Americans and Costa Ricans.

The theory of free trade makes economic sense, but political and other forces within nations tend to restrict international trade in an effort to protect special interest groups. Here are two examples: 1) The oil producing export countries (OPEC) form cartels to regulate the production of oil and prices and 2) the United States establishes tariffs and quotas to protect some domestic industries from foreign competition. This prevents U.S. citizens from purchasing foreign imports at the lowest prices. If free trade were allowed, the price of all goods and services would be lower. Will low priced foreign goods cause some Americans to lose their jobs? Yes, in the short-run inefficient American companies and their employees will be displaced as low priced foreign goods displace higher priced domestic goods. However, in time, the locally displaced resources should flow into industries where America has a comparative advantage and these industries will expand and absorb the displaced resources.

Some people support self-sufficiency on the grounds that national defense requires a country to be able to stand alone and not depend on other countries for vital products. Other people counter this argument by stating that no nation can become truly self-sufficient in all products and that any attempt to do so will result in a national defense that will be weak.

In today's world each country attempts to maximize its own welfare by cooperating with other nations on some occasions and not cooperating at other times. The result is an international economy that is constantly in flux as political and economic events cause alliances to shift back and forth. This in turn causes national economies to shake and roll as international events unfold. As these international events unfold, national and local real estate markets feel the impact. For example, the lower value of the dollar versus other foreign currencies, in the late 1980's, attracted many foreign investors to the bargain prices of United States real estate. This investment by foreigners stimulated the United States real estate market, driving up prices and adding to profits and commissions.

Question: What should happen to this process when the value of the dollar rises?

Answer: Investments by foreigners should slow down as prices of U.S. real estate will appear too high. This is because the foreign investor must put up excessive amounts of foreign currency to convert to the high valued dollars needed to purchase U.S. real estate.

THE ECONOMIC THEORY SOUNDS GOOD, BUT . . .

Thus far, we have stressed the interaction of supply and demand in perfectly competitive markets and in a pure capitalistic system.

But the real world is not so simple. Many of the markets in the United States are imperfect, either due to trade restrictions or because the buyer or the seller is in a superior position and can influence price and output. The automatic corrections that take place in a perfectly competitive market do not always work in imperfect markets. Furthermore, our mixed capitalistic system grants a role to the government that also disturbs the pure capitalistic concept of supply and demand.

Nevertheless, our study of the "perfect" system permits us to understand the basic mechanics of capitalism. We must remember also that, although we have imperfect markets and some government control of resources, the main economic philosophy in the United States is still capitalism. Individuals do have the right to own property, run businesses, compete, and earn profits. But these rights are not absolute: the principles of pure capitalism have been modified to reflect social as well as private rights. This point is discussed in the next chapter, which examines the role of the government in the economy.

REVIEWING YOUR UNDERSTANDING

Markets and Prices

1. If supply stays the same but demand decreases, what will happen to price? To the amount supplied?

2. If the demand remains the same but supply increases, what will happen to price? To the amount supplied?·

3. If the main industry in your town goes out of business, what effect will this have on the price of homes? In terms of supply and demand, what has occurred?

CHAPTER SUMMARY

Economics is a social science that examines how people use and allocate scarce resources. There are several ways of solving the problems of what will be produced, how it will be produced, and for whom it will be produced. A capitalistic economy leaves the decisions to private individuals operating in competitive markets. Command or socialistic systems look toward government for the decision making. The United States operates under a mixed capitalistic system, using both government and private enterprise to make economic decisions.

All economies need four elements, known collectively as the factors of production, in order to produce goods and services: land, labor, capital, and entrepreneurship. In a capitalistic economy, these factors are privately owned and must be paid for before being used.

The payment for land is called rent, for labor it is called wages, for capital it is called interest, and for entrepreneurship it is called profit. When rent, wages, interest, and profits are received, they are called income. Income is earned by individuals when they sell the factors of production. The earned income is then spent to purchase goods and services produced by these same factors of production. Thus, our economy has a circular flow, of which imports and exports from international trade are a part.

The prices paid in a competitive economy are determined in markets through the interaction of supply and demand. Demand is the total quantity that buyers are willing to purchase at a given set of prices, in a particular market, at a particular time. The law of demand states that the lower the price, the more consumers will buy; the higher the price, the less they will buy.

Supply is the total quantity that sellers are willing to sell in a particular market, at a particular time, at given prices. The law of supply states that producers will offer more products for sale as prices increase and less as prices decrease. The law of supply is based on the profit motive.

It is the interaction of supply and demand which determines the prices paid and the quantity produced in a competitive economy. Certain influences cause either supply or demand to change. When this occurs, prices and output also change. Understanding how market changes influence price and output is essential for real estate investors.

IMPORTANT TERMS AND CONCEPTS

Balance of payments	Factors of production
Balance of trade	Flow of the economy
Capitalism—pure and mixed	Free trade
Changes in demand	Law of demand
Changes in supply	Law of supply
Command economy	Market
Comparative advantage	Rate of exchange
Demand	Rent, wages, interest, profits
Economics	Supply
Equilibrium point	

REVIEWING YOUR UNDERSTANDING

1. A social science concerned with how people produce, distribute, and consume goods and services is:

   a. history
   b. economics
   c. geography
   d. political science

2. Famous capitalist who wrote The Wealth of Nations:

   a. Karl Marx
   b. John Stuart Mill
   c. Thomas Jefferson
   d. Adam Smith

3. The major economic decisions are made by a government committee, but minor economic decisions are left to private individuals. This describes:

   a. pure socialism
   b. mixed socialism
   c. mixed capitalism
   d. pure capitalism

4. All of the following are principles of pure capitalism, *except*:

   a. private property
   b. laissez-faire
   c. public ownership of basic resources
   d. open and competitive markets for goods and services

5. The payment for entrepreneurship is called:

   a. profit
   b. wages
   c. interest
   d. rent

6. In the circular flow of the U.S. economy, individuals go to the resource markets as sellers and to the product markets as buyers.

   a. true
   b. false

7. According to the Law of Demand, the higher the price of homes, the more likely that:

   a. the number of homes built will increase
   b. people will buy new homes
   c. the number of home sales will decline
   d. the number of homes built will decline

8. In a purely competitive real estate market, if the demand by renters for apartments increases, while the number of apartment units available for rent decreases, apartment rents should:

    a. increase

    b. decrease

    c. remain in equilibrium

    d. become static

9. The principle of capitalism states that goods and services are produced for people who:

    a. need them

    b. desire them

    c. wish for them

    d. effectively demand them

10. In international trade, the price that the currency of one nation brings in terms of the currency of another nation is known as:

    a. balance of payments

    b. rate of exchange

    c. balance of trade

    d. principle of comparative advantage

Chapter 3

Government's Role in the Economy

Preview

This chapter summarizes the role played by the government in our economy. Section 3.1 explains the major reasons why the government has joined business and consumers as a full partner in the operations of our economy. Section 3.2 shows how economists measure the performance of our economy using national income accounting and changes in business activity. Section 3.3 introduces fiscal and monetary policy, the tools used by the government to help fight the ills of inflation, recession, and unemployment. When you have completed this chapter you will be able to:

1. Discuss why the government's role in our economy has been expanding.

2. Define gross national product and label the phases of a business cycle.

3. Describe the trend in national real estate cycles.

4. Define and explain the two main tools used by the government to fight economic problems.

3.1   THE REAL WORLD OF MARKETS AND GOVERNMENT

The pure capitalism of Adam Smith, which we analyzed in the previous chapter, is not the capitalism that exists in the United States or in any other country. Most of our resources are manufactured and sold in imperfect markets.

Imperfect markets arise when a small group of buyers or sellers is able to influence directly the price and output of a good or service. This control may be in the form of an exclusive patent, ownership of a scarce commodity, or control of a transportation route. Control may also be obtained through extensive advertising or by other means.

When a small group of sellers can eliminate competitors, they can manipulate the market and generate abnormally high profits. On the other hand, when a small group of buyers can manipulate markets, profits may be driven so low that sellers fail to realize any return on their investments.

In the 1890s, to help balance the inequities created by imperfect markets, the U.S. government passed antitrust legislation and created regulatory agencies. The Sherman Antitrust Act, passed in 1890, forbade combinations that restricted competition between businesses. The Interstate Commerce Commission, created in 1897,

SPECIAL INTEREST TOPIC

Types of Imperfect Markets

Monopoly—A market in which there is only one seller.

Oligopoly—A market in which there are only a few sellers.

Monopolistic competition—A market where a large number of sellers compete, but through advertising and promotion, each attempts to convince consumers that one brand is better than another. If successful, the seller then can charge a slightly higher price for his or her product.

Monopsony—A market in which there is only one buyer.

Oligopsony—A market in which there are only a few buyers.

regulated the practices of monopolistic sellers of interstate products. The trend from the 1890s to the 1970s was increased government regulation over business activities.

Beginning in the 1980s some "deregulation" has occurred, to reverse what many feel has been too strong a government role. Some felt that tight government regulations put a damper on businesses' ability to expand output and create jobs. The airline, trucking, and other transportation industries have been deregulated, as have many areas of the banking industry. Whether deregulation is good or bad is a debate that is rooted in both political and economic ideologies.

GOVERNMENT INTERVENTION IN THE ECONOMY

Government spending, regulatory agencies, welfare programs, zoning, planning, and environmental constraints are a few examples of current government intervention in economic affairs. Some of the reasons given to justify why the government should become a full partner in the operations of our economy follow.

1. Capitalism has a tendency to create imperfect markets; if they remain unchecked, a misallocation of resources can occur. Government intervention is needed to assure a reasonable degree of competition to prevent one economic group from dominating others.

2. Although the threat of war has lessened, international peacekeeping requires that government control some economic resources and personnel for defense needs.

3. Citizens have set certain social goals that can best be achieved by a nonprofit institution. Most of these goals include care for those who are unable to provide for themselves: the aged, the infirm, and the disadvantaged. If the government is to achieve these social goals, it needs more economic resources.

4. Citizens have requested that the government attempt to prevent economic instability. In other words, we have asked the government to fight inflation, recession, and unemployment. To do this the government needs economic power.

5. Finally, some observers note that more and more voters are turning to the government for services once provided by private enterprise. To provide such services, the government must expand its economic activity.

FLOW OF THE ECONOMY—THE GOVERNMENT INCLUDED

Figure 3.1 illustrates how the government fits into the flow of the economy. It is important to know how the government partici-

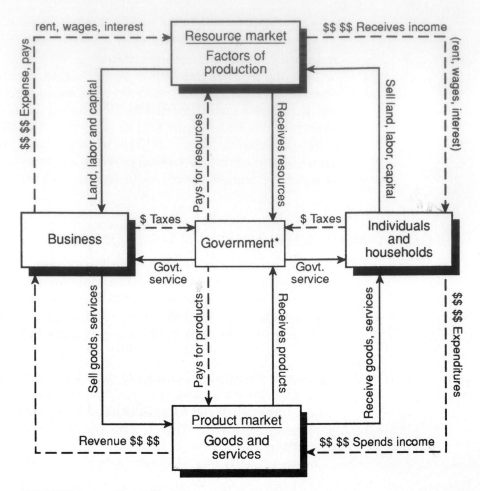

FIGURE 3.1   Simplified flow of the economy showing government's role.
* The payments to the government in this model are called taxes, but include all forms of income flow (taxes, borrowing, fines, and fees).

pates with individuals and businesses in the flow of money, goods, and services.

In Figure 3.1, note how individuals and households pay taxes to the government and in return receive government services. Business also pays taxes and receives government services. To provide the needed services demanded by individuals and business, the government must purchase factors of production from the resource market and goods and services from the product market. The money for these purchases comes mainly from the taxes paid by households and business. Students should attempt to visualize this illustration as a continuous flow of money and goods, a system that is always moving and always changing.

REVIEWING YOUR UNDERSTANDING

The Real World of Markets and Government

1. How does a monopoly differ from pure competition? Why are most monopolies regulated by the government?

2. If most real estate brokers charge the same commission rate, is the real estate business noncompetitive? How do real estate brokers compete?

3. Why does the government intervene in the economy?

4. If the government increases taxes, what impact will this have on the flow of the economy?

3.2   MEASURING THE PERFORMANCE OF THE ECONOMY

Just as a mechanic measures the condition of an automobile by checking various factors, the economist uses diagnostic tools to check the condition of the economy. When all the reports are in, the economist, like the mechanic, recommends any needed repairs. Unlike the mechanic, however, the economist may differ from his or her colleagues about what must be done to bring the economy back into good working order, but as we pointed out earlier, economics is not an exact science.

Local real estate markets are heavily influenced by economic changes in the immediate area. However, local economies are in turn influenced by the general trend of the national economy. Understanding the causes of changes in the national economy will help you to understand what impact these changes will have on your community.

NATIONAL INCOME ACCOUNTING

One way to gauge the state of the national economy is to compare the output and income generated in the present year to that of past years. To do this, economists have developed several measurements including the measurement called *gross national product*, frequently referred to as GNP, and defined as *the total market value of all goods and services produced in an economy during a given time, usually in one year.*

If you add up the final retail price of all goods and services produced in a year, the total dollar amount would be the GNP. Gross national product is compiled by the U.S. Department of Commerce and is reported on a monthly basis. When comparing GNP in one year with past years, one must be sure that the figures have been adjusted to omit the distortion of inflation. For example, if the GNP increases by 2 percent, but prices have inflated by 6 percent, the real GNP has decreased by 4 percent. GNP adjusted for inflation is called *real GNP*.

WHERE DOES GNP GO?

The gross national product of the United States is used by consumers, business, government, and foreign markets. Goods and services purchased by consumers are called *personal consumption expenditures*. Business buying is called *gross private domestic investment*. Government purchasing of GNP, simply called *government*, includes federal, state, and local government buying.

Other nations also purchase a portion of our GNP, which is called exports. We, in turn, purchase a portion of the GNP of foreign nations, and this is called imports. If we export more than we import, foreigners have purchased more GNP from us than we have purchased from them. This calculation is called *net export*.

In recent years, our purchase of imports has exceeded our sale of exports, so GNP showed a minus balance in this category. With the recent publicity regarding foreign trade, it should be noted that net exports only represent about 3–5 percent of GNP. Table 3.1 shows the breakdown of GNP for selected years.

As shown in Table 3.1, GNP increased between 1980 and 1989. When adjusted for inflation, however, the increase is less than what the raw figures indicate.

TABLE 3.1   GNP Expenditures (billions)

Gross National Product	*1980*	*1985*	*1989*
A. Current Dollars	2,732.0	4,014.0	5,200.8
B. Real GNP (1982 dollars)	3,187.1	3,618.7	4,117.7
Components			
Personal Consumption Expenditures			
A. Current Dollars	1,732.6	2,629.0	3,450.1
B. Real (1982) Dollars	2,000.4	2,354.8	2,656.8
Gross Private Domestic Investment			
A. Current Dollars	437.0	643.1	771.2
B. Real (1982) Dollars	509.3	637.0	716.9
Government Purchases of Goods and Services			
A. Current Dollars	530.3	820.8	1,025.6
B. Real (1982) Dollars	620.5	731.2	798.1
Net Exports			
A. Current Dollars	32.1	−78.0	−46.1
B. Real (1982) Dollars	57.0	−104.3	−54.1

Source: U.S. Department of Commerce. Real GNP is current dollar GNP adjusted for inflation using 1982 dollars.

If real GNP increases, the national economy is growing, and optimism and spending are adding to prosperity. However, it should be noted that increases in real GNP measure only the growth in physical output and income. They do not measure the quality of life or the equality of the distribution of output and income.

OTHER INCOME MEASUREMENTS

In an effort to study in detail the performance of the economy, economists have devised many other measurements. A few of the important measurements for real estate purposes are personal income, disposable personal income, and discretionary income.

Interesting Controversies

Does GNP really stand for gross national pollution?

Environmentalists point out that economic growth represented by GNP does not take into consideration the pollution caused by the manufacturing of goods. They argue that a standard of living should include the quality of life, not just material possessions. Two dilemmas arise: how do we increase economic growth without increasing pollution, and how do we measure the quality of life?

Does an increase in GNP mean more goods and services per person?

One argument advanced by the advocates of zero population growth is that if real GNP remains the same while population declines, our standard of living will rise rapidly with a minimum increase in environmental damage. Looking at the equation below, what will happen if real GNP increases, but our population increases at a faster rate?

$$\frac{\text{Real GNP}}{\text{Population}} = \text{Goods and services per capita (standard of living)}$$

Personal income is the total income earned by individuals after business taxes have been paid but before personal taxes are paid.

Disposable personal income is income after the payment of personal taxes. It is often called take-home pay. Disposable personal income is closely watched because it is an important measure of consumer purchasing power for all basic needs, including housing. If take-home pay increases faster than the rate of inflation, consumers may have more money to spend on various items, including housing.

Discretionary income is the amount of money people have after the payment of necessities. Payments for basic housing, food, clothing, and transportation are subtracted from disposable personal income, leaving income that can be spent any way people wish.

An increase in discretionary income means that our society is becoming more affluent and that we are in a position to spend more on luxuries. The successful operation of travel and leisure facilities, such as restaurants, theaters, motels, vacation homes, health clubs, and tourist attractions, is tied to adequate levels of discretionary income.

KEEPING UP WITH NATIONAL INCOME

Changes in GNP, personal income, disposable personal income, and discretionary income are important for real estate agents and investors. An increase in personal disposable income could mean that consumers are better able to qualify for mortgage loans or that tenants can now afford higher rent levels.

An increase in discretionary income could mean that raw recreational land might be more in demand and that tourist-oriented real estate, such as ski facilities, could be developed. Increases in real GNP mean that industrial and commercial properties will be in demand as business activities expand.

Information about these changes can be found in such publications as *Business Week* or *The Wall Street Journal*. In addition, most public libraries carry the *Survey of Current Business*, published by the U.S. Department of Commerce. Free publications on the economy can be obtained by writing to the regional Federal Reserve Bank.

FOREIGN OWNERSHIP OF U.S. BUSINESSES AND REAL ESTATE

The amount of foreign ownership of U.S. businesses and real estate has risen in the 1980s and early 1990s. Some of the reasons are:

1. The flight of capital out of politically unstable countries.

2. The decline in the value of the dollar relative to some other currencies, beginning in 1986, has made U.S. prices a bargain as opposed to the prices for similar items in those foreign countries.

3. Politically, the U.S. Congress and the president had been unwilling, until 1991, to face the reality of the budget deficit by cutting government spending or raising taxes. The easy short run "fix" had been to increase government borrowing to cover the deficit. The large U.S. budget deficit has forced the government to borrow heavily, thereby forcing up interest rates. These high U.S. interest rates have attracted foreign capital seeking a greater rate of return than can be found in other countries. In essence, foreign investment has been helping finance the U.S. budget deficit.

4. The growth rate of the U.S. economy in the late 1980s out-stripped many of the economies of the U.S. trading partners, generating higher interest rates and rates of return. This in turn attracted foreign investors. A slow down in the economy in the 1990s could reverse this trend.

5. The United States represents a large homogeneous consumer market. U.S. citizens spend a large percentage of their personal income: consumption is high, saving rate is low. Foreign business interests wish to gain a foothold in this consumer market. One way is to purchase existing U.S. businesses that are currently serving these markets. Another way is to increase the shipment of foreign products to the U.S.

COMPOSITION OF FOREIGN INVESTMENT

According to 1988 figures from the Department of Commerce, the origins of the foreign investors in ranking order were British, Japanese, and Canadian. In California, Japanese, Koreans, and Hong Kong Chinese have been the dominant foreign investors.

With all the publicity regarding foreign ownership of U.S. businesses, it should be pointed out that Americans have been buying the assets of foreign countries for decades. Now that the trend is somewhat reversing, some people are uncomfortable.

3.3   CHANGES IN ECONOMIC ACTIVITY

Since the Great Depression of the 1930s, real GNP has generally been on the rise, although this upward movement has fluctuated. The up-and-down movement in economic activity can be labeled seasonal fluctuation, a business cycle, or a long-term secular trend.

Seasonal fluctuations are short-term changes in business and economic activity that occur within the year, resulting from either weather or custom. For example, housing construction declines in the winter months, retail sales increase at Christmas time, and travel increases in the summer.

Business cycles are the recurrent expansions and contractions in general business activity that take place over a period of around two to nine years.

Long-term secular trends refer to economic changes that occur over an extended period of time, perhaps 50 years or more. Some examples of secular trends include a reduction in family size, a shorter work week, an increase in per capita income, and an increase in suburban housing.

As real estate investors observe economic change, it is important that they classify the change as seasonal, cyclical, or secular. If a person acquires real estate in a community that has severe seasonal changes, he or she must be prepared to support the investment when vacancies rise in the off-season. Apartments in college-dominated communities must generate enough income in nine months to help offset the loss of income in the summer recess. Ski resorts must generate enough extra income during the winter and spring to pay necessary expenses during the summer and fall.

Cyclical changes are especially important for a real estate investment. Business cycles cover economic activity changes that occur over a two- to nine-year period, and this corresponds with the average length of time that a real estate investor keeps an investment. Business cycles measure changes in employment, income, output, and prices (see Figure 3.2). All of these have a significant influence on the success of an investment, especially in its early years. Vacancy ratios and rental rates are closely tied to changes in employment, income, and prices.

Long-term secular changes are also important for real estate purposes. The time span of secular trends can run 50 or more years. Secular changes will be the major influence on long-term value changes.

CAUSES OF BUSINESS CYCLES

There are many theories about the cause of business cycles. Although economists are continually debating the merits of each

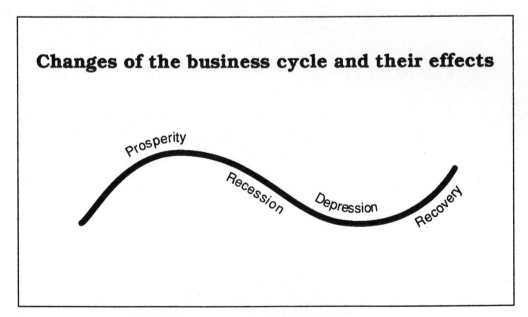

Changes of the business cycle and their effects

FIGURE 3.2   Changes of the business cycle and their effects. Prosperity = boom times, high activity, high employment, increased income and prices. Recession = decline from high point, unemployment increases, real GNP declines. Depression = massive decline in sales, very high rate of unemployment. Recovery = depression or recession bottoms out, employment and sales increase. In the real world, a business cycle is not as even as the diagram above. Many cycles go from recession to recovery without a depression. More time is usually spent in the recovery-prosperity phase than in the recession-depression phase.

theory, most agree that no single factor is the sole cause of business cycles. Instead, cycles are caused by a combination of the factors listed below, and the combination or "mix" varies with each swing in business activity.

Business cycles can be caused by the following:

1. War and other international conflicts.

2. The introduction of new innovations that create new industries. *Examples would include radio in the 1920s, television in the 1950s, computers in the 1960s, and electronics in the 1980s.*

3. Erratic spending patterns of consumers, business, and government. *There is a tendency for consumers, business, and government each to have periods of spending followed by periods of saving. This causes irregular supply and demand patterns.*

4. Changes in the amount of money and credit in circulation. *When money is plentiful and interest rates are low, spending tends to increase. When money is scarce and interest rates are high, spending tends to decline. In short, some economists believe that incorrect monetary policy causes business cycles.*

5. The psychological frame of mind of business people and consumers. *If people are optimistic about the future, investment and spending will usually occur. If people are pessimistic, caution will prevail and business activity declines.*

FORECASTING CHANGES IN ECONOMIC ACTIVITY

What a person does today is greatly influenced by what he or she thinks will occur tomorrow. One purchases real estate, for example, on the basis of what one feels will happen to property values in the future.

Economic forecasting is one way of reducing this inherent uncertainty. If investors can anticipate the direction of economic change, they will have a better idea of what lies ahead. Then they can decide whether they should take steps to protect their real estate investments from a shortage in income or an increase in expenses. In addition, economic forecasting can help investors decide whether now is the time to capitalize on a new investment opportunity.

Economic forecasting is an art, not a science. It is impossible to predict the future with absolute accuracy. Nevertheless, educated guesses are possible and are almost always better than blind plunges. Real estate students are encouraged to be aware of forecasts that are published by government agencies, financial institutions, economic research companies, and major universities. One can contact any of these institutions for monthly economic newsletters, many of which are available to interested parties at no or nominal charge.

REAL ESTATE CYCLES

If we have national business cycles, do we also have national real estate cycles? Does real estate activity move through phases of prosperity, recession, depression, and recovery? Real estate markets clearly do have their ups and downs; however, the patterns are irregular.

A review of U.S. economic history shows that until the 1940s, real estate construction activity fluctuated severely, experiencing great booms and deep depressions. On the average, these cycles took approximately 18 years to move through the four phases of prosperity, recession, depression, and recovery. This 18-year cycle is known as the *long real estate cycle*.

Since the 1940s, economists have not been able to find clear signs of this long real estate cycle. Instead, they have located another, much shorter real estate cycle that takes perhaps three to six years to move through all four phases. This new cycle is called the *short real estate cycle*.

Longer run trends in real estate activity appear to be influenced by gradual changes in population, age distribution, marriage rates, income levels, construction costs, tastes, and transportation patterns. Short-run trends in real estate markets are heavily influenced by the availability and cost of mortgage money.

Most real estate purchases require the use of borrowed funds. If these funds are available at reasonable interest rates, real estate activity increases. If these mortgage funds are available at very high interest rates, real estate activity declines. Every drop in housing construction since World War II can be somewhat attributed to the availability and cost of mortgage money.

Does this mean that the old long real estate cycle is dead? There is no definite answer, and economists are still debating the question. It is obvious that national real estate activity since 1945 is closely tied to changes in the mortgage market. More details on this important topic can be found in Chapter 4, *Money, Credit, and Real Estate*.

REVIEWING YOUR UNDERSTANDING

Measuring the Performance of the Economy

1. If you knew that in the next five years the economy would experience prosperity with rapid inflation, would you invest in real estate today or would you wait for a couple of years? Why?

2. Assuming fixed interest rate loans, does unanticipated inflation benefit mortgage borrowers or mortgage lenders?

3. What influences long-run trends in real estate activity? Short-run trends?

3.4 GOVERNMENT TOOLS TO FIGHT ECONOMIC PROBLEMS

One of the prime responsibilities of the federal government is to maintain economic stability by limiting the adverse effects of unemployment, inflation, and recession. This section discusses the major tools the federal government uses to fight declines in GNP and economic activity. The same tools can be used to fight inflation caused by excessive spending.

FISCAL POLICY

Fiscal policy is the government's use of taxing and spending power to help counteract recession, unemployment, and inflation. When the economy is in a recession, an increase in government spending may create a demand for more land, labor, and capital. This generates more income for individuals in the form of rents, wages, and interest. Some of this added income will be saved, but much will be spent in the marketplace. This increase in spending should stimulate economic activity.

In addition to direct government spending, the economy can be stimulated if the government cuts taxes. A general tax cut will give consumers more disposable income and give businesses more after-tax profits. Some of this additional income and profit will be spent, thereby stimulating economic activity.

Government spending to fight recession should not be financed by an increase in taxes, since a tax increase would reduce private income at the very time an increase in spending is needed. Instead, the government frequently finances additional spending by going into debt. When government spending exceeds government income, it is called *deficit spending*.

When our economy is producing at full capacity and employment is high, we are in the prosperity phase of the business cycle. If consumers, business, and government continue to spend, pushing demand beyond the economy's ability to supply, then prices will rise, causing inflation.

Inflation is harmful because it drives up prices without increasing output. The uncertainty about price changes causes business and consumers to act hastily, to become dismayed, discouraged, and confused. This eventually causes major disruptions in all segments of the economy. The government can fight inflation by cutting back on government spending or increasing taxes. This will reduce disposable income and demand, thereby reducing the pressure on prices. The combination of reduced government spending and increased taxes can create a situation where government income exceeds government spending, resulting in a *budget surplus*.

THEORIES AND THEORETICIANS

National Archives

John Maynard Keynes (1883-1946)

John Maynard Keynes, a British economist, is considered the founder of the "new economics." Keynes published his *General Theory of Employment, Interest, and Money* in 1936 and instantly started the "Keynesian Revolution."

Prior to Keynes, traditional economic theory held that there was a natural tendency for the economy to stabilize at full employment. Any unemployment would only be temporary since the economy would soon adjust itself to a full employment balance.

Keynes' work pointed out that, contrary to traditional theory, the economy can reach a balance at less than full employment. And unless steps were taken by the government to stimulate the economy, the unemployment would become permanent. Thus, Keynes shocked traditional capitalists by advocating government intervention into private economic affairs in order to preserve the capitalist system. Today, economists are debating whether Keynesian theory is relevant in today's globalized market-driven economy.

In his private life, Keynes was a successful and shrewd business investor. He is reported to have made over $2 million (in 1930 dollars!) through speculating in bonds and international currency by devoting one-half hour of his time, before breakfast, to these private business ventures.

SPECIAL INTEREST TOPICS

Stagflation: Inflation During Recession

Traditional fiscal and monetary tools were designed to fight economic problems such as rising prices and overemployment during periods of excessive prosperity and declining prices and unemployment during periods of recession. But in the 1970s, a new economic phenomenon was identified—inflation during recession—and the term *stagflation* was coined to label it.

How do you fight stagflation? If you attempt to fight recession by increasing spending, you add to inflation. If you attempt to fight inflation by reducing spending, you prolong the recession. Stagflation ceased in the 1980s, but economists are currently debating whether stagflation will return in the 1990s.

Automatic Stabilizers

Our economic system has some built-in stabilizers that tend to dampen large swings in the business cycle without waiting for governmental action. Two prime examples are the progressive income tax and unemployment insurance. During periods of prosperity, the amount of income taxes you pay could rise faster than your increase in wages. This reduces your ability to spend, while building up a surplus of money for the government. Also during prosperity, contributions to the unemployment insurance program increase, while unemployment claims fall, creating a larger surplus.

When the business cycle is heading for a recession, the process reverses itself. As your income declines, the amount of income tax you pay drops, leaving you with proportionately more money to spend. Also, those left unemployed by the recession can obtain money by filing unemployment claims.

Both of these processes move opposite to the business cycle and are called *automatic stabilizers*, meaning that they work without requiring direct government action.

MONETARY POLICY

In addition to fiscal policy, the government can use monetary policy to counteract recession, unemployment, and inflation. The government uses monetary policy when it increases or decreases the supply of money in an effort to stabilize the economy.

During periods of recession, the government may increase the supply of money, which in the short run may lower interest rates and increase the availability of credit. With easier credit, the government hopes that consumers and businesses will borrow for expenditures and business expansion. This could generate employment and help fight the recession.

However, excessive long-run expansion of the money supply will

THEORIES AND THEORETICIANS

AP/Wide World Photos

Milton Friedman—Free Market Giant

Milton Friedman, formerly of the University of Chicago, is one of America's foremost economists. A Nobel Prize winner in economics, Friedman is a free market advocate who believes that government's role should be limited to maintaining an environment where competition and free choice are allowed to flourish.

In Friedman's view, the free market is the best allocator of social and economic well being. Friedman stresses that the common person has faired better under capitalism, as opposed to communism, socialism, or fascism.

As a monetarist, Friedman points out that the money supply is a prime determinant of economic stability, and that the Federal Reserve Board has caused chaos by constantly turning on and off the money machine. A steady increase of the money supply at a rate equal to the real growth of GNP is the best way to wring out inflation and maintain a stable economy, in Friedman's view.

eventually increase interest rates as inflation causes lenders to "index" or increase their interest as a hedge against inflation.

During periods of inflation, the government can use monetary policy to curb spending by reducing the supply of money and credit. A reduction in the supply of money will usually drive up interest rates. High interest rates discourage borrowing, which in turn will reduce spending. As spending declines, the pressure is taken off prices, and inflation may recede.

Monetary policy is carried out by a government agency called the Federal Reserve Board. Chapter 4 is devoted to the Federal Reserve System, money, and its effect on the real estate industry.

THE THEORY SOUNDS GOOD, BUT THERE ARE SOME PROBLEMS

In theory, fiscal and monetary policy can "fine tune" the economy to prevent recession and inflation. However, in the real world, fiscal and monetary tools run into some problems. Most of these problems can be placed into two broad categories: political and structural.

Fiscal and monetary policies are enacted by the government. The governmental process is essentially political because governmental representatives must be elected. Critics point out that either Congress, the president, or both will often delay appropriate fiscal measures that conflict with current political realities. In times of high prosperity, for example, fiscal theory suggests that taxes be increased and government spending be cut to create a budget surplus to help pay off previous budget deficits. But if an election is coming up, these actions may be delayed for fear that higher taxes or cutting someone's favorite government program might prove unpopular at the polls. Thus, budget deficits tend not to be reduced, but rather increased, even during a booming economy.

Even the monetary policy of the Federal Reserve Board is not immune to political pressure, despite its theoretical independence. The Federal Reserve Board is a creature of Congress and, realistically, can be abolished or altered by an act of Congress. So, for better or worse, economics frequently must give way to politics.

The second major problem is structural. Neither fiscal nor monetary policies can be changed very rapidly. Fiscal policy must be enacted by Congress and approved by the president. The legislative process is long and drawn out. By the time the policy is enacted, it sometimes is too late to be effective.

On the other hand, monetary policy can be changed more quickly because the Federal Reserve Board does not have to contend with congressional red tape. Once enacted, however, monetary change takes a great deal of time to work its way into the economy. Indeed, it may be six months or more before changes in the money supply begin to influence economic decisions.

REVIEWING YOUR UNDERSTANDING

Government Tools to Fight Economic Problems

Use fiscal and monetary tools to answer the following:

1. If the economy is in a recession, should the government increase or decrease taxes? Government spending? Money supply?

2. When should the government have deficit spending? Why? Should the government ever have a budget surplus (take in more taxes than it spends)? When?

CHAPTER SUMMARY

Today, the government is deeply involved in private economic affairs. Imperfect competition, international conflicts, nonprofit social goals, and a desire to maintain economic stability are some of the reasons why the government has become a full partner in the operations of our economy.

Economists have tools to measure the state of the economy. The most common measurement is gross national product (GNP) which measures the total value of goods and services produced in a year. Other measurements include personal income, disposable personal income, and discretionary income. These measurements may all be on a total or per capita basis.

Increases in GNP do not occur at a constant rate, but rather in up and down movements. These fluctuations in economic activity are either seasonal, cyclical, or long-term secular trends. Most attention centers around business cycles, but to date no single theory is universally accepted as explaining the causes of business cycles.

In addition to business cycles, there are real estate cycles, which can be classified as either long or short. Since the 1940s, the short real estate cycle, caused by changes in the availability and cost of mortgage credit, has been the most obvious. It is important for real estate investors to understand business and real estate cycles and to forecast their swings, because these cycles give a better idea of what lies in the future. Investors can then decide whether they should take steps to protect their investments.

Fiscal and monetary policies are the tools that the government uses to fight the problems of inflation, unemployment, and recession. Fiscal policy means the use of government spending and taxation to counteract economic ills. Monetary policy refers to changes in the supply of money to encourage or discourage consumer spending and business investments.

IMPORTANT TERMS AND CONCEPTS

Business cycles

Discretionary income

Disposable personal income

Fiscal policy

Gross national product (GNP)

Imperfect markets

Long-term secular trends

Monetary policy

Personal income

Real estate cycles

Real GNP

Seasonal fluctuations

REVIEWING YOUR UNDERSTANDING

1. A market in which there are only a few sellers is called a(n):

    a. monopoly

    b. oligopoly

    c. monopsony

    d. oligopsony

2. In the flow of the economy, government needs to generate money to pay for the benefits society demands from government. Government raises revenue by all of the following, *except*:

    a. borrowing

    b. taxes

    c. fees

    d. labor

3. The total market value of all goods and services produced in the economy in a given year is called:

    a. gross national product

    b. personal consumption expenditures

    c. net export

    d. gross private domestic investment

4. The slope downward from the peak of a business cycle is called:

    a. depression

    b. recovery

    c. recession

    d. prosperity

5. The rise in foreign ownership of U.S. businesses and real estate is caused in part by:

   a. greater growth rate of foreign economies

   b. disorganized U.S. consumer markets

   c. reduction in the U.S. budget deficit

   d. flight of capital seeking a safe haven

6. In the short run, real estate cycles tend to be most influenced by changes in:

   a. mortgage interest rates

   b. death rates

   c. age brackets

   d. cost of construction

7. The government's use of spending and taxing as a tool to control swings in the business cycle is called:

   a. automatic stabilizers

   b. fiscal policy

   c. monetary policy

   d. foreign policy

8. The government's use of money, credit, and interest rates as a tool to control swings in the business cycle is called:

   a. automatic stabilizers

   b. fiscal policy

   c. monetary policy

   d. foreign policy

9. During times of recession, the government can attempt to stimulate the economy by:

   a. decreasing government spending

   b. increasing taxes

   c. increasing interest rates

   d. increasing the supply of money

10. During times of rapid inflationary prosperity, the government can attempt to slow down the economy by:

   a. increasing government spending

   b. decreasing taxes

   c. decreasing interest rates

   d. decreasing the supply of money

Chapter 4

Money, Credit, and Real Estate

Preview

Money and credit have a critical effect on real estate activity. This chapter expands our explanation of economic principles and the role of the government in the economy by examining money's role in economic transactions. Section 4.1 discusses the functions of money and how it is created. It also examines the subject of inflation and its impact on the real estate market. Section 4.2 reviews the way that the Federal Reserve System controls the money supply in an effort to maintain economic growth and full employment without inflation. Section 4.3 emphasizes the impact that changes in the money supply has on real estate activity. The appendix discusses the savings and loan crisis. When you have finished this chapter you will be able to:

1. Explain what money is and describe how banks and other depository institutions create money.

2. Understand the purpose of the Federal Reserve System and describe three main tools it uses to regulate the flow of money and credit.

3. Discuss the impact that Federal Reserve policies have on real estate activity.

4. Outline the events that led to the savings and loan crisis.

49

Your understanding of money and credit will allow you to anticipate changes in the real estate market and explain to your clients the relationship between current real estate market conditions and shifts in the money supply.

4.1   THE SUPPLY OF MONEY

There is more to making money that just inking the printing presses. Most money in America is neither in coins nor bills; most money has been created by banks and other depository institutions in the form of demand deposits. This section explains the uses of money, the different types of money, and how money is created. Understanding the money supply is an important tool for understanding real estate economics.

WHAT IS MONEY?

1. *Money is a medium of exchange.* It allows people to exchange goods and services without the need to revert to a barter (or swap) system.

2. *Money is a measure of value.* It is used to compare the worth of unlike items. What is a home worth in relation to an automobile? What are the services of a physician worth as compared to the services of a plumber? Under a barter system, we might say that ten automobiles equal one home or two plumbers equal one doctor. Under our monetary system, each item is measured in dollars: an automobile, $20,000, a home, $200,000, a plumber, $40,000, a doctor, $100,000, and so on.

3. *Money is a store of value.* It is a way to save your wealth. If you choose not to buy goods and services immediately, you can store your right to spend later by saving money. But there are some risks. For example, what happens to your money during periods of inflation? Does it increase or decrease in value?

4. *Money is a standard of deferred payment.* It is used to describe what a debtor owes a creditor. If you buy now and pay later, the amount you owe is expressed in money.

WHAT MAKES "GOOD" MONEY?

Gold, silver, corn, cattle, and shells have been used as money at one time or another. Contrary to popular belief, money does not have to be a precious metal. Anything that is universally accepted by society can be used as money. In a practical sense, money should be *portable*, so that it is easy to carry; *durable*, so it will not lose its value by wearing away; *divisible*, so it can be broken down into smaller units; and *stable*, so that it will not radically change in value.

MONEY TODAY

Today, there are three types of money in the United States: *coins*, *paper currency*, and *checking accounts*. Pennies, nickels, dimes, quarters, half-dollars, and dollar coins make up our coin system. The metallic value of coins is less than their face value. If the value of the metal should exceed the value of the coin, people would tend to hoard the coins and then illegally melt them down in order to sell the metal. Coins account for approximately 2 percent of our total money supply.

Paper currency ($1, $5, $10, and other bills) makes up approximately 25 percent of our total money supply. These bills, issued by the Federal Reserve, are essentially promissory notes. Federal Reserve notes circulate as money and will continue to do so as long as people have faith in the strength of the government. Contrary to popular belief, our paper money is no longer backed by gold in Fort Knox, Kentucky. The only thing backing our currency is the strength of the government.

The rest of our money supply, some 73 percent, consists of checks drawn against checking accounts—bank money. *In economic terms, checking accounts are called demand deposits.* When you write a check, you are transferring a portion of your bank deposit to a third party. The bank must pay this money upon demand. No time delays are allowed, hence the term *demand deposit.*

DEPOSITORY INSTITUTIONS CREATE MONEY

Only the federal government may legally mint coins and print paper currency, but depository institutions such as banks and savings and loan associations can legally create demand deposits or checks. At one time only commercial banks could issue checks and create money. But the Depository Institutions Deregulation and Monetary Control Act of 1980 plus other laws now allow various depository institutions, namely savings and loan associations, to also issue checks and create money. For simplicity, all depository institutions will simply be referred to as "banks."

Banks create money because of a concept known as *fractional reserve banking.* Federal law requires that the bank must set aside a reserve for each deposit received. These reserves cannot be used to meet withdrawals, but rather are used to give the Federal Reserve Board control over the money creating ability of banks.

SPECIAL INTEREST TOPIC

Tangibles in Times of Uncertainty

During rapid inflation and/or political unrest some people abandon paper currency and seek refuge in tangibles, such as precious metals, art, antiques, real estate, and so on. The key is to find some item that has a limited supply which cannot be easily expanded. As people swarm to these tangibles, their prices skyrocket. If the panic subsides, the price of the tangible levels off or declines.

This trend can be seen in some South American countries. There, runaway inflation has driven many South Americans to acquire tangibles outside their own countries, such as U.S. real estate.

Speculators capitalize on the trends by attempting to purchase on the low side and then ride the upswing and sell just before the market declines. If, on the other hand, prices continue to rise, the tangible may become a good long-term hedge against inflation.

HOW FRACTIONAL RESERVES CREATE MONEY

To see how banks actually create money, let us assume that federal law requires that 20 percent of each deposit in checking accounts must be kept as a reserve. The remaining 80 percent can be used to create a loan. Actual reserve requirements are less than 20 percent and they vary with the size of the institution's deposits. Twenty percent is used here because it is easily divisible.

Now let us assume that $1,000 is deposited into Bank A. Bank

A will put $200 in reserve and loan out $800 to Mr. X. Mr. X will take the $800 and spend it. The receiver of this money will probably deposit the funds into Bank B. Bank B now has an $800 deposit, of which $160—20 percent—is kept in reserve, and $640 is loaned out to Ms. Y. Ms. Y spends the $640 and the receiver deposits the money into Bank C. Bank C now has a $640 deposit of which $128 is kept in reserve and $512 is loaned out. In theory, this process continues until all funds are exhausted. Table 4.1 illustrates this process.

A single $1,000 deposit under a 20 percent reserve requirement can expand to become a $5,000 deposit, $4,000 of which is loaned out. In essence, the banking system has created additional purchasing power (demand deposits). This has the same effect on spending as increasing the amount of coin and paper money.

In the real world, does this creation of bank money always occur at a constant, smooth rate? Not usually! Some banks differ in their reserve policy (choose to hold more reserves than required by law) and the amount of loans available from each deposit varies between banks. In addition, "leakage" occurs when people fail to deposit money in banks. Going back to Table 4.1, what would happen if the borrower of the $640 from Bank B buys merchandise, and the store owners put the $640 under their mattress instead of depositing the money in Bank C?

FEDERAL DEPOSIT INSURANCE

With only a fraction of actual deposits in reserve, won't a bank or other savings institution fail if depositors panic and attempt a "run" on the bank by trying to withdraw all their savings? Prior to the establishment of the Federal Deposit Insurance Corporation (FDIC) this was a distinct possibility. The FDIC is a federal agency, backed by the full faith of the U.S. government, that insures depositors up to $100,000. If a bank or savings and loan association fails, the government will pay insured depositors up to $100,000 to cover their lost savings. The key here is insured savings. Some securities issued by banks and thrift institutions are not insured by the FDIC and a subsequent institution failure could result in a total loss of money invested in these types of securities. See the appendix, *The Eco-*

TABLE 4.1 How Banks Create Money

Banks	Deposits	Reserves	Loans
Bank A	$ 1,000.00	$ 200.00	$ 800.00
Bank B	800.00	160.00	640.00
Bank C	640.00	128.00	512.00
Bank D	512.00	102.40	409.60
Bank E	409.60	81.92	327.68
All other banks together	1,638.40	327.68	1,310.72
TOTALS	$ 5,000.00	$ 1,000.00	$ 4,000.00

nomic Impact of the Savings and Loan Crisis, at the end of this chapter.

TOO MUCH MONEY CAN CAUSE INFLATION AND HARM REAL ESTATE MARKETS

As the money supply expands, interest rates tend to drop and credit becomes easier to obtain. This stimulates spending and increases the demand for resources, goods, and services. But a point is reached where additional increases in the money supply will stimulate demand beyond the ability of the economy to increase supply. *The result will be inflation—a rise in general prices—too much money chasing too few goods.*

Inflation hurts people on fixed incomes, creditors, and workers who are unable to gain wage increases to offset inflation. Inflation also harms real estate markets. However, the federal government gains during inflation, because inflation often pushes people into higher income tax brackets. This is, in effect, a "hidden" tax.

REAL ESTATE MARKETS AND INFLATION

In periods of inflation, mortgage lenders are hurt because the money they receive from loan repayments is worth less than the money they originally loaned. Thus, to protect themselves during periods of rapid inflation, mortgage lenders increase interest rates. An increase in interest rates causes monthly payments to increase, thereby preventing some potential buyers from qualifying for loans. This reduces the demand for real estate.

Inflation can cause some depositors in thrift institutions, such as savings and loan associations, to withdraw their funds and seek higher returns in other parts of the money market. This sometimes reduces the money available for mortgages.

During inflation, the cost of the components of construction (land, labor, and materials) rises. This increases the cost of construction and drives some people out of the housing market.

SPECIAL INTEREST TOPIC

Classifications of the Money Supply

For monitoring and analysis, the Federal Reserve classifies the money supply as follows:

M1 = coins, paper money, and demand deposits

M2 = M1, plus items that can quickly be converted to money, such as small savings accounts, CDs, and money market accounts.

M3 = M2, plus large CDs of over $100,000

DEMAND-PULL INFLATION

COST-PUSH INFLATION

Two Types of Inflation

Demand-Pull Type

"Too much money chasing too few goods." Sellers are producing at full capacity and find it impossible to expand supply. Additional demand, fed by easy money and liberal fiscal policy, drives up prices. This type of inflation is curbed by reducing government spending and by reducing the money supply in order to slow down demand to the point where supply and demand are balanced.

Cost-Push Type

Prices are pushed up because production costs (land, labor, and capital) are increasing.

Controversy: Do strong labor unions force wages up, causing business to raise prices? Or does business raise prices, forcing unions to seek higher wages? Economists are still trying to find a solution to this type of inflation. Government wage and price controls have been used, but their success is debatable.

Increased prices also drive up the cost of purchasing the basic necessities of life. In effect, this reduces discretionary income— money for luxuries and leisure. A decline in discretionary income has harmful effects on the recreational and leisure real estate markets, such as vacation homes, motels, and tourist attractions.

Finally, inflation strikes at the basic core of decision making. Uncertainties about price changes cause businesses and consumers to act hastily, to become dismayed, discouraged, and confused. Ultimately, this causes major disruptions for all sectors of our economy.

THE IMPORTANCE OF CONTROLLING THE SUPPLY OF MONEY

As discussed in the previous chapter, an increase or decrease in the money supply can be used to counteract fluctuations in our economy. However, there is always the danger that too much money can cause an inflation, while not enough money can bring on a recession.

Section 4.2 discusses who controls our money supply and how it is done. Before you proceed, review your understanding of the following.

REVIEWING YOUR UNDERSTANDING

The Supply of Money

1. How has the Federal Deposit Insurance Corporation (FDIC) strengthened our banking system?

2. If all banks keep 10 percent of deposits in reserve, what are the maximum deposits and loans that can be generated if a new $1,000 deposit is taken into the system?

3. If the economy is in a recession, and assuming you had the power, would you increase or decrease the percentage of reserves that banks must keep to back each deposit? Why?

4. How can too much money create inflation? What problems does this cause for real estate brokers?

4.2   THE FEDERAL RESERVE SYSTEM

The Federal Reserve System regulates most of our money supply. This section explains the tools available to the Federal Reserve and illustrates how these tools can counteract economic imbalances.

PURPOSE OF THE FEDERAL RESERVE SYSTEM

The purpose of the Federal Reserve System (hereafter referred to as The Fed) is to regulate the supply of money and credit in order to achieve economic growth without inflation and unemployment. In short, The Fed views itself as a "money doctor," attempting to cure or prevent economic sickness by controlling the flow of money and credit.

The Fed was established by Congress in 1913. The system consists of 12 regional reserve banks and a seven-member Board of Governors located in Washington, D.C. (see Figures 4.1 and 4.2). Each governor serves a 14-year term, in the hope that long-term appointments will insulate the governors against political pressures when making economic decisions.

HOW THE FEDERAL RESERVE ATTEMPTS TO CONTROL THE MONEY SUPPLY

Section 4.1 described how depository institutions create money by using fractional reserve banking. The amount held in reserve, you will recall, could not be loaned out. Control over the percentage of reserves, therefore, would constitute control over the money supply: an increase in the percentage of reserves causes a decrease in the money supply, while a decrease in reserve percentages will result in an increase in money and credit. This is exactly how The Fed operates. Using specific tools (frequently referred to as "weapons"), The Fed attempts to control our money supply by manipulating bank reserves.

MAJOR TOOLS OF THE FEDERAL RESERVE

The Fed controls bank reserves by using the following major tools.

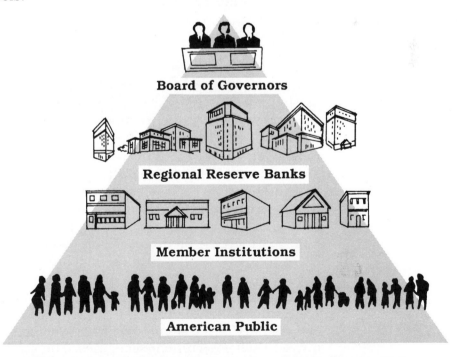

FIGURE 4.1   The Federal Reserve System. *Source: The Federal Reserve.*

FEDERAL RESERVE MAP OF THE UNITED STATES

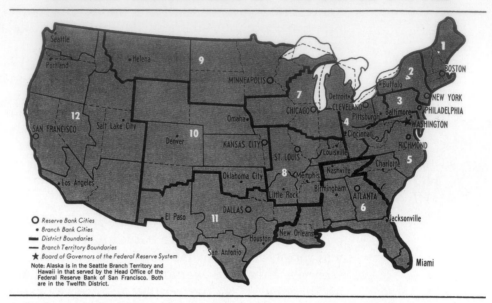

FIGURE 4.2   Federal Reserve map of the United States. *Source: The Federal Reserve.*

1. Changes in the reserve requirements.
2. Open-market operations.
3. Changes in the discount rate.

Changes in the Reserve Requirements

All depository institutions are required to keep a certain percentage of each deposit as reserves. The percentages are established by law. But the Board of Governors of the Federal Reserve have the right to vary the percentages within a certain range. These reserves are kept at the regional Federal Reserve Bank. If the Fed feels that easy money and credit are feeding inflation, it can raise the reserve requirements, which will force banks to restrict their lending, as money must be diverted from loans to cover the shortage in reserves. This action is designed to decrease the amount of money in circulation, drive up interest rates, and eventually lessen inflation by slowing down spending.

What will happen if The Fed decreases the reserve requirements? Will this increase or decrease the money supply? Will this raise or lower interest rates? Trace the steps to check your understanding.

Open-Market Operations

As part of its money-management tools, The Fed is allowed to buy and sell government securities. The public (private citizens and financial institutions) also may buy and sell government securities as a form of investment. When The Fed buys government securities from the public, the seller of these securities (the public) receives The

Fed's check, which the seller then deposits in a local bank. The local bank forwards the check to The Fed for payment. When The Fed receives its own check, it increases the reserves of the local bank by the amount of that check. The local bank now has more reserves than are required and therefore can grant more loans. *Thus, when The Fed buys government securities from the public, it increases the money supply by increasing bank reserves, which in turn will support more loans.*

What happens to the money supply when The Fed sells government securities to the public? The money supply tightens up, which increases interest rates and discourages borrowing. To help review your understanding, let us trace what happens when The Fed sells government securities.

When government securities are sold, an individual purchases them by writing a check on his or her local bank. The Fed receives the buyer's check and subtracts it from the reserve account of the local bank. The local bank now has fewer reserves and therefore must constrict its lending. *So when The Fed sells government securities, it decreases bank reserves, which in turn decreases the bank's ability to grant loans.*

Once again we notice that the ultimate effect is a change in the money supply by manipulating bank reserves. But The Fed has still another important tool—changes in the discount rate.

Changes in the Discount Rate

When you need a loan, you frequently go to your bank. Where does a bank go when it needs a loan? One possible place is the Federal Reserve. The Fed is considered a banker's bank. When you borrow from your bank, you pay interest. When a bank borrows from The Fed, it is charged an interest rate known as the *discount rate*.

By decreasing the discount rate, The Fed can encourage banks to borrow. The borrowed funds will increase the local bank's deposits and reserves, which allows for the expansion of loans. An increase in the discount rate will discourage banks from borrowing, which will decrease the amount of money available for loans.

FEDERAL FUNDS RATE

Although not technically listed as a major tool of The Fed, the federal funds rate is one of the most closely watched indicators as to the current thinking of the Federal Reserve people. What is the federal funds rate? When one bank is at its maximum loan to reserve requirement, it cannot grant additional loans to expand business until its reserves are increased. Or if the bank has granted too many loans relative to its existing reserves, it must by law either call in some loans or increase its reserves. One way to solve these problems is to borrow excess reserves from another bank which currently is not granting additional loans. The *federal funds rate*, then, is the rate of interest one bank charges another for the overnight use of excess reserves.

The Federal Reserve, in its effort to fight inflation or recession, increases or decreases the money supply to keep the federal funds rate among banks in a certain trading range. If The Fed wishes to allow the economy to expand, it may allow the federal funds rate to drop below the trading range. This will encourage one bank to borrow the excess reserves of another and use the reserves to grant more loans which should expand the economy. If The Fed wishes to slow the economy, it may tighten up the money supply and force the federal funds rate to rise. This will discourage one bank from borrowing excess reserves from another bank, thereby not granting additional loans. This will tend to keep the economy from expanding.

A SUMMARY OF THE MAJOR FEDERAL RESERVE TOOLS

Changes in the reserve requirement, open-market operations, and changes in the discount rate allow The Fed to control the supply of bank money. Of these tools, the most commonly used is that of open-market operations.

To increase the money supply, The Fed will either decrease the reserve requirement, buy government securities, decrease the discount rate, or use some combination of all three.

To decrease the money supply, The Fed will either increase the reserve requirements, sell government securities, increase the discount rate, or use some combination of all three.

REVIEWING YOUR UNDERSTANDING

The Federal Reserve System

1. Why does the Federal Reserve system view itself as a "money doctor"?

2. If The Fed wishes to stimulate demand in an effort to fight a recession, would it increase or decrease bank reserves? What should it do under open-market operations? Under the discount rate?

3. Why are the governors of the Federal Reserve System appointed for 14 years? Who is the current chairman of the Federal Reserve System?

4.3   THE ACTIONS OF THE FEDERAL RESERVE BOARD AND THEIR EFFECTS ON REAL ESTATE ACTIVITY

This section explains how the money supply and The Fed's attempt to regulate it can influence the real estate market. The section also points out that the cycle for real estate will not always be in step with the general economic trends.

TIGHT-MONEY POLICIES AND REAL ESTATE

The Fed institutes a restrictive monetary policy in order to combat inflation. Inflation itself is frequently caused by excessive private demand, government deficits, or a swollen money supply.

When The Fed fights inflation, it tightens up the money supply, which in turn causes interest rates to rise as government agencies and corporate borrowers bid against one another for the shrinking money supply. Higher interest rates cause funds to flow out of depository institutions, as savers go elsewhere seeking higher rates of return. Depository institutions have the biggest share of home mortgages. Thus, when savings institutions lose funds, mortgage lending decreases, and the real estate market heads into a recession. The economic term for the outflow of funds from depository institutions into corporate and government notes is called *disintermediation*.

As a result, when The Fed tightens money to combat inflation, housing is one of the first economic sectors to feel the pinch. This frequently brings cries of "discrimination" from the real estate industry.

DOES THE FED DISCRIMINATE AGAINST HOUSING WHEN IT TIGHTENS MONEY?

Does The Fed really discriminate against housing? In the purest sense, the answer is no. When The Fed decreases the money supply, it does not single out just the real estate market and crimp only housing funds. Historically, real estate mortgages in tight-money markets are usually unattractive investments because they are long-term loans bearing low to moderate fixed interest rates.

During periods of prosperity and inflation, interest rates for other investments tend to rise. Many savers and institutional lenders refuse to lend on low-paying, long-term mortgages and instead are attracted to high-yield, short-term business loans. As the demand for funds continues to exceed the supply, interest rates on Treasury and federal agency instruments also increase, and disintermediation takes place. The Fed does not specifically discriminate against housing; rather, the structure of the mortgage market tends to defeat itself in tight-money situations.

EASY-MONEY POLICIES AND REAL ESTATE

During periods of economic slowdown, The Fed attempts to head off a recession by easing the money supply. An increase in money and credit may cause spending to increase, and this expansion will ideally bring an increase in employment.

As money and credit become more plentiful, interest rates tend to decline. These lower interest rates do not immediately attract business borrowers because the economic turndown still leaves a lingering feeling of pessimism. Meanwhile, private savings may increase as uncertainty causes people to become cautious and to restrict their spending.

SPECIAL INTEREST TOPIC _____

U.S. Addiction to Foreign Capital

As noted earlier, politically the U.S. Congress and the president have been unwilling to face the reality of the budget deficit by cutting government spending or raising taxes, or some combination of the two. The easy short run "fix" has been to increase government borrowing to cover the deficit. A substantial amount of this borrowing has come from foreign investors. This need for foreign capital gives rise to a couple of questions: does the dependence on foreign capital reduce The Fed's ability to influence U.S. interest rates? If so, does this mean that The Fed's ability to use monetary techniques to help control the U.S. economy has been weakened? Although it is too soon to tell for sure, it appears that trends in the financial markets in Japan and Europe (both large buyers of U.S. bonds) have a strong influence on U.S. interest rates. This in turn makes The Fed's job more difficult. High or low interest rates in foreign markets will have an impact on what U.S. interest rates must do to attract foreign investors to help finance the U.S. budget deficit. High interest rates could be counter to The Fed's wishes. For example, the U.S. economy could be in a slump. Monetary policy calls for lowering interest rates to stimulate production and jobs in such a situation. But lower interest rates would discourage foreign investors, thereby forcing Congress and the president to cut government spending or raise taxes. This would tend to depress the economy even further. This is just another example of what impact the globalization of financial markets has on domestic economies in the 1990s.

Financial institutions find that savings are piling up. The Fed is making more money available, but few businesses are borrowing. So lenders look more favorably at real estate mortgages as an outlet for funds. As money moves back into the mortgage market, the demand for housing, which was previously suppressed by a lack of credit, begins to pick up, and the real estate market slowly recovers.

RECOVERY IN THE REAL ESTATE MARKET NORMALLY PRECEDES A RECOVERY IN THE NATIONAL ECONOMY

Because of the size and impact of the construction industry, an increase in home building helps to lead the economy out of a recession. As home construction picks up, employment, income, and spending increase. This in turn generates even more activity, and the general business cycle heads for recovery.

However, if spending and demand rise beyond the equilibrium point, inflation will recur. If this happens, The Fed may tighten up the money supply, and the mortgage market will start to lose funds, causing real estate activity to decline.

The real estate market (cycle) in the short run tends to travel somewhat opposite to the general business cycle. When the general economy is at the top of a boom, real estate activity is usually already declining because of a tightening of credit. When the general economy slows down, real estate activity may increase as funds flow back into the mortgage market.

MORTGAGE MARKET REFORMS

With the introduction of adjustable rate mortgages, money market certificate accounts, and a vastly improved secondary mortgage market, savings institutions are becoming somewhat insulated against excessive disintermediation. Starting in the mid-1970s, both the general economy and the real estate market prospered simultaneously for the first time since World War II. However, these mortgage market reforms have driven up the cost of money for savings institutions and the higher costs are being passed to mortgage borrowers in the form of higher interest rates.

REVIEWING YOUR UNDERSTANDING

The Actions of the Federal Reserve Board and Its Effects on Real Estate Activity

1. How do tight-money policies of the Federal Reserve System influence the real estate market?

2. What causes disintermediation from savings and loan associations? How does this affect real estate markets?

3. Why does a recovery in the real estate market usually precede a recovery in the national economy?

CHAPTER SUMMARY

Money acts as a medium of exchange, a measure of value, a store of value, and a standard for deferred payment. There are three types of money: coins, paper currency, and demand deposits (checking accounts). Demand deposits are by far the most important part of our money supply.

Although only the federal government may legally mint coins and print currency, our banks and other depository institutions create checking account money. Banks create this money by fractional reserve banking.

The amount of money in circulation has a tremendous influence on the performance of our economy. Too much money and credit can create inflation, while too little can cause a recession. In an effort to control the flow of money and credit, Congress established the Federal Reserve System (frequently referred to as The Fed).

The Fed attempts to control our money supply by using three main "tools": changes in the reserve requirements, open-market operations, and changes in the discount rate. All of these tools control the credit-creating ability of banks by manipulating the amount of money banks must keep as a reserve. If a bank's reserve rate is high, the bank can lend less money. If a bank's reserve rate is low, the bank can lend more money.

If The Fed feels that there is too much inflation, it will attempt to tighten up the money supply. It does this by increasing the reserve requirements, raising the discount rate, or selling government securities in the open market. As the money supply tightens, one of the hardest hit areas is the real estate market. Tight money and high interest rates make mortgage credit scarce and expensive. This makes it difficult to buy or build a home, and activity in the real estate market declines.

On the other hand, if our economy is heading for a recession, The Fed may increase the money supply. This encourages more spending and helps to slow the recession. An increase in the money supply is called an "easy money" policy. During the early periods of easy money, activity in the real estate market picks up as interest rates decline and mortgage credit becomes more plentiful. Because of the size and impact of the construction industry, an increase in home building helps to lead the economy out of a recession.

However, if spending and demand rise beyond our economy's ability to supply goods and service, inflation recurs. If this happens, The Fed may again tighten up the money supply so that funds flow out of the mortgage-lending institutions (disintermediation). This will cause a drop in real estate activity, and once again it becomes difficult to buy and sell homes. Understanding the impact that changes in the money supply have on local real estate activity is one of the most important concepts for successful real estate investments.

IMPORTANT TERMS AND CONCEPTS

Changes in the discount rate

Changes in the reserve
   requirement

Demand Deposits

Disintermediation

Easy-money policies

Federal funds rate

Federal reserve system

Fractional reserve banking

Inflation

Measure of value

Medium of exchange

Open-market operations

Store of value

Tight-money policies

REVIEWING YOUR UNDERSTANDING

1. Which of the following *is not* considered a function of money?
   a. medium of exchange
   b. measure of value
   c. standard of deferred payment
   d. standard of tangible asset

2. The greatest percentage of the U.S. money supply is represented by:
   a. checks
   b. coins
   c. paper currency
   d. certificates of deposit

3. If the banking system is using a ten percent reserve requirement, an initial $1,000 deposit can expand to a maximum of how much in new loans?
   a. $1,000
   b. $5,000
   c. $9,000
   d. $10,000

4. If the Federal Reserve wishes to expand the money supply it could:
   a. increase the reserve requirements
   b. raise the discount rate
   c. buy government bonds
   d. increase the federal funds rate

5. The rate of interest that one bank charges another for the overnight use of excess reserves is called:
   a. prime rate
   b. discount rate
   c. federal funds rate
   d. commercial rate

6. The flow of funds from thrift institutions to the general money market is called:
   a. reintermediation
   b. disintermediation
   c. run on the bank
   d. recapitalization

7. Which of the following actions by The Fed tends to raise interest rates?

    a. selling government securities

    b. lowering the discount rate

    c. decreasing reserve requirements

    d. reducing the federal funds rate

8. The increase in the use of foreign capital tends to motivate Congress and the president to solve the U.S. budget deficit problem.

    a. true

    b. false

9. Which government agency insures savings accounts at approved depository institutions?

    a. Federal Reserve System

    b. Federal Home Loan Bank

    c. Federal Deposit Insurance Corporation

    d. Federal Trust Association

10. Which of the following is true?

    a. U.S. paper currency is not backed by gold.

    b. Inflation is always good for real estate because prices go up.

    c. Government deficits decrease the government's need to borrow.

    d. All economists agree that monetary policy is better than fiscal policy for controlling the economy.

APPENDIX: The Economic Impact of the Savings and Loan Crisis

BACKGROUND

By the early 1980s excessive inflation during the previous decade had placed the savings and loan (S&L) industry in a financial bind. High interest rates were being paid by banks and money market funds to attract depositors, but savings and loans were prohibited by law from paying interest above a low passbook account rate. Thus, deposits were flowing out of S&Ls into other investments. In the meantime the savings and loan industry was saddled with a huge inventory of low fixed interest rate mortgages made in earlier years. The resale value of these loans was low because of the discount needed to increase the yield to the level demanded by investors. In short, the asset value of the entire industry was declining and it looked like the real estate market, which was closely tied to the savings and loan industry, was heading for trouble.

THE PROPOSED SOLUTION

Deregulating the savings and loan industry and allowing its owners and managers to compete in the general marketplace, as did banks and other financial institutions, was the proposed solution. This in turn should stimulate the general economy and boost the real estate market. The following major events set this proposed solution in motion:

1. In 1980, Congress passed the Depository Institutions Deregulation and Monetary Control Act. This law, in a series of phases, lifted interest rate ceilings for S&Ls and allowed the industry to issue checking accounts and certificates of deposits, grant commercial real estate and consumer loans, acquire stocks and bonds, and own and operate real estate development companies and mutual funds, and many other ventures.

2. In 1981, Congress passed the Economic Reform Act to stimulate the economy, which was in a recession. One of the main provisions of this act was favorable accelerated depreciation for real estate investors. This in turn started a boom in new residential, commercial, and industrial development. The savings and loan industry was heavily involved in financing these projects. Many projects were built on speculation, without a buyer or tenant under contact. This was especially true in the rapidly expanding mountain and southwest states.

3. In 1982, Congress passed the Depository Institutions Act (Garn Bill) which continued the trend of deregulation, and had another important feature. This law allowed real estate lenders to enforce due-on-transfer clauses, thereby allowing lenders to call their existing low interest rate loans when a property is transferred to a new owner, rather than being stuck with the loan via a loan assumption.

4. After much promotion, real estate lenders were able to convince the public to accept the concept of adjustable rate mortgages (ARMs). This helped to protect the value of the lender's portfolio by passing the risk of future inflation to the borrower and away from the lender. In addition, an ever sophisticated secondary market allowed lenders to package and resell their existing mortgages faster and not be stuck with unwanted inventory.

These events plus others placed savings and loan associations on an equal footing with other financial institutions, giving S&L owners and managers the economic freedom to go to the marketplace and generate profits.

WHAT HAPPENED?

Why do we have a savings and loan crisis? Why did Congress need to pass the "bailout" legislation known as the Financial Institutions Reform Recovery and Enforcement Act of 1989 (FIRREA)? Did deregulation fail? Did the "free market theory" fail to work?

It will be many years before these questions will be fully answered, but here are some concepts to consider.

1. The collapse of oil prices led to the economic crash in the "oil patch" and mountain states (Texas, Louisiana, Oklahoma, Colorado, and Utah), which in turn led to massive real estate foreclosures and other business failures. After a decade of oil shortages, who in the late 1970s and early 1980s dreamed that we would have an oversupply of oil in the mid-1980s? Had oil prices remained stable, might the savings and loans in these regions still be solvent?

2. Did deregulation really create a free market? Savings and loan managers were able to use government insured deposits to invest in various ventures. Thus, a case can be made that there was not a free market. If government deposit insurance was not available, a depositor would scrutinize the financial background of the savings and loan association before depositing savings, just like a prudent investor would in any other non-guaranteed investment. With no government insurance, it is likely that savings depositors would have avoided the weak, poorly managed institutions, thereby depriving those institutions of the funds needed to make investments. Instead, depositors placed money with institutions knowing that it did not matter if they were good or bad because the government would guarantee up to $100,000 worth of savings.

3. If the government was going to maintain the deposit insurance program, would it not be prudent for the president and Congress to provide adequate funds for the inspection and examination of savings institutions? Instead, it has been reported that the budgets of the bank and savings and loan examiners were cut during the 1980s. This made it easier for crooked owners and managers of S&Ls to loot the institutions. It also allowed incompetent, but not necessarily dishonest, managers to operate longer.

4. Another question is being asked: Did pressure from savings and loan association trade groups, along with their PAC fund contributions, generate political favors that added to the crisis?

5. It must be pointed out that many savings and loan associations were financially solid and profitable throughout this period. Apparently deregulation and free market forces worked for these institutions.

As with many economic issues, there are no clear cut answers to the questions posed by the S&L crisis. Economists will be debating its causes for many years to come. Politicians, industry leaders, and consumer action groups will be pointing fingers. But in the end, the U.S. taxpayer will foot most of the bill.

Chapter 5

Important Economic Features of Real Estate

Preview

This chapter sketches the basic economic features of real estate. A more in-depth analysis of residential, commercial, industrial, and rural real estate markets will be presented in later chapters.

Section 5.1 discusses the major differences between a perfectly competitive market and typical real estate markets. Section 5.2 outlines how real estate markets react when the demand for real property changes. Section 5.3 presents a short discussion on the advantages and disadvantages of foreign ownership of U.S. real estate.

Chapter 5 completes Part One, *Basic Economic Background for Real Estate Analysis*. When you have completed this chapter you will be able to:

1. List five reasons why a real estate market is considered to be imperfect.

2. Describe why real estate markets need the services of real estate professionals.

3. Discuss why the supply and use of land is considered fixed in the short run.

4. Describe how an increase or decrease in demand influences the value of real estate.

5.1   ECONOMIC CHARACTERISTICS OF REAL ESTATE MARKETS

A market was previously defined as a place where buyers and sellers meet to exchange items of value. The character or makeup of a particular market influences the level of prices paid. In a perfectly competitive market, there are numerous buyers and sellers, each assumed to be knowledgeable and free to move in or out of the market at will. Neither party has control over the market. Because the products being sold are assumed to be alike, buyers will always select the one offered at the lowest price. In such a perfect market, prices would be established purely by the principles of supply and demand.

In practice, most markets are imperfect. Some of the characteristics of a perfect market are either missing or distorted, preventing the principles of supply and demand from operating efficiently.

Are real estate markets perfectly competitive or are they imperfect? The answers may be found in Table 5.1, which compares the characteristics of a perfect market and a typical real estate market.

Table 5.1 shows that real estate markets are imperfect. The essential characteristics are: real estate buyers and sellers are usually uninformed about real estate values and trends in the marketplace; the transfer of real property requires a legal and technical knowledge not possessed by the average citizen; each real estate parcel is separate and unique from all other parcels; and the location of the land cannot be moved to capitalize on better market conditions in other geographic areas. All of these things create an imperfect market for real estate activities.

DOES THIS MEAN THAT THE PRINCIPLES OF SUPPLY AND DEMAND DO NOT WORK IN REAL ESTATE MARKETS?

No, the principles of supply and demand are still an important factor influencing the value of real estate. However, it is important to recognize that the principles operate differently in real estate markets. In a perfectly competitive market, supply and demand react quickly to changes in market conditions. *In real estate markets, supply cannot respond quickly to changes in market conditions.* Let us examine why.

TABLE 5.1   Perfect Markets Versus Typical Real Estate Markets

Characteristic	Perfect Market	Typical Real Estate Market
1. Number of buyers and sellers	Many participants; no monopoly, oligopoly, or monopolistic competition.	Few participants; seller controls during a "seller's" market, buyer controls during a "buyer's" market.
2. Product knowledge and market exchange	Buyers and sellers are highly knowledgeable; the exchange takes place with ease.	Buyers and sellers are not knowledgeable; the exchange is legalistic, complex, and expensive.
3. Standardized products	All products are alike and interchangeable; there is little difference between products of different sellers.	Each parcel of real estate is unique and separate from all others; no two are exactly alike.
4. Mobility	Products can be transported to capitalize on more lucrative markets.	The location is fixed; a real estate parcel cannot be moved to another more profitable location; a real estate market is local, not regional or national.
5. Size and frequency of purchase	The item purchased is small and relatively inexpensive; it is purchased frequently.	Real estate is purchased infrequently (rarely more than four or five times in a lifetime); a home represents the largest single investment made by the average family.
6. Government's role	Government plays little if any role; laissez-faire prevails.	Government plays a dominant role in encouraging or discouraging real estate development through the use of fiscal and monetary tools and by use of other controls, such as zoning, environmental, and health codes.
7. Prices	Prices are established by the smooth action of supply and demand.	Prices are influenced by the interaction of supply and demand, but this interaction is not smooth; a lack of knowledge by either the buyer or seller can distort the prices paid.

The Supply of Land Is Fixed

One of the most fundamental principles of real estate economics is the recognition that the total amount of land is fixed. The land surface cannot be increased or decreased according to the whims of demand. However, the *intensity of land use* can change, and in time this will increase or decrease the supply of real estate. For example, it may be impossible to increase the number of acres within your community, but you can increase the number of homes per acre. If home construction increases, this will generate an increase in the supply of homes, but not necessarily an increase in the supply of land.

In the Short Run, Land Use Is Also Fixed

Any change in the intensity of land use takes time. If the demand for residential or other real estate projects were suddenly to increase, developers would need considerable time to acquire land and obtain permits and financing. The state and local permit process could take years.

Once a building is constructed, it tends to have a long life, regardless of the short-run changes in the real estate market. For example, if the demand for homes declines, a builder with an unsold supply of houses will not demolish them simply because the demand for the homes has diminished. Instead, the homes will sit vacant on the market until they are sold. If they remain unsold, eventually the lender will foreclose and then sell the inventory at discount prices.

A Fixed Supply Means That Real Estate Prices Fluctuate with Demand

If the supply of real estate is fixed, short-run current market prices and rents will be determined by changes in demand. When the demand goes up, prices and rents rise as buyers and renters attempt to outbid one another for a fixed supply. When the demand goes down, prices and rents decline because a decrease in demand creates some vacancies, and owners and landlords attempt to fill these vacancies by lowering prices.

REVIEWING YOUR UNDERSTANDING

Economic Characteristics of Real Estate

1. Why is a real estate market classified as "imperfect"?

2. What is meant by the statement, "The supply of land is fixed, but in time the number of real estate uses can be increased"?

3. If in the short run the supply of real estate is fixed, what happens to prices and rents if demand increases? If demand decreases?

5.2   HOW THE REAL ESTATE MARKET REACTS TO CHANGES IN DEMAND

An increase in the demand for real estate will generally have the following consequences.

1. An increase in demand will reduce existing real estate vacancies.

2. This reduction in vacancies will be followed by an increase in rents and prices, assuming no rent controls, as more people continue to bid for the fixed supply.

3. As demand pushes rents and prices up, a point is reached where investors and builders, motivated by profit potential, are drawn into the construction market.

4. Assuming favorable economic and governmental conditions, new construction takes place slowly, and the supply of real estate increases gradually.

5. As this new construction overtakes the increase in demand, vacancies begin to rise.

6. This increase in vacancies causes a fall in rents and prices. Price and rent declines may not be readily apparent, but instead show up as rent concessions, or favorable seller financing.

7. With lower rents and prices, the difference between building costs and sales prices begins to narrow, and profits disappear. This process is accelerated by the fact that increased construction actively forces up building costs, catching profits in a squeeze between rising costs and falling sales prices.

A decrease in the demand for real estate will generally have these consequences.

1. A decrease in demand causes an increase in vacancies.

2. The increase in vacancies will cause rents and prices to decline.

3. With lower rents and prices, people can now obtain more spacious quarters at no increase in costs. This may absorb the vacancy. If not, the continued vacancy will eventually force property owners to abandon their properties, allow them to go to foreclosure, or demolish the structures.

4. The real estate market will remain in this state until demand once again increases.[1]

[1] *A Teacher's Guide for Real Estate Economics*, California Department of Real Estate, prepared by Dr. William Hippaka, pp. 142–43, 1974, Sacramento, CA.

WHAT CAUSES SUPPLY AND DEMAND FOR REAL ESTATE TO CHANGE?

Changes in real estate demand are caused by changes in population, income, availability of mortgage credit, personal lifestyles, and governmental actions. Long-run changes in supply result from changes in the rate of construction, conversion, demolition, and from governmental actions.

However, the cause of change can vary for each type of real estate market. The reasons for changes in the supply or demand for residential real estate are often different from the reasons for changes in commercial, industrial, or rural real estate. The specific causes for changes in supply and demand will be examined in detail in Chapter 9, *Housing Markets*; Chapter 10, *Commercial and Industrial Markets*, and Chapter 11, *Rural and Recreational Real Estate Markets*.

FOREIGN OWNERSHIP OF U.S. REAL ESTATE[2]

In the last decade, major segments of real estate have shifted from being controlled by local developers, lenders, and agents, to a global international business with many foreigners playing a key role. Foreign investors initially acquired fully leased commercial properties with triple "A" tenants at excellent locations in major U.S. cities. Foreigners were perceived to be overpaying for the properties and driving up prices in the local real estate market. But now some foreign investors have either purchased or founded U.S. based real estate companies to acquire and manage their properties. Foreign development companies are also beginning to create projects from the ground up rather than depend upon existing buildings. Foreign investors are now considered marketwise, and are paying local market prices.

The entire issue of foreign ownership of U.S. businesses and real estate has emotions running high. Here are some of the advantages and disadvantages frequently quoted by persons on both sides of this issue.

Advantages of Foreign Ownership

1. Generates income for U.S. real estate owners who sell. This income is reinvested to stimulate the economy and provide additional employment.

2. Provides tax revenue to the government from the profits on the sale. This helps cover some of the budget deficit without raising tax rates or cutting government spending programs.

3. Generates commissions and fees for the real estate industry.

[2] Information based on Lawrence Bacow,"The Internationalization of the U.S. Real Estate Industry," Cambridge: Massachusetts Institute of Technology, 1989. For a copy and price, contact Director of Publications, MIT Center for Real Estate Development, Building W31–310, Cambridge, MA 02139.

Disadvantages of Foreign Ownership

1. Makes U.S. less self-sufficient and more dependent upon foreigners.

2. Gives the government less incentive to solve the budget deficit problem by providing a short-run "quick fix" using foreign capital instead of reducing government spending or raising taxes.

3. High prices keep local investors out of the real estate market.

No matter where a person stands on the issue of foreign ownership, it should be pointed out that U.S. citizens have been buying assets of foreign countries for decades. Americans supported free trade when they were buying into foreign countries; now that the reverse is true, some U.S. citizens are lobbying for restrictions.

THE ROLE OF THE REAL ESTATE PROFESSIONAL[3]

In perfectly competitive markets, there is no need for the services of a real estate professional or any other third party. Buyers and sellers are assumed to be fully knowledgeable and able to handle all transactions themselves. Because the real estate market is highly imperfect, the real estate professional has a major task: to help overcome these imperfections.

Real estate professionals can provide the following services.

1. Increase buyer and seller knowledge by:
   a. Providing current market information regarding selling prices and rents,
   b. Advising clients on investment opportunities,
   c. Providing information on alternative methods of financing and helping to close the transaction.

2. Increase the number of market participants by persuading owners to offer their property for sale and by encouraging people to acquire real estate. These efforts can increase the number of buyers and sellers and help to reduce one of the major problems of a real estate market—too few participants.

---

[3] *A Teacher's Guide for Real Estate Economics*, California Department of Real Estate, prepared by Dr. William Hippaka, pp. 142–43, 1974, Sacramento, CA.

REVIEWING YOUR UNDERSTANDING

How the Real Estate Market Reacts to Changes in Demand

1. If the demand for apartments increases, what will happen to vacancy rates? The price of apartment buildings?
2. Will an increase in real estate demand raise mortgage interest rates in the short run? In the long run?
3. If contractors build too many homes, what will happen to sales prices? Why?
4. As a broker, you have been asked by a consumer group to justify the need for the services of a real estate agent. What are some things you should point out?

CHAPTER SUMMARY

Real estate markets have unique economic characteristics that separate them from other markets. For example, real estate buyers and sellers are usually uninformed about real estate values and market trends. The transfer of real property requires a legal and technical knowledge not possessed by the average person. Each real estate parcel is unique, isolated, and tied to a single, fixed location. Real estate is purchased infrequently and often represents the largest single investment an individual will ever make. Once a real estate use is established, it tends to have a long physical and economic life.

These characteristics create a need for an expert to advise the uninformed. The expert's role is filled by real estate professionals who provide buyers and sellers with the market information needed to make rational real estate decisions.

The analysis of any real estate market requires the understanding of some basic facts about the supply and demand of real estate. The supply of land per se is fixed—it cannot be expanded. The supply of land usage is fixed in the short run. Thus, changes in current real estate values usually are the results of shifts in demand, not in supply.

Changes in demand result from changes in population, income, credit, lifestyles, and governmental action. Long-run changes in the supply of real estate structures are influenced by the rate of new construction, conversion, and demolition. However, each segment of the real estate market, whether residential, commercial, industrial, or rural, reacts differently and therefore must be analyzed separately. Recently an increased rate of foreign ownership of U.S. real estate has created debates regarding the "selling of America."

IMPORTANT TERMS AND CONCEPTS

Fixed land supply

Fixed short-run land uses

Real estate demand changes

Real estate market characteristics

Real estate professional's role

REVIEWING YOUR UNDERSTANDING

1. Which of the following is a characteristic of an imperfect real estate market?

   a. many and equal numbers of buyers and sellers

   b. highly knowledgeable buyers and sellers

   c. all products are alike

   d. fixed location

2. In a real estate "seller's market:"

   a. supply exceeds demand

   b. prices are declining

   c. there are many qualified buyers but few properties are for sale

   d. mortgage interest rates are very high

3. One of the key economic features of real estate is:

   a. relatively fixed supply

   b. fixed demand

   c. mobility

   d. low unit cost

4. An increase in demand will have what short-run impact on real estate prices and rents?

   a. prices and rents should decrease

   b. prices should decrease, but rents should increase

   c. prices and rents should increase

   d. prices should increase, but rents should decrease

5. The use of real estate brokers tends to make the real estate market:

   a. less perfect

   b. more imperfect

   c. more perfect

   d. does not influence the market one way or the other

6. Multiple listing services of a local real estate association tend to make the real estate market:

   a. less perfect
   b. more imperfect
   c. more perfect
   d. does not influence the market one way or the other

7. If the demand for commercial real estate increases, but "no growth" controls prevent new construction, rents per square foot in the short-run should:

   a. increase
   b. decrease
   c. remain the same
   d. shift downward

8. All of the following can influence the demand for real estate *except*:

   a. population
   b. mortgage interest rates
   c. rates of construction
   d. lifestyles

9. "Six months free rent" as a concession is in reality a(n):

   a. reduction in rent
   b. sign of an increase in the need for more construction
   c. sign of an increase in demand
   d. sign of a decrease in supply

10. Foreign ownership of U.S. real estate:

   a. provides needed capital for U.S. citizens
   b. in the short run increases government revenues
   c. helps maintain real estate prices
   d. does all of the above

Chapter 6

Regional and Community Analysis

Preview

In a pure sense there is a technical difference between a *community*, a *city*, and a *town*. In an effort to simplify, however, the three terms will be used interchangeably to refer to a centralized location where people live and work. A *region* will refer to a group of communities in a surrounding area. This chapter examines the factors that contribute to the location and economic health of a community. Section 6.1 discusses the origins of communities and describes how these origins affect the development of the community. Section 6.2 explores the reasons that cause a city to either grow or decline. Section 6.3 outlines techniques used to forecast a region's economic growth. When you have completed this chapter, you will be able to:

1. Discuss how communities are formed.
2. List the economic factors that cause communities to change.
3. Describe the major tools used to forecast a region's economic growth.
4. Locate data sources that help you forecast your community's economic growth.

6.1   THE ORIGINS OF COMMUNITIES

Economic activity has a major effect upon the location of a community and the value and use of real estate within the community. Once the roots of a community are understood, and current local economic trends interpreted, a forecast can be made of what might happen to the value of real estate within the community.

THE HISTORY OF COMMUNITIES

Early human beings lived as nomads. They migrated with the seasons and the availability of natural foods or wild game. In time, they selected caves or other shelters in areas that they visited repeatedly. They began to build simple structures at the stages in their journey. This style of life was typical of the California Indian tribes before the Spanish arrived.

At some point, early people began to build small clusters of dwellings in fixed locations; these were the earliest towns. Knowledge of these early people is very limited. It is believed that the first towns arose around 7000 B.C. in the valleys of the Tigris and Euphrates rivers, known as Mesopotamia, now part of Iraq. From the long history of communities, two important themes emerge: the reason why the original town location was selected and the reasons for the economic survival of the town after its beginning.

WHAT DETERMINES COMMUNITY LOCATION?

Every community faces the initial decision of where to locate. The factors that influence the choice of a site depend on why the community is being formed. Among early nomads, important factors often included water, sources of food, and protection from enemies. Later, the factors sometimes involved social reasons; for example, sites chosen for their religious significance or for governmental motives like regional development. But the majority of community sites appear to have been chosen because of their commercial significance. Commercial influences result in the formation of three types of towns:

1. The central town,
2. The transportation service town,
3. The special-function town.

Central Towns

A community that is a central town performs a variety of services for a surrounding area. Such communities tend to be evenly spaced throughout the productive countryside, each surrounded by the hinterland, or "tributary area," which it serves. Thus, when forest land is converted to agriculture, the growing population provides an opportunity for the start of a series of such central market towns. The California Central Valley and the American midwest are examples of areas with many central market towns.

Transportation Service Towns

In the second category are towns performing services along transportation routes. These towns seek locations, called nodes. Among the many types of nodes are those at a "break-cargo" point, which is a place where a shift in the transportation system or route, or an obstacle, requires the unloading and reloading of the transport vehicle. At this point, the goods being carried can be repackaged ("break-bulk"), processed, wholesaled, or otherwise manipulated more easily than elsewhere. Possible break-cargo points include ports, major rail intersections, freeway intersections, river forks, and mountain passes. Points where transportation systems require service also function in a similar manner, as shown by the many old railroad watering stops in the western United States, such as Ogden, Utah, and San Bernardino, California.

Special-Function Towns

The third type of commercial city concentrates on one special function or service, such as mining, government, or retirement. Examples of special-function towns include resort towns (e.g., Palm Springs), lumbering centers (e.g., Eureka, California), government towns (e.g., Washington D.C.), and university towns (e.g., Davis, California).

REASONS FOR AMERICAN CITY LOCATION

A study of American cities indicates a range of reasons for community origin. Some towns, such as Fort Bridger, Wyoming, were originally protection sites. Rossmoor (a senior-citizen development in Walnut Creek, California) is a more recent protection community.

Salt Lake City was a religious community created at a site chosen to provide protection by distance and isolation. Break-cargo points include such ocean ports as San Francisco Bay, Seattle, and San Diego. River forks were factors at Sacramento and Stockton, California; Denver, Colorado and Truckee, California owe their origins to mountain passes. The first plat of Los Angeles (Figure 6.1) suggests that the river and the ford over it were important to the early town's location.

HOW THE TOWN'S ORIGIN FITS IN

There are several keys to explaining a town's origin. Topography (the shape of the earth's surface) often influences where towns are located. For example, protection-type communities tend to be located at sites that offer some security, such as islands or mountaintops.

Moreover, all towns must have some contact with the world around them. The transportation systems then in use, combined with local topography and the town's purpose, determined where the initial town was sited. It may have been at the ship landing, the

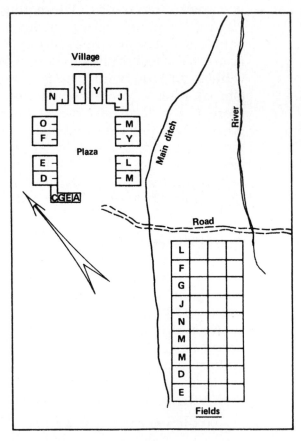

FIGURE 6.1 First plat of Los Angeles. *Source:* Richard M. Hurd, *Principles of City Land Values.* New York, The Record and Guide, 1903, p. 39.

railroad station, or the stage depot. This location is the point of contact with the outside world and becomes the focal point for the new town's growth.

The origin of a town, and the factors that influence its location, will shape the placement of buildings and streets in early years. In turn, these original buildings and streets have a major impact upon the shape and layout of the town, many years later, as it matures into a city. Therefore, in order to understand the factors that form a town's size, shape, and layout, a person must know the reason for the town's origin. Once the reasons for the town's origin are known, a person can better understand its growth pattern. When a city's growth pattern is understood, a real estate investor is better able to predict future paths of growth. These growth patterns, plus a reading of the area's mandated general plan, provide the information needed to analyze real estate investment opportunities.

REVIEWING YOUR UNDERSTANDING

Origins of Communities

1. What determines a town's location?
2. What are the three types of commercial cities? Give some local examples of each.
3. How does transportation affect the location of communities?

6.2   WHY THE COMMUNITY GROWS

The continued survival of communities requires that the residents' needs for food, clothing, shelter, and other necessities are met. Very few communities are completely self-sufficient. Therefore, each community must be able to pay for the imported goods that it needs. It must export goods, earn money, and use the money to buy needed imports.

THE COMMUNITY AS AN ECONOMY

Economic success is so essential to the continued existence of a community that economists are frequently hired to study and forecast the community's economic health. They pay particular attention to how a community develops export goods and services to pay for its imported goods and services. This is very similar to the principles of international trade that exist between countries. All businesses and employees are separated into two broad categories. Companies that produce goods and services locally to be shipped outside the community or region are called *basic industries* or *basic employment*, and companies that produce goods and services locally for use by people within the community or region are called *local* or *secondary industries or employment*. Economists then analyze the trends within these two categories to forecast the economic strength and growth potential for the community and its surrounding region.

The Need for New Export Jobs

Economic success for a community can take several forms. The simplest would be continued survival of a fixed population at a fixed standard of living. More complex forms would involve either growth in population ("volume" changes), growth in the economic welfare of individuals ("per capita" changes), or both.

Community survival without population or income change is not common in American society because the rate of births and immigration has been higher than the rate of deaths. These increasing numbers of people must be housed and fed. Communities have expanded their economic capacities in order to provide these necessities.

Outside forces, moreover, tend to upset the stable economic existence of the community. For example, the advent of the automobile created new jobs in some towns but eliminated jobs (such as making buggy whips) in other towns. As a result of changes in technology, tastes, resources, or other factors, all goods and services have somewhat limited lifetimes. New goods and services must be developed to replace those that become obsolete and unwanted. Thus, even the stable town finds itself in a race to encourage new jobs. Projected natural increases in population require further job (and export) increases if the new workers are to be employed.

Where Do Export Goods and Services Come From?

In the early days of a town's existence, its export opportunities are restricted by the community's limited size and capabilities. Often, the only possible export is some simple local resource, such as cattle, grain, ores, timber, or fish. For other communities, the only available export may be labor skills, exported for the day or the week or the year. When the workers bring their earnings back, the money supports the community. This is evident today as Mexican nationals work in the U.S. and return and/or send money to their families in Mexico.

As the community grows, additional resources can be developed into export items. Quite often, the resource itself requires processing that can be done locally, leading to the export of processed goods instead of raw materials. In turn, the processing develops local skills, which are a new marketable resource.

If the shift in exports from resources to processed goods is successful, towns that were originally formed for resource exploitation can still survive when the resource is exhausted by having the raw materials shipped to local processing plants with a skilled work-force.

A complex example is Detroit, which was a wheat-shipping port many years ago. Its workers learned how to repair broken steam engines of wheat ships, then how to make needed spare parts, and finally how to make entire engines. They became so expert at man-ufacturing steam engines and similar machinery that early automo-bile designers were drawn there for technical help with engine designs.

This analysis of community economic growth focuses on the products or services that are developed. Readers will find *The Economy of Cities*, by Jane Jacobs, a fascinating presentation of this type of analysis. She suggests that two main growth methods are impor-tant. The first method generates new export products. The second method develops local production of goods that were previously im-ported. When this happens, the product is no longer imported or the import quantities are reduced. In turn, this change frees export earn-ings that can be used to buy some other needed imports. In the Detroit example, workers learned to make spare parts that had pre-viously been imported. This was a key step in the evolution of Detroit from a port to a manufacturing center.

Production Efficiency

The efficiency of production is a third path to economic growth. A fixed work force could export more goods if local manufacturing could increase its productivity. This would mean obtaining more production without the use of added labor, but rather by using so-phisticated equipment. However, this path to economic growth may be resisted by workers. The increase in productivity acts to reduce the number of workers needed for a particular productive level. This means firings, retraining, and change, which some firms and work-ers resist. From society's view, however, increased productivity is good because the freed worker can be used to produce other goods and services. Thus the total amount of goods and services available to the community can grow without any increase in the numbers of workers.

Modern Growth

There have been studies in recent years of the economic growth of American towns. Because the data available are limited, the stud-ies examine the growth of employment rather than the growth of goods and services produced. The studies show that two main fac-tors are significant to regional economic change.

The first factor is the growth rate of an area's export industries. Much of the recent emphasis in community economic growth has been on the "glamour" industries—those with rapid business growth. Every growing community, for example, has sought to at-tract electronics manufacturing plants because of their growth rate and limited pollution.

TABLE 6.1 Industrial Location Factors

Raw Materials	cost_____availability_____
Selling Markets	near_____far_____
Transportation	cost_____availability_____
Labor	cost_____quality_____quantity_____
Water	cost_____quality_____quantity_____
Energy	cost_____quantity_____
Community Attitude	positive_____negative_____
Taxes	high_____low_____
Site Cost	high_____moderate_____low
Environmental Controls	restrictive_____moderate_____

The second major factor in regional economic change is the shift of an industry from one location to another. This shift can occur whether the industry's nationwide activity is growing or declining. At the new location, however, the industry will grow in local employment and earnings. For example, the cotton-growing and ginning industries have moved from the southeastern United States to the southwestern region. Changes in technology, population, and available natural resources have been the major influences upon such shifts of location. Table 6.1 lists several factors industries look for when seeking a new location.

A SUMMARY OF REGIONAL AND COMMUNITY GROWTH THEORY

In general, especially for smaller regions or communities, community growth requires increases in basic employment, usually by the generation of new export goods and services. These new exports and their production are created either by the expansion of existing firms or by the addition of new businesses. The factors that influence industrial locations, discussed at length in Chapter Ten, are summarized here.

When considering locations, industries generally seek the least expensive access to needed inputs and outputs. This means access to the inputs of land, labor, capital, and entrepreneurship and to its output markets.

For each community, the availability of land, skilled labor, raw materials, business skills, and final markets is fairly fixed at any one time. Many communities will not have the resources or skills that particular industries need, but over a period of years, changes in technology, natural resources, population, and community attitude can alter the desirability of the community for industrial locations.

SETTING COMMUNITY GOALS

Each community or region has a choice of economic futures: to decline, to hold stable, or to grow. The decision is sometimes made politically, as when the area votes for or against community growth.

At other times, the decision is an economic one as the demand for local products and skills either increases or decreases.

Growth in Population

One choice concerns the level of population growth. An increase in export production is the most common path toward population growth. However, issues of pollution and changes in lifestyles are often raised.

Clearly, every community must encourage new ideas, new products, and/or new fields of work to replace those that decline. In the process, it is hard to stop with just enough replacement jobs. Indeed, the small town with a rapidly growing new-employment category may find population growth all but impossible to stop. On the other hand, when natural resources are depleted, say in a lumber region, the forces for population decline may be hard to arrest.

Growth in Welfare

The second type of economic change for a community is to improve its income per person—its per capita welfare. There are wide variations across communities and states in per capita income. Some of these are explained by differences in population composition, such as comparing the ages of people in the area, since per capita income could be lower in a town with many young children than in a town with mostly older couples. A population composed of workers with limited skills or limited education, for example, has a lower per capita income than one with advanced skills.

However, the type of employment in the town is the main force in differences between the per capita income of towns. The higher per capita incomes are found with high-salaried occupations. These are usually industries with a large amount of machinery, technology, and other capital investment in relation to the numbers of workers. On the other hand, industries that are "labor-intensive" usually seek out existing low-wage locations. This means that past differences in community income levels tend to get reinforced in the future. Low-income communities are chosen as locations for industries that need low wages, while higher-income communities often have skills or facilities that attract high-wage industries.

However, the factors that influence all new community jobs are important. Many of them, such as technology or transportation changes, can produce major new higher-income opportunities in low-income areas. For the individual community, the important factor in both population and per capita growth is an awareness of its weaknesses and strengths as a business location and a willingness to respond to opportunities.

Trying to Diversify

Finally, the community may have other economic goals besides those involving population or per capita growth. One example is of a single firm or industry being so successful that it dominates the entire town. If it ages and declines, it will drag the town down with it.

As towns develop skills drawn from their early resources, their industries tend to specialize in these resources and skills. This is desirable because these skills become major exports. However, if these skills become obsolete because of new materials or processes, entire towns can be put out of work. Thus, most communities today prefer not to be one-industry towns. They prefer a *diversification* of companies, industries, and job types.

REVIEWING YOUR UNDERSTANDING

How the Community Grows

1. Why must each economic community usually have some export trade? Why must there be new products or services to export?
2. How does a community generate new exports?
3. Explain the difference between growing industries and shifting industries. How do they choose locations?
4. What are the two factors influencing changes in per capita income?

6.3 HOW TO STUDY A COMMUNITY

The economic study of a community or a region can be approached informally or formally. Most businesspeople and investors are continually watching community progress for signs of strength or weakness. Informally, they are watching the forces of supply and demand when they observe population, employment, and income changes. Although keen observation and instinct are invaluable investment tools, concrete economic studies can provide a factual basis for improved judgment decisions. This section reviews traditional ways used to analyze community growth, stressing the two major techniques now used for regional study: economic base analysis and input-output study. The section ends with a discussion of sources of information on regions and communities.

TRADITIONAL COMMUNITY ANALYSIS

A number of supply and demand factors have been traditionally used to study and analyze communities. Analysis of supply factors has emphasized the inventory of existing structures and their size, price, age, and condition. The cost of new construction, availability of suitable land, zoning, financing, and utilities have also been considered important.

The most important demand factor is population, both in total numbers and by age, education, or other categories (population demography). Population change is the focus of growth. Because people must have jobs, employment characteristics of the town are also studied, including wage rates, types of jobs, and unemployment rates.

BASIC EMPLOYMENT

The most important long-term influence upon a community's population and employment is its basic or export employment. Because basic employment differs from one town to another, towns can be classified according to the dominant type of basic employment.

Some towns concentrate on industry, some on commerce, some on resorts, some on government, and some on resources. There are several classification systems; one, distinguishing towns as central places, transportation-service centers, or special-function cities, was introduced in Section 6.1.

These classifications indicate the major activity in the town's economic base. This information can be combined with data on community origin to see how basic employment has changed since the community was founded. In turn, it is important to discover what factors have caused the changes in basic employment.

All this information is necessary in order to forecast the future

SPECIAL INTEREST TOPIC

The Multiplier Effect

Economists who study basic employment have found that all towns do not have the same proportion of workers in basic or export jobs. This proportion varies with the size of the community as shown below.

Community Size	Number of Local Jobs Added for Each New Basic Job
Very large cities	2.0
100,000 people	1.0
50,000 people	0.5

The ratio of local to basic jobs is significant. An addition of 100 new jobs in basic employment will actually have a greater effect upon total employment. This is called the *multiplier effect*. It is easy to see why chambers of commerce want to obtain large, new manufacturing plants in their communities, because of the multiplied effect on total employment and the increase in retail sales.

of a region and the communities within it. Understanding past changes in the economic base will help forecast future changes. Even knowing the current economic base may tell something about the area's future. This is particularly true of extractive resource regions, whose future depends on the size of reserves of timber, oil, fish, or whatever resource is harvested.

REGIONAL ECONOMIC STUDIES

Studies of regional economic forces must often be very general. The factors previously discussed give only a general picture of the region's economy. Such broad studies can often be helped by reference to formal economic studies if any are available. The two main formal techniques of regional study are the *economic base study* and the *input-output study*. Each has a number of versions and adaptations.

The *economic base study* forecasts population growth by forecasting basic employment. The starting data are the present jobs in the area broken down by export and non-export companies. The first step is to forecast how employment in each basic industry in the region will change, either by assigning some fraction of the nationwide growth in that industry or by projecting past local trends of employment. The forecasts of employment by industry are then totaled to make a forecast of basic employment for the region.

The next step is to convert the forecast of basic employment to total employment, using the ratio or multiplier of export to local employment. Next, the forecast of total employment is converted to a population forecast for the total community by using the ratio of workers to people (the labor force participation rate). In turn, population forecasts can be converted to land-use forecasts or other specialized studies.

These economic base studies require enormous amounts of data and analysis and are therefore quite expensive. They are not practical for small communities and would not be reliable simply because a single new factory could move into town for reasons impossible to predict. For the large community or region, however, the studies have value.

The *input-output study* was developed more recently. In this type of study, researchers examine the resources that go into the economic activity of the community (inputs). They then calculate the goods and services (outputs) of the producing sectors of the community on the basis of where they are distributed or shipped. Outputs that are used locally as inputs for other producers must be identified separately.

As you can see, input-output analysis requires extensive amounts of data, which can rarely be obtained. When the data are available (usually for very large regions), this method provides a full understanding of what happens in the economy of the region. For instance, the dollar amounts of all imports and exports can be determined. The production of various industries is totaled, as well as the breakdown of customers by product. In this way, one can see the flow of money through the community. This is one of the major features of input-output analysis.

SPECIAL INTEREST TOPIC

"Where Are We Moving To?"

Sunbelt USA

The "sunbelt" states of the South and West have experienced major growth due to their pleasant climate, city dwellers desire to escape urban congestion, excellent retirement communities, tourist attractions, and the shift in new jobs in aerospace and other technologies. In the case of the South, the lack of unions, lower wages, and inexpensive real estate were initial factors. Today the cost differentials are not as great as they once were.

The losers in this shift have been the Mid West (rustbelt) and some Northeastern states. Recently, some of these "loser" states have grouped together to provide a united political front in an attempt to stem the flow of business and government projects to the sunbelt states.

Rocky Mountain High

The mountain states such as Colorado and Utah experienced economic growth and gains in population in the 1970s and early 1980s. Jobs and alternative lifestyles led the growth. However, the decline in resource extraction (oil and shale) in the mid 1980s slowed down the rapid growth of many of the mountain states. In some of these states over-building has glutted the residential and commercial real estate markets.

Pacific Northwest and Green Acres

Extreme Northern California, Oregon, and Washington with their forests and plentiful rain, have been attracting both people and industries. In the state of Washington, especially the Seattle-Tacoma area, there has been rapid growth. These cities have been selected by various rating agencies as the most "ideal" in the United States.

U.S. Census Bureau Data

According to the U.S. Census Bureau, for the years 1980–1989, the ten fastest growing states, by percentage, in ranking order were: Nevada, Alaska, Arizona, Florida, California, New Hampshire, Texas,

Georgia, New Mexico, and Utah. The fastest growing large metropolitan region in the United States was the Riverside-San Bernardino area in California.

Gate Keeping Syndrome

In rapidly growing areas there is a tendency for "old timers" to resent the "new comers." Once the newcomers get in they try to keep out the "new" newcomers. In addition, a large portion of Western land is owned by the federal government. Environmental groups are attempting to lock up a vast portion of this land to preserve the natural environment. These and numerous other factors are creating controversy. There are hundreds of polarized groups all fighting one another to press their own viewpoint.

SOURCES OF DATA

The major sources of information about current and past conditions are the United States Census Bureau publications, including the most recent and earlier censuses of population, housing, and manufacturing. State and federal labor and employment offices are good sources of added data, as are state and local chambers of commerce. Research publications from banks, universities, and regional Federal Reserve banks are also very helpful.

In general, only the larger areas have been studied and reported on. However, the scope of this coverage is improving. Some county and city planning departments and regional planning groups now have or are developing elaborate and detailed data centers.

Future forecasts have most often been available from state and federal agencies, although some were produced as regional studies. Regional forecasts of specific types (especially transportation) are now available for many regions, and they are being updated and expanded. Various specialized forecasts (transportation, land use, pollution, water demand, and sewage) are being combined. The errors of some earlier forecasts are also being reviewed as planners seek to improve forecasting accuracy.

REVIEWING YOUR UNDERSTANDING

How to Study a Community

1. Why is the economic base important in studying a region?
2. What is an input-output study?
3. What is the "multiplier effect"?

CHAPTER SUMMARY

This chapter stressed that the purpose of regional and community analysis is to understand the economic activity in the area and its direct effects upon the supply and demand for real estate.

The origin of communities results from the combination of site characteristics and commercial or social factors. Commercial factors play a more important role in cities founded recently both in America and throughout the world. The origin of a city has tremendous influence on the layout of major buildings and street patterns in subsequent years.

Community growth depends on economic factors because communities are not self-sufficient; they need many imported goods. Volume growth of a city, practically speaking, is often limited by the growth of jobs that produce goods or services for export. These export earnings, in turn, pay for the necessary imports. Exports at the time of a city's origin were usually related to the community's material resources, but in time the skills learned from handling these resources became more important.

Community studies examine such factors as basic employment, population, income, and other specific land-use factors. The two major types of such studies are economic base studies and input-output studies, and there is a variety of source material available for persons wishing to engage in community analysis.

IMPORTANT TERMS AND CONCEPTS

Basic (export) employment

Break-cargo (break-bulk) point

Central-place town

Demography

Economic base analysis

Input-output analysis

Service (local) employment

Special-function town

Transport-service town

REVIEWING YOUR UNDERSTANDING

1. A town formed at a "break-cargo" point is called a
   a. central town
   b. transportation-service town
   c. special-function town
   d. economic town

2. Growth of a region is most closely tied to what kind of jobs?
   a. local
   b. secondary
   c. basic
   d. internal

3. In terms of economic base analysis, a computer manufacturing company would be considered what kind of business?
   a. export
   b. import
   c. secondary
   d. local

4. In terms of economic base analysis, a residential real estate brokerage business is what kind of business?
   a. export
   b. basic
   c. manufacturing
   d. secondary

5. If a region's population expands rapidly, while jobs and government welfare decline, the per capita standard of living as measured by goods and services will probably:
   a. decrease
   b. increase
   c. remain the same
   d. escalate

6. If the multiplier effect for a local economy is 1 export job creates 1.5 secondary jobs, an increase in 100 basic export jobs should create a total of how many new jobs in the area?
   a. 100
   b. 150
   c. 250
   d. 350

7. When selecting a new location for a factory, a company will usually check which of the following items?

    a. environmental requirements

    b. community attitudes

    c. transportation systems

    d. all of the above

8. The underlying principle of economic base analysis states that for a region to grow economically, it must:

    a. export more than it imports

    b. import more than it exports

    c. increase secondary business faster than basic business

    d. decrease basic industries

9. Which could be cited as disadvantages of economic growth?

    a. more people

    b. traffic congestion

    c. additional pollution

    d. all of the above

10. One advantage of economic growth is more:

    a. goods and services

    b. jobs

    c. financial security

    d. all of the above

Chapter 7

Community Growth Patterns

Preview

This chapter describes how a community takes physical shape, how land use determines the community's layout, and where its population settles. Section 7.1 explains the factors that determine land use patterns. Section 7.2 illustrates basic city growth patterns. Section 7.3 describes what happens to growth patterns as the community population increases. When you have finished this chapter, you will be able to:

1. List the major forces influencing the shape, layout, and density of a community.

2. Describe how each force affects the future shape of the community.

3. List the basic patterns of community growth.

4. Explain how land use in a community is a dynamic, evolving pattern that can be studied to forecast the path of growth.

7.1   LAND USE PATTERNS

The initial reason for establishing a community often determines the shape of the community, the pattern of land use, and even how land is allocated among users. In the many cities laid out by the church in medieval Europe, church leaders made land use decisions, primarily for religious reasons. Similarly, in cities whose original function was to protect the residents, military and police considerations dictated the location of shops, homes, and manufacturing sites.

However, as stressed in Chapter Six, communities that continue to develop must become economically successful, whatever the reasons were for their initial location. Therefore, economic motives will influence how land is allocated among competing land users.

HOW ECONOMICS DETERMINES LAND USE

In a market economy there is competition among the various buyers of each product. In the absence of controls, goods and services go to the highest bidder. There is a similar competition among potential users of a site, and land goes to the user who is willing to pay the highest price. Appraisal books call this the "highest and best use."

According to the *principle of highest and best use*, the best use of land is the legal use that will produce the highest capitalized net income return to the land after allowing for the cost of the building. In most cases, this means that the quality of a site is determined by how much rent it will bring, and possible tenants are considered according to how much rent each could pay at that site.

WHY PATTERNS?

Even though land use is determined by the rent paying ability of different legal users, why do communities form patterns of land use? The answer seems to be that a set of rules affects each possible use of land differently. Thus, similar users cluster together at favorable locations, even with the absence of government zoning. Commercial users cluster with other commercial users, homeowners locate near other homeowners, and so on.

WHAT ARE THE RULES?

A series of rules appear to control the economic process of developing land-use patterns.

Rule 1: Competition of Uses

When a number of different potential users seek the same site, the competition raises the asking price until the most profitable use at that location is able to generate the needed rent. Thus, it is rent-paying ability that determines land use.

Rule 2: Economics of Succession

If a site is vacant and open to all legal uses, development will usually be for the most profitable use. However, if there is a building on the site, a user who can occupy the existing improvements has an advantage over other users. The improvements will be demolished only when a new use is profitable enough to pay for the site, the old building, the demolition cost, and the cost of the new building.

Rule 3: Comparative Advantage

Each site has unique advantages and disadvantages for particular uses. Some locations may have favorable natural endowments (raw materials, climate, topography, water, etc.) Other locations may have access to many buyers or to by-product materials from other facilities. Still other locations might have good schools, suppliers, favorable government regulations, or other institutional advantages.

The advantages and disadvantages of a particular site will give a comparative advantage to whichever land use gets the greatest net benefit from that unique set of advantages and disadvantages.

Rule 4: The Rule of Imperfection

The ideal pattern of land use rarely exists because the information needed to make a perfect decision is often not available. Unwise property development or unusual social or political situations will also interrupt the highest and best use. Sometimes the community will interfere with the market (by zoning, etc.) to avoid disruptions that market forces would otherwise cause. Thus, land-use patterns are never completely perfect or completely predictable.

Rule 5: Principle of Change

Nothing is static or fixed; therefore, the highest and best use is always changing. Technical, social, and economic changes continually alter the structure of the community and the pattern of ideal land use.

These five economic rules are important determinants of land-use patterns. Every community furnishes repeated examples of each rule. The student should particularly think about *comparative advantage*—why each use is located where it is. Examples: Industrial users cluster together because favorable utilities and transportation routes are nearby. To locate elsewhere could incur additional costs that can cut into profits or drive up prices with the danger of losing sales. Retail stores group to form a "one stop" shopping convenience. Homes are built near one another because water and other needed services are nearby and already in place.

THE NONECONOMIC FACTORS IN LAND USE

In addition to economic forces, other factors involving social or political forces influence land-use decisions. Political influences take the form of decisions carried out by state and local authorities executing the law, while social influences operate more subtly through group pressures. Political, social, and economic determinants of land use can operate independently of each other.

Political or legal effects on land-use decisions result from community attitudes on land use expressed through the police power and the power of eminent domain. Police power refers to the right of the community to regulate private behavior in order to protect the public's health, safety, and welfare. Eminent domain is the right of the community to buy for full value any site that the community needs to use. Zoning laws provide one of the most noticeable examples of police power. This topic is so important that most of Chapter Thirteen is devoted to political land-use controls.

Social controls on land use are less noticeable than political or economic ones. The past forms of social control involved unwritten understandings or common viewpoints that certain land-use decisions will or will not occur. Past examples of such unwritten rules included ethnic neighborhood limits, the importance of downtown stores over neighborhood stores, and the superiority of detached homes over multiple-unit structures. Such social controls could influence both political and economic decisions. They are separated to point out that they are based on social notions, opinions, and/or biases rather than on any kind of objective, established, factual bases. Social controls are becoming less influential as political controls replace them.

REVIEWING YOUR UNDERSTANDING

Why There Are Land Use Patterns

1. The three major community forces that influence the land-use system are economic,_____ , and _____ (fill in).

2. How does competition influence land use?

3. List the five rules of economic land-use allocation. Explain each.

THE IMPORTANCE OF TOPOGRAPHY

Von Thünen simplified everything by assuming that villages were located on flat plains and that they used the transportation systems of 1826: walking, pack animals, and slow carts. These two assumptions were important to his conclusion. His central concern was the importance of transportation cost or effort, and his pattern of uses provided people with the easiest access to those places they had to go to most often or most urgently.

However, when a town site is not level, the round pattern begins to change. For example, if a town had its origins as a protection site and is located on top of a ridge, with steep slopes on two sides, there will be little economic activity on these steep slopes. The town would be strung out along the ridge top in each direction, and its circular shape would become a ribbon. This is one example of the effect of topography upon city shape. Topography—the shape and slope of the land—changes the shape of cities in several ways.

Topography may explain the town's location. Similarly, topographical features can attract added development or impede growth. Features that are attractions to growth include pleasant lake shores, level land, and—for their views—gentle hills. Features that are barriers to growth include steep hills, ravines, marshes, swamps, and river banks. Von Thünen's concept of a round city assumed a town on a level site. As we introduce topography, the shape changes. Figure 7.2 shows how topography modifies the round city shape.

TRANSPORTATION

Topography also has an obvious effect upon transportation. It is easier, cheaper, and faster to travel on level land than up or down steep hills. The circle city developed in the first part of von Thünen's

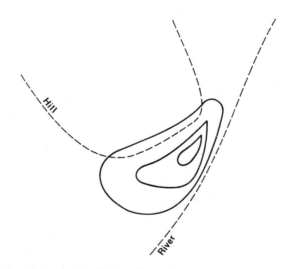

FIGURE 7.2   The influence of topography upon the circular city.

work was based on transportation by foot, pack animal, or cart. These are all transportation systems that we would describe as slow and dispersed or *random*. "Random" means that one can go from any place to any other place with equal ease. Later, von Thünen's study explores the effect of other systems of travel.

Twentieth-century communities have transportation systems that von Thünen did not foresee. The influence of each on city shape differs. The automobile driven on a city street is a random transportation system similar to a person on foot, but it is capable of moving far greater distances in the same time period. Automobile cities, therefore, tend to be circular like von Thünen's but extremely spread out, with lower population density.

Street cars and subways, on the other hand, cannot move randomly; they must move along rail lines. They are "linear" or "axial" transportation systems. Such rail systems, however, are strongly influenced by topography. Freeways are a combination of the two types of transport: the car itself tends to give a circular shape to the city, but freeways produce a series of linear extensions. Simple examples of these are illustrated in Figure 7.3. When we add modern transportation systems to von Thünen's simplified model of a community,

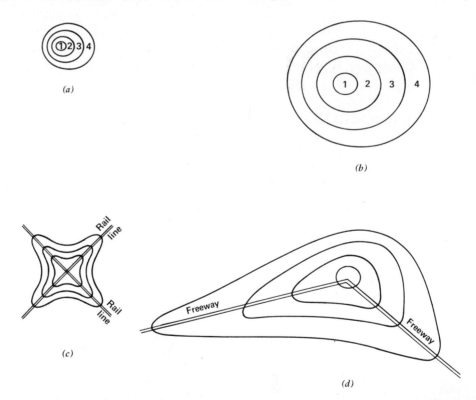

FIGURE 7.3   Effects of transportation on city shape for cities with 100,000 people. (*a*) Small size due to foot transportation; round shape by random access. (*b*) Large size due to auto transportation; round shape by random access. (*c*) Small size due to streetcar transportation; star shape from linear access.(*d*) Large size due to auto transportation with two freeways; linear shape from linear access.

we see that *the transportation system or systems in use will affect the density of the town as well as its shape.*

THE EXISTING TOWN-ORIGINS

The fourth factor that influences community structure is history: how was the community first built? When the first building was erected, it influenced where the second building would be—probably close to the first, but not too close. When the first store was built, it is likely that it was located in the center of the existing housing cluster. Similarly, when the first government structure was built, it was usually located in the middle of the existing community. The town probably grew around its center—shops next to shops, homes next to homes, and offices next to offices.

This type of development occurred because there is a locational advantage for each type of land use at some particular location. Each new user wants the same locational advantages that existing competitive users have. This means that the community's origin continues to play a major part in the location of new buildings because the new buildings tend to develop near existing buildings. This, then, is the tremendous power of the existing investment in the community to draw additional investment toward it. In time, this original area will have built up a commanding number of economic and cultural attractions for many land uses. Only very high land prices or traffic congestion stops the constant pressure of new uses seeking to obtain these existing locational advantages.

REVIEWING YOUR UNDERSTANDING

Looking at the Structure of Communities

1. List the four dominant factors in community shape. Give an example of each.
2. How does each of these four factors influence the population density of a town?
3. List four examples of how topography influences a town.

7.3   MODERN CITY GROWTH PATTERNS

This section combines the four factors of accessibility, transportation, topography, and origin with the additional elements that appear in the larger community. The result is a fairly realistic model of the pattern of land use in American communities.

PROXIMITY VERSUS ACCESSIBILITY

If the community grows, population exerts greater and greater pressures upon the downtown central zone. These growing pressures involve larger numbers of people seeking to work, shop, and visit in this central area. Congestion increases (whatever the transportation system) until the advantages of the downtown area—its accessibility and central location—begin to disappear. For the person who lives on the edge of town and needs to buy a dozen eggs, the shopping trip downtown becomes uneconomic. At some point, it becomes feasible for some types of land uses to leave the downtown and move to the outskirts to gain better access to their outlying customers. This movement can be a gradual creep, one store moving a little further out than the last, or a sudden "leapfrog" to the city's fringe.

This process illustrates the continual tug-of-war between two influences. The first, proximity, comes from the original location of the town, the high investment in existing building, the central location of the city center, and its proximity to the entire community. These factors represent the established, the fixed, and the past. The second is accessibility (the original reason for the central core) and the influence of transportation and transportation change upon accessibility. These factors speak for change and the future.

Each land-use decision throughout the community involves a weighing, often consciously, of these two factors. Should we put the building in the safe location near where the last one was built? Or should we pioneer further out along the transportation routes that have emerged in recent years? Quick investor response to the San Francisco Bay Area Rapid Transit System (BART) in the late 1960s is an excellent example of a new transportation system bringing shifts in the balance between proximity and accessibility, and the system's impact on real estate values. When new transportation systems are initiated in other metro areas the same investor response and favorable impact on real estate values will take place. Outlying suburban areas tend to benefit most when a new transportation system is created because of improved accessibility to the central core. All of the station locations along the route also benefit because of the increased traffic exposure and accessibility.

THE COMPLEX CITY

As the community gets larger, it requires more than one transportation system. Most communities now combine linear types of transportation with random types: subways and automobiles, for instance. Even in communities on level ground, with streets forming a grid, some streets will be one-way and some will be widened, arterial routes. These changes introduce linear features into an otherwise random street pattern.

Each use that moves away from the downtown along a linear route pulls the circular shape of the community with it. Sometimes a use will leapfrog, or jump still further out, as most shopping centers have done. These in turn become mini-downtown areas with their own forces of proximity (also called "gravity" or "centrality") flowing out in mini-circles around them, as shown in Figure 7.4. Because these leapfrogging users of land are primarily seeking better accessibility to customers, they usually locate near an intersection of two or more transportation routes. This may be where two arterials meet, at a major freeway off-ramp, or (best of all) at a freeway–freeway intersection. Such locations can become complete new downtowns, able in turn to ignore accessibility, because of the drawing power that their growing mixtures of uses create.

ENTER THE WEDGE

Our analysis so far has involved a town that has no better or worse side. Thus, we have assumed that you and I would live anywhere in the residential ring that lies on the outskirts of town. This is not so in practice, and one example is our preference for locations that are easier to reach. Homer Hoyt's classic 1939 study, *The Structure and Growth of Residential Neighborhoods in American Cities,* concluded that higher-priced homes took the first choice of acreage in the outskirts of town. Localities of such houses tended to cluster

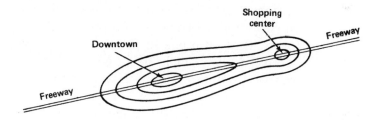

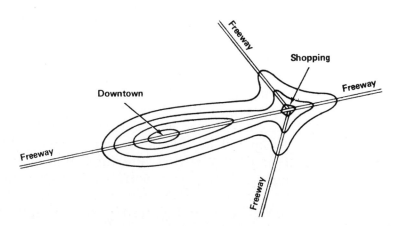

FIGURE 7.4   (a) The effect of a suburban shopping center on community shape. (b) The added effect of a second freeway.

into one segment of the outer circle. As the community grew, and as new houses were added in the suburbs, the higher-priced homes were added just beyond the existing high-priced areas. In this fashion, the higher-priced sector became a wedge. Medium-cost and low-cost homes sort themselves out similarly. The medium-cost homes typically seek to be near prestige locations, leaving the poorest area for development of lower-priced homes. In fact, one author called these poorer areas "sinks," because they are often areas with poor drainage. Hoyt mapped the shifts in location of better residential areas in a number of American cities; several of his maps are reproduced in Figure 7.5.

Hoyt then pointed out that the retail district in the town follows the higher-priced homes. As these homes concentrate to one side of the town and move out toward the suburbs in a wedge, the better residential shops move to that side of the downtown core. The wholesale and manufacturing uses generally orient themselves out of the way of such high-priced commercial uses. This sorting process often leaves manufacturing located on the side of the downtown core closest to the area of low-priced homes.[2]

Hoyt further found that the wedge shape of the high-priced home area endured for a long time. Its direction of movement was toward the higher ground, but it also moved away from areas that were impossible to build on or that involved such dead-end developments as running out the end of a peninsula or up against a river bank. He found that changes in the direction of high-priced home movement occurred very slowly because of the long life of real estate improvements. He noted that industry and manufacturing tended to be close to such transportation sources as waterfronts, railroads, airports, and highways. Retail business, on the other hand, might be found at highway intersections and at any similar population cluster away from highways.

POLITICAL AND SOCIAL FACTORS

As we indicated earlier, we rarely find an ideal community growth pattern. Part of the reason is that factors like topography have subtle effects because they are based on people's *feelings* about topography. A good example is that hills and high ground can be an attraction to growth, especially of high-priced homes, and can also be a barrier to growth because of the high utility and transportation costs associated with getting there. The question of whether a particular hillside will be an attraction or a barrier to growth is difficult to predict. Moreover, the amount of attraction may change as transportation, utility systems, and people's tastes change.

The process is also complicated by factors other than the "big four"—accessibility, transportation, topography, and community or-

---

[2] Contrary to Hoyt's theory, in some industrial cities old abandoned factories have been turned into shopping malls and condominiums. The success of these projects has varied.

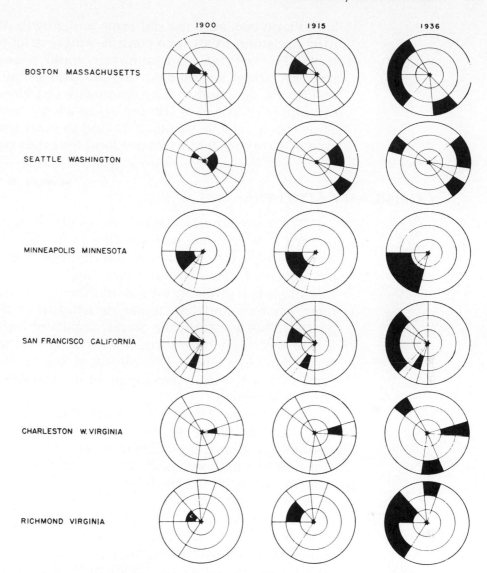

FIGURE 7.5 Shifts in location of fashionable residential areas in six American cities, 1900–1936. Fashionable residential areas indicated by solid black. *Source:* Hoyt, *The Structure and Growth of Residential Neighborhoods in American Cities.* Washington, D.C., Federal Housing Administration, Government Printing Office, 1939, p. 115. This study is considered a classic by modern urban planners.

igins. Politics and political factors also influence community location and direction of growth. In some instances, political boundaries of cities are absolute barriers to growth, with no construction permitted outside the city limits. Sometimes these limitations are county boundaries, and growth of the city or community in that direction may be blocked. In other instances, city and county boundaries are not the problem. Instead, growth is hampered by boundaries of sewer or water districts.

Political factors are not limited just to the boundary problem. Communities establish master plans to express community feelings about land use, land-use patterns, and growth patterns. These planning decisions create land controls and restrict or direct growth patterns. For example, a community could pass an ordinance that reserves prime flat land for agriculture, despite its suitability for residential development. A community can also state what types of structures it desires or the density at which development can occur. Thus, there may be insufficient land to meet market wishes for one type of structure and excessive land for other types.

COMMUNITY ATTITUDES

There are other social influences upon the community's growth pattern and land-use pattern. One is the community's attitude toward transportation systems, alternatives, and change. The refusal of voters in a dense urban area to approve the financing of a rapid transit system probably means that the transportation system will be more random and less linear or axial than if the financing had passed. This will affect the overall density of the region and the clusters of secondary downtowns, or secondary concentric centers, that occur in a large region. The refusal of San Mateo County in the San Francisco Bay Area to participate in the Bay Area Rapid Transit System is an example.

Even individual decisions can influence community growth patterns. An example is the farmer whose property is on the community's outskirts, in the path of development. Should this farmer hold and farm the land well past the time developers seek to use it, development pressures will be directed toward other available lands to the sides or beyond. The farmer could create a large island or barrier to growth. In other cases, however, the farm owner whose land is somewhat remote from development may become eager to sell, and by skillful merchandising, vigorous promotion, and use of politics, the farmer may encourage development far earlier than would otherwise be the case.

THE RESULTS

Thus, there are many factors that influence community growth patterns. Their effects, and the end result, are complicated and interwoven. It is possible, however, to describe how these forces interact, and the best description is the widely quoted statement by the pioneer urban economist Richard Hurd in his *Principles of City Land Values* (1903):

Cities originate at their most convenient point of contact with the outer world and grow in the lines of least resistance or greatest attraction, or their resultants. The point of contact differs according to the methods of transportation, whether by water, by turnpike or by railroad. . . . The influence of topography, all-powerful when cities start, is constantly modified. . . . The most direct results of topography come from its control of transportation. . . .

Growth in cities consists of movement away from the point of origin in all directions, except as topographically hindered, this movement being due both to aggregation at the edges and pressure from the centre. Central growth takes place both from the heart of the city and from each subcentre of attraction, and axial growth pushes into the outlying territory by means of railroads, turnpikes and street railroads. All cities are built up from these two influences, which vary in quantity, intensity and quality, and resulting districts overlapping, interpenetrating, neutralizing and harmonizing as the pressure of the city's growth brings them in contact with each other. . . . Residences are early driven to the circumference, while business remains at the centre, and as residences divide into various social grades, retail shops of corresponding grades follow them, and wholesale shops in turn follow the retailers, while institutions and various mixed utilities irregularly fill in the intermediate zone, and the banking and office section remains at the main business centre. Complicating this broad outward movement of zones, axes of traffic project shops through residence areas, create business subcentres, where they intersect, and change circular cities into star-shaped cities. Central growth, due to proximity, and axial growth, due to accessibility, are summed up in the static power of established sections and the dynamic power of their chief lines of intercommunication.[3]

Each sentence in this quotation has great significance. Reread the passage and take each sentence as a full, separate thought. Stop at the end of the sentence and ask yourself what it means in terms of the cities and communities that you have known. It is striking that Mr. Hurd was so successful in capturing the dynamic combination of factors in such clear language so long ago.

OTHER VIEWS

Comments by Burgess, Hoyt, and others do not seem to disprove or take a position opposing what Hurd said but rather emphasize one view or another of the complicated whole. For example, Harris and Ullman suggested in 1945 that the dominant concept in city shape was that of *multiple nuclei*. Their thought was that each land use responds in a different way to topography, transportation, and other influences. Similar uses tend to cluster together in nuclei, illustrated in Figure 7.6. The city thus created appears to be star-shaped. The multiple-nuclei concept explains how uses become located in different places in the community.

[3] Richard M. Hurd, *Principles of City Land Values* (New York: 1903), pp. 15–16.

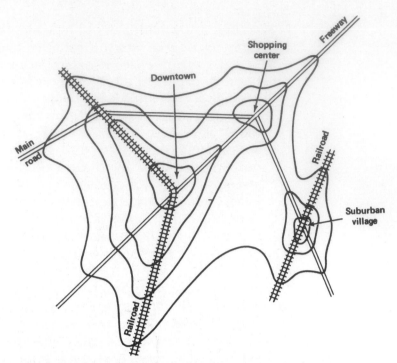

FIGURE 7.6   "Multiple nuclei" in city growth patterns

Others have stressed socioeconomic linkages and have pointed out that locational desires of families are the force in shaping cities. Families choose their residential location for social and economic needs. Businesses and public facilities follow them in order to be of service. This humanistic viewpoint of community shape, however, falls short of analyzing the factors that influence family residential choices. These turn out again to be amenities of location, topography, transportation, and political and social constraints on growth. Again we find a viewpoint that seems to restate Hurd.

Richard Nelson suggested in 1958 that there are four urban models. The largest is the metropolitan commercial center, which he calls *Commerce City.* Next in size is the medium-sized city, which he calls *Center Town.* Third is the rural trading area (*Countyville*) and fourth is the dormitory suburb for a larger city (*Forest Lake*). He suggests that land-use patterns in Countyville are predominantly the circular-zone concepts of von Thünen and Burgess. Sector (wedge) theory seems to become more relevant or visible in the larger Center Town. The largest community, Commerce City, shows the patterns described by the sector theory and also begins to demonstrate the multiple-nuclei concept. His fourth model, Forest Lake, is a satellite community, unlike the other three. It has a layout that will vary as determined by its relationship to its parent city.

In 1972, Barlowe suggested that suburban areas surrounding large cities increasingly show a land-use pattern of large grids. In these grids, the major avenues and cross-streets are lined with commercial and industrial uses or sites, while the enclosed superblocks and the interior streets are reserved for residential uses. Figure 7.7

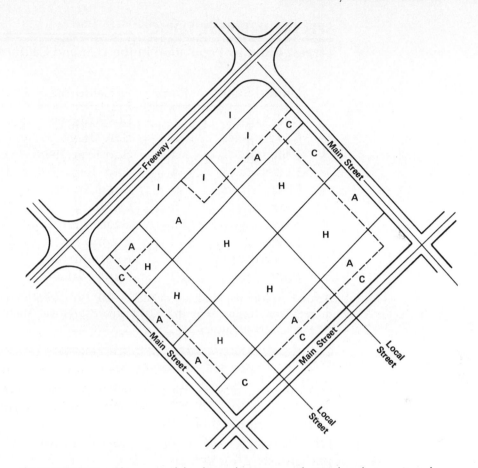

FIGURE 7.7   The superblock grid system of city land use. Land-use codes: I, industrial; C, commercial; A, apartments; H, houses; *Source*: After Barlowe, *Land Resource Economics*, 1972. Prentice Hall, Inc. Englewood Cliffs. N.J.

illustrates this pattern. Both Nelson and Barlowe sharpened our perception of how communities are structured. Nelson's four cities, in particular, seem to agree with the California experience. Both Nelson and Barlowe are consistent with the model that Hurd presents.

THE EFFECTS OF TRANSPORTATION CHANGE

Nevertheless, there are ways in which Hurd's language cannot help us understand today's city. One major change since his time has been the effect of transportation upon manufacturing and wholesale activities. Airfreight, trucks, and freeways have freed wholesalers from the need to locate close to their retail customers. Indeed, many wholesalers now service an entire state, a region, or sometimes an entire country from one warehouse. These shifts in wholesale location do not violate Hurd's general concepts, but his language about the specific location of wholesalers is generally no longer valid.

Manufacturing, too, has thrown off its former ties to the railroad line and has gone beyond the need to locate in the center of the

SPECIAL INTEREST TOPIC

Largest Cities by Population in the U.S. and California

United States	Rank	California
New York	1	Los Angeles
Los Angeles	2	San Diego
Chicago	3	San Francisco
Houston	4	San Jose
Philadelphia	5	Long Beach
Detroit	6	Oakland
San Diego	7	Sacramento
Dallas	8	Fresno
San Antonio	9	Anaheim
Phoenix	10	Santa Ana

Source: Statistical Abstract of U.S. 1989, Bureau of Census, Department of Commerce, Washington D.C. and California Statistical Abstract 1988, Department of Finance, Sacramento, CA.

community, where the railroad yard and unloading spurs were located. Once freed from these constraints, manufacturing can follow other locational factors. One is a need for inexpensive land as industrial factories shift to single-story buildings. The addition of worker parking heightens this need.

The ties that once bound many types of land use to the inner zone are now weak. In the past, both wholesale and manufacturing had to be located in the central community in order to have reasonable accessibility to their shipments, to their customers, and to needed technical assistance like patent lawyers, banks, etc. The transportation revolution of the twentieth century has liberated these land uses from the central zone.

Another significant force, and one that is critical for the future, is the explosion in our communications capabilities. Although the telephone and the mail were present in 1903, the era in which many businesses required physical proximity to their customers (because interactions between people required a physical meeting) is at an end. Suburban movement of office buildings is one recent example of this change. The photocopying and FAX machines are both a cause and a result of this major swing. In many downtown areas today, the remaining establishments consist primarily of specialty retail stores and those wholesale and office occupations that require face-to-face contact, such as jewelry or fashion clothes wholesaling and lawyers, who must negotiate directly.

These changes, which expand and extend the ideas Hurd presented, produced results that he did not foresee. The bursting concept first expressed by Babcock in the 1930s is another notion not anticipated by Hurd. Babcock notes that a new use need not locate adjacent to the most recently built similar use. Rather, it is possible for it to leapfrog over intervening uses to a new location, in advance of the gradual linear movement of the community toward that location. Shopping centers are our premier example of bursting. Suburbanized office buildings, research parks, and manufacturing plants also illustrate the concept. This change has resulted from the tremendous increase in mobility that the automobile has given American society, although this is a change in the scale of mobility rather than a difference in the type of mobility. It allows us to go further, faster, and in more directions than any other transportation system. What impact pollution caused by automobiles will have on this trend are not yet apparent, but change certainly will occur.

REVIEWING YOUR UNDERSTANDING

Modern City Growth Patterns

1. What is meant by proximity and accessibility as forces in shaping cities? Give an example of the influence of each in your town.
2. Explain how the home location preferences of high income people influence the layout of towns.
3. Give five examples of how political and social factors can influence town shape and layout.
4. What does the concept of multiple nuclei mean? What effect do they have on the shape of towns?
5. Give five examples of the ways that the car and truck have changed the shape and layout of towns.

CHAPTER SUMMARY

This chapter has discussed how the community gets its shape, layout, and population density. The patterns of community development are important because they tell what factors have influenced land uses and changes. When we forecast future changes in land use, our understanding of these past and present forces and changes is our major tool.

The major forces influencing community growth patterns are (1) accessibility, (2) transportation, (3) topography, and (4) community origins. For any given parcel of land, one use has a comparative advantage over all other uses because of the effects of these forces. This comparative advantage is reflected by the amount of rent that the highest and best use is able to pay. Nearby sites, which have similar usefulness, attract similar uses to them. This leads to clusters or nuclei of similar uses.

In addition to economic forces, political actions and social pressures affect land-use decisions. Public land-use controls and eminent domain are the two most common types of political forces. Social pressures are varied but are a main influence on land use. All three forces spring from "we, the people," but in different ways, with different effects and mechanisms.

Small towns tend to have simple land-use patterns, generally a series of concentric rings of different land uses. Larger cities develop pie-shaped wedges that expand through several rings. This results from the gradual development of a higher-priced side of town or sector in the residential and commercial rings. When we turn our view to large metropolitan areas or complexes, we see that a number of small concentric communities grow until they meet. The resulting pattern of land uses has a number of centers, both from suburban downtowns and from new clusters around major transportation intersections. Each center or nucleus will have rings of uses around it, but each center may serve a specialized function.

In each case, the location of land uses seems to be the result of the competition between the drawing power of the existing buildings and the changing accessibility to people that is provided by growth of the community and its transportation system. The former is dominated by the origins and early transportation features of the town, while the latter owes much to topography, social and political influences, and the current transportation systems.

IMPORTANT TERMS AND CONCEPTS

Accessibility

Comparative advantage

Competition of uses

Concentric growth

Economic succession

Growth:

  Attraction

  Residence

Linear (axial) growth

Multiple nuclei

Topography

REVIEWING YOUR UNDERSTANDING

1. When land is allocated to the legal user who pays the highest price, economists call this the principle of:

    a. comparative advantage

    b. highest and best use

    c. economic succession

    d. change

2. The impact that zoning has on community growth patterns is what type of force?

    a. economic

    b. physical

    c. social

    d. political

3. The circular or concentric theory of growth has the city growing:

    a. around the downtown central core

    b. along transportation lines

    c. from several points such as suburban shopping centers

    d. from the highest to the lowest topographic points

4. The multiple nuclei theory of growth has the city growing:

    a. around the downtown central core

    b. along transportation lines

    c. from several points such as suburban shopping centers

    d. from the highest to the lowest topographic points

5. The growth of a community along transportation lines such as freeways or rail routes is best described as:

    a. spatial

    b. axial or linear

    c. sporadic

    d. circular

6. In real estate land use, accessibility means:

    a. similar zoning

    b. ability to get in and out of a site

    c. social factors that determine use

    d. nearness to other businesses

7. According to the classic study by Homer Hoyt, *The Structure and Growth of Residential Neighborhoods in American Cities*, higher priced homes tend to be built:

    a. on flat land

    b. near transportation systems

    c. near industrial parks

    d. on hillsides

8. The physical shape of a city can be changed by:

    a. new transportation systems

    b. topography

    c. new technology

    d. all of the above

9. No-growth policies by city governments are an example of what type of force?

    a. political

    b. economic

    c. physical

    d. social

10. The future growth patterns of large U.S. cities will be heavily influenced by:

    a. transportation systems

    b. environmental concerns

    c. telecommunications systems

    d. all of the above

Chapter 8

Neighborhoods: Clusters of Land Use and Value

Preview

Chapter Eight describes the clusters of similar land uses and values called "neighborhoods." Section 8.1 illustrates how to locate neighborhood boundaries and then stresses how important neighborhoods are to individual property values. Section 8.2 describes how the study of neighborhoods can be used to identify changes that are taking place. Section 8.3 analyzes neighborhood decay and the tools used to reverse the decline. When you have completed this chapter, you will be able to:

1. Define "neighborhood," and explain how to locate the boundary of neighborhoods.

2. Discuss how neighborhoods influence real property values.

3. List the four forces that affect neighborhood change.

4. Describe the process of neighborhood decay.

This information will help you to analyze the strengths and weaknesses of neighborhoods in your local community.

8.1   THE NEIGHBORHOOD AS A FOUNDATION OF VALUE

Chapter Seven discussed how growth starts with the origins of the community and creates a predictable pattern of land uses. This section shows how neighborhoods make a bridge between those community land-use patterns and the values of individual parcels.

WHAT IS A NEIGHBORHOOD?

A neighborhood is a cluster of properties of relatively similar land use and value. Neighborhoods also frequently have occupants with similar characteristics: in residential areas, occupants may have similar income levels, education, and status.

Neighborhoods exist because topography, transportation, and social and political influences have different effects on each type of land use. Thus, similar uses will be influenced in similar ways and will tend to cluster together. On the other hand, land uses can conflict, such as an airport locating in a residential neighborhood (see Figure 8.1). This potential problem is addressed by zoning ordinances, which restrict land uses in a zone to a few narrow categories. Variances are granted only when the applicant shows that they are not injurious to the primary categories. Similar controls can be found in private deed restrictions.

NEIGHBORHOOD LOCATION AND PROPERTY VALUES

There is an old saying that there are three factors that determine the value of a property— "location, location, and location!" This saying emphasizes that real estate has a fixed location, which means that the value of an individual parcel is determined by the features or forces that surround it.

The value of a property is also a function of the physical property itself. That is, a large house on a large lot is worth more than a small house on a small lot, assuming that all other factors are the same. Other physical characteristics of the property, such as age, condition, quality, charm, renovation, mechanical features, and special equipment, are also part of what gives that property its value. How-

FIGURE 8.1   A conflict in land use of an unsatisfactory residential neighborhood. *Source: Flying Magazine.*

ever, the example of a brand-new automobile assembly plant in the middle of the Sahara Desert is used by many appraisal teachers to illustrate the relative importance of the physical property versus its surroundings. In this case, despite the newness, excellent condition, functional layout, and quality materials of the assembly plant, the plant is not worth much because it lacks necessary features around it such as utility and transportation systems, availability of skilled workers, raw materials, and markets for its products.

Another example is that of building identical homes on different sites. One site may be very close to downtown, while another may be in an older suburb on the last available lot. A third site may be in a new suburb surrounded by similar newer homes. Finally a fourth site might be in a rural area on a lot in a farmer's field. Although the houses are identical and were built by the same builder at the same time, each will have a different market value because of its individual location.

Defining Location

If property value is heavily influenced by location, the question is asked, What is location? *Location is the sum of all the topographical, transport, and other influences on land use that characterize a particular neighborhood or nucleus.* Location means almost the same thing as neighborhood. Location refers to the proximity to transportation, employment, shopping, and desired cultural facilities, and the influence of any nuisance that is found in the area. Location is also the sum of all the characteristics of the people who are present in the neighborhood. When we refer to the neighborhood, we are emphasizing the general characteristics of the area. Location refers to how these characteristics apply to a specific site.

NEIGHBORHOOD BOUNDARIES

Where does one neighborhood end and another begin? Neighborhood boundaries occur where the location starts to change. In some cases, a neighborhood boundary will be sharply defined, as by a lake, river, marsh, freeway, or similar distinct barrier to development. In other cases, neighborhoods lack such sharp boundaries; instead there is a gradual merging of neighborhoods. Sometimes two adjacent neighborhoods could be considered as one because they differ only slightly in their characteristics. On the other hand, one could subdivide any neighborhood by using minor differences between its several parts. You can see that "neighborhood" is not a precise term, and that boundaries are usually not exact.

The type of boundary also varies for different types of neighborhoods. For example, the neighborhood for central financial office buildings in larger cities may be set by the cluster of the existing financial office buildings.

Industrial developments tend to have defined boundaries set up by the zoning ordinance or at the point where the existing industrial park stops. If the industrial district has a mixture of other uses in it, however, the boundary becomes uncertain. For example, many older central industrial areas have industrial buildings and residential buildings mixed together. This type of mixture has characteristics that could make it a neighborhood of its own, separate from adjoining areas that contain only industrial buildings.

Thus, neighborhood boundaries are usually defined by geographic features, political boundaries of some kind, or by transitions in the existing pattern of land use. The boundaries are often vague and imprecise; however, most local observers would generally agree about the area that is considered to be a neighborhood.

REVIEWING YOUR UNDERSTANDING

Neighborhoods as Foundations of Value

1. What determines the boundary of a neighborhood?
2. How small can a neighborhood be? How large?
3. What do occupants of a neighborhood have in common?

8.2 NEIGHBORHOODS AS BAROMETERS OF CHANGE

Although a neighborhood is a collection of relatively similar occupants, structures, and uses of land, there are slight differences among properties in the neighborhood. These variations could be among the lots, structures, occupants, or locations. When the forces that determine land use in the community are changing, their effects will be noticed first in those places that are most vulnerable to change. When the small changes over the months are similar, it indicates that the neighborhood is responding to the new forces pushing on it. An example would be conversions of homes to small offices along a busy street.

FORCES FOR CHANGE

All forces for neighborhood change can be described as physical, economic, social, or political. Within these broad headings, there are several different possibilities.

Physical Factors

Physical factors for neighborhood change include the effects of time and the elements. They include weather—from routine fading and settling to the sudden tornado or flood, as well as earthquakes, slides, soil creep, and fault creep. Fires can be a physical factor for change as can pollution.

Political Factors

Political factors that cause neighborhoods to change range from taxation to education. They include the effects of a radical city council upon a conservative neighborhood and of a traditional city council upon an unorthodox neighborhood. Examples of these effects can include the willingness or failure to provide the level and type of police and fire support that the neighborhood seeks. Political factors can combine with physical issues; one example is governmental land-use controls in neighborhoods that use septic tanks.

Social Factors

These can consist of national or local factors, or a variety of lifestyle and age factors. Examples include the type of conflict faced by a neighborhood with predominately older residents when younger couples move in. The conflict can be over children playing, rock guitar amplifiers, residence upkeep, or other issues that result from the differences in the characteristics of younger and older households.

Social conflicts can be among the most destructive to neighborhood stability. They are exceeded only by the physical catastrophes (fires, floods, etc). At various times in the past, changes in the nationality, race, or religion of neighborhood occupants have panicked owners into hasty flight. Fortunately, such an extreme reaction is rare today.

Economic Factors

The most obvious economic factor that causes neighborhoods to change is the *steady transition of a neighborhood* to lower-income use as its structures get older. Although this is not a rule throughout the life of a neighborhood, this concept will be true during most of its existence. A second economic factor is that *locations will vary in their economic stability*. Thus one neighborhood might be heavily occupied by workers from nearby electronics or auto factories. A swing in the business cycle within this neighborhood may cause more variation in the unemployment rate than another neighborhood occupied by people with a more varied mixture of jobs.

Transportation influences are a third economic factor. Because income differences affect the transportation capabilities of households, a bus strike, for example, will have different economic impacts on different neighborhoods. Closure of a bus company can have a permanent effect on one neighborhood's values but have no effect on another neighborhood that is also served by the bus line. The residents of the latter had the means to seek other transportation while the others did not. The effects of a transportation change upon a neighborhood involves the social class of the occupants as well as their income levels. For instance, in a downtown high-income apartment, automobile ownership may be as low as in a low-income residential neighborhood, leaving both areas dependent upon public transit.

Combinations

Physical, political, economic, or social factors can become involved with each other. Protection from floods is surely a political issue and a social responsibility. Damaging civil riots may involve all four factors in a most complex and distressing pattern. Nevertheless, it is helpful to categorize these factors in order to understand the forces at work in a neighborhood. Table 8.1 provides an outline of the forces for neighborhood change.

TYPES OF NEIGHBORHOOD CHANGE

As stated earlier, neighborhoods are a sensitive barometer of change in a city. The effects of change will be different in residential, commercial, or industrial neighborhoods. Nevertheless, the following broad categories suggest what to look for as signals of a changing neighborhood.

Condition

Age is an inescapable physical force creating change in every neighborhood. Regardless of the category of land use, there is a constant struggle to maintain the condition of the real estate. Stable, unchanging neighborhoods almost always appear well maintained. Other neighborhoods show signs of trouble when conditions deteriorate and repairs accumulate. This is a warning that at some future time more rapid change must occur.

Turnover

Surprisingly, a stable neighborhood does not necessarily mean stable ownership. The reason is that, like buildings, owners and occupants age. If there is no turnover in owners, then their average age gets steadily older. This increasing age has implications for use,

TABLE 8.1   A Summary of the Forces for Neighborhood Change

Physical	Social
Time	Conflicts
The elements	Age
Weathering	Lifestyles
Tornados	Demography
Floods	Ages
Earthquakes	Household sizes
Fires	
Pollution	**Economic**
	Job stability and diversity
Political	Aging of buildings
Facilities	Transportation cost and availability
Provided	
Omitted	
Taxes	
Amount	
Kind	
Philosophies	

maintenance and the demand for neighborhood properties. Will there be adequate future demand when owners' ages force the sale of an increasing number of properties? A reasonable level of turnover, then, is a sign of a stable neighborhood age balance. Too much turnover, however, represents a response to some unpleasant neighborhood force.

What is a "normal" turnover rate? The level will differ for owners of different property types. Downtown commercial properties usually have the slowest turnover rates, while residential districts vary widely, depending upon the age, income, and employment characteristics of the occupants.

Use Change

Changes in property use cause neighborhoods to change. When change in use start to occur, the first changes are usually at the boundaries of the neighborhood. This may involve demolition of a house for construction of a new store, for example. Often, however, the early changes do not involve demolition but rather conversion to another use. In the above example, instead of demolishing the house, it might be converted to an office or to a light commercial use like a dressmaker's shop or a preschool nursery. Not all changes occur, even if they are economically feasible. Many possible use changes will be regulated by the zoning ordinance, and a use permit, a variance, or rezoning would be needed. Neighborhoods often try to resist change by blocking these use changes politically.

Density of Occupancy

Sometimes when it is not feasible or legal to change the use, a more subtle change will occur—an increase in the density of use. A homeowner may rent out rooms; an industrial manager may sublease an unused portion of a plant; a store owner may sublease space for an affiliated venture; an office tenant may seek someone to share space. Increases in density are another way to get more income from an existing structure. This desired increase in income suggests that the previous income of the structure was inadequate to cover its costs, perhaps because the previous use was no longer successful at this location. These density changes are usually temporary, until economic conditions change enough to justify a full conversion in use or else a return to the prior use. In either case, however, the meaning is clear: the neighborhood is changing its characteristics, whether for better or worse.

THE MEANING OF IT ALL

What does all this change mean? How does it affect real estate markets and values? The most important concept to realize is not whether a change is for better or worse, but that a change is occurring. Once it is recognized that a neighborhood is changing, these changes can be studied to determine the forces causing the shift. Consider changes as signals for the future—predictors of the direction of real estate values. Common indicators of neighborhood change are turnovers, shifts in usage, increases in density, and increases or decreases in upkeep and maintenance. An understanding of the patterns of city growth, outlined in Chapter Seven, should be combined with an understanding of the forces of neighborhood change. This combination will help to forecast the investment potential of individual properties within the city and neighborhood.

REVIEWING YOUR UNDERSTANDING

Neighborhoods as Barometers of Change

1. List four forces that produce neighborhood change. Give two examples of each.
2. List five visible effects of neighborhood change.

8.3   AS NEIGHBORHOODS AGE

The song says, "That old man river, he just keeps rolling along." Like a river, aging is a constant force for change. The changes that age imposes on neighborhoods affect every neighborhood regardless of use.

PROGRESSIVE DECAY

Age exposes property to the weathering effects of the elements and to wear and tear from use. Unless care and maintenance are applied, buildings deteriorate and decay with age. The comment has been made that houses do not wear out but neighborhoods do. Do neighborhoods die? Like people, do neighborhoods have a life cycle of childhood, maturity, and decline?

It is obvious that some type of a "life" sequence does occur in all neighborhoods. In its childhood, a new neighborhood will have only a few new buildings. The remaining area will be vacant lots or older, preexisting uses. As a neighborhood advances to adulthood, most of the land will have been developed and the initially high rate of new construction will slow down. Some construction may continue for several years as the last remaining lots are slowly developed. During the maturing or middle-aged stage of a neighborhood, building conditions generally remain good. Occupancy is typically stable, and the properties generate adequate income.

In time, however, the community changes. These changes begin to have their effect on the neighborhood, and neighborhood decline sets in. Deteriorated buildings and other signs of decay are noticeable. This sequence can be observed in many neighborhoods, but the age of the neighborhood does not seem to be closely related to the time in the sequence. Areas such as Georgetown in Washington, D.C., are several hundred years old and have never been more desirable than they are now. Other areas appear to pass maturity and turn downward in 25 years, as in some of the lower-priced residential subdivisions built in the 1960s and early 1970s.

The End Result

We should note that neighborhood life cycles do not lead inevitably to the same result. In some cases, a declining neighborhood is redeveloped for a new use. This might involve the commercial expansion of the downtown area or expansion of nearby industrial areas. The conversion to a new use can be accomplished by private money, or it can be aided by governmental urban-renewal programs.

In other cases, a neighborhood simply continues to decline. The dying process continues and produces a neighborhood that is truly a social horror. In some extreme cases, the neighborhood becomes so miserable that many city blocks of property are totally abandoned.

WOW! WHAT HAPPENED?

Most interesting, however, are older deteriorated neighborhoods that neither change uses nor slide into blight. At some point, some factor or group of factors emerges to produce a slow, gradual stabilization of the neighborhood and even reverse its decline. Remember that the properties are still aging; weather and constant use are still beating them down. The process that stabilizes such a neighborhood *must* be positive and forceful to overcome the continuing pressures of time!

This process of stabilization is not well understood, but is very significant to the real estate community. Here is why. When a city's population is growing, there is ample economic pressure to convert a deteriorating older neighborhood to new land uses. But when the city's population is not growing or even is declining, then there tends to be no demand for new land uses. So the alternative of converting an old decaying neighborhood to a new use would not be present. Enduring the deteriorating slums, the other alternative, is an even worse answer. So the process of neighborhood recovery, then, is critical if society is to have pleasant stable older neighborhoods in cities with stable or declining population.

THE REHABILITATION CYCLE

The evidence suggests that in a number of older American residential neighborhoods, property has repeated the same cycle a series of times. Let us review the steps of this cycle. Each cycle has started with neighborhood properties well maintained, modernized, and occupied by stable uses. The cycle then turns to a gradual decay of the neighborhood, with all the effects noted earlier.

This leads to a period when the neighborhood has deteriorated and prices of properties have fallen. In some instances, prices will sink quite far before the recovery begins. The neighborhood has a high turnover of low-income persons. Density is high and maintenance is low. Illegal uses can be common, and abandoned properties are noted, often in the center or heart of the neighborhood.

The Recovery Period

The cycle then enters a recovery period, attracting new occupants who are different in income levels and density of occupancy from present occupants. This change usually appears first on one side of the neighborhood, toward the better-maintained or more attractive areas that are adjacent. These new occupants rehabilitate and remodel the structures that they buy and occupy (see Figure 8.2). They will be pioneers who show the way to additional buyers, so that a gradual renaissance of the neighborhood occurs. Prices begin to rise at this stage, and enthusiasm grows, often to an evangelical pitch! This is the rehabilitation phase of the neighborhood cycle.

However, over the years the enthusiasm wears off. As the forces of aging continue, the neighborhood reaches a mature state again and starts to deteriorate once more. This cycle of decay and rebirth can be repeated indefinitely unless it is interrupted by a major change in land use.

The American Experience

Many older American cities have experienced such repeated rehabilitation cycles. In some cases, the cycle has had a very wide swing, from decayed slum to prestige address. Certain examples are well known, such as Georgetown in Washington D.C., and Back Bay in Boston. Others are not well known and could be only a few blocks in area. Some swings of the cycle may only be ripples: a small and unnoticed deterioration of some houses for several years, and then a gradual recovery. Nearly every major article on housing rehabilitation now mentions a new neighborhood where this cycle has been observed.

History shows that residential neighborhoods need not deteriorate into slums; that deterioration, once begun, can still be stopped. However, there is still the question of how to halt or reverse deterioration.

It is well to remember that American cities are far younger than those in some other areas of the world. Our understanding of neighborhood aging and the feasible life of structures is less complete than those who have wrestled with the problem for 2,000 years (as Rome has) or 4,000 years (as Cairo has).

FIGURE 8.2   Signs of neighborhood recovery. Boston Redevelopment Authority.

LEARNING TO FIGHT DECAY

How is neighborhood decay arrested and rehabilitation encouraged? What is this magical process that can fight off the forces of aging? Indeed, not every decaying neighborhood can be preserved. To try would be to try to freeze change or to deny that change exists and is real! Neighborhood declines that should *not* be reversed might include areas on the fringe of a growing downtown commercial area, where land conversion is feasible. Another example is a neighborhood so influenced by a new transportation system that it is best to encourage change.

SPECIAL INTEREST TOPIC

Neighborhood Preservation: Two Viewpoints

1. *Government aid:* When a community decides that a neighborhood should be preserved, then the resources of the entire community should be put to work. One could just wait to see if the neighborhood recovers by itself, but many do not. Instead, an active effort is required. Aging and obsolescence can be countered by maintenance and remodeling. Property owners who are willing to do this should be encouraged and provided with the necessary funds by loans or outright grants and other public assistance. Owners or tenants who refuse to maintain their properties must be persuaded to do so by social pressure or legal force.

2. *Free market approach:* Keep government out of the neighborhood preservation business! The free market of supply and demand will be a better determinant of the highest and best use of land than will a government agency. Given a reasonable amount of time, the profit motive will stimulate maintenance of an existing use or a transition to a more economically feasible use. Government's track record of mandated neighborhood preservation is a tale of waste, mismanagement, blown up housing projects, and silly economics.

Imagine an older residential section that has had a new rapid transit station placed in the middle of it. The traffic, noise, and congestion from the station can destroy the residential amenities that single-family residential owners require. The transportation shift also changes the characteristics of the neighborhood's location by changing its accessibility. This could change the neighborhood's use from private homes to new apartments and apartment conversions. These uses are oriented to the easy transportation access and are historically more tolerant of congestion and noise.

Destabilizing Forces

Forces other than age also contribute to neighborhood decline. In many communities, for example, the master plan and zoning ordinance show older residential neighborhoods as intended for some other use. This is a policy statement that the neighborhood is to be changed. It is a serious error if, in fact, the community seeks to stabilize and save the existing use of the neighborhood.

In addition, many people have commented that property taxes often work against neighborhood stabilization. They point out that a professional tax assessor is required to reevaluate a remodeled property because of its higher value. However, this leads to a higher tax, which penalizes the person who remodels and continues to occupy the building. Assessors have also usually placed low values on slum properties because the owner can demonstrate limited property income and major deterioration. Deteriorated property thus usually has much lower taxes than rehabilitated buildings in the same neighborhood.

In many communities, the process of change has included population shifts. In some cases, there has been extreme antagonism between the group departing the neighborhood and the group entering. Such hostile transitions often hasten neighborhood deterioration during the months or years of change.

Another problem is where market pressures or the individual idiosyncrasies of owners introduce clashing uses into a neighborhood. With some effort, the community could try to minimize the destructive effects of market pressures upon other uses. If the land use in a neighborhood is going to change, for example, from residential to commercial, the changes should be encouraged first at the edges of the neighborhood, where the impact will be less noticeable. The heart of the neighborhood could be fully protected from the change for a while. Thus the new use can be gradually phased in without years of growing blight and neighborhood problems.

A Summary of Preservation

The foregoing discussion highlights how the forces of change put pressure upon a neighborhood and what stabilizing actions are available. Fighting neighborhood decay involves locating the negative forces in time to correct the problem or to fight the negative influence. Just who should fight decay, government or private enterprise, is debatable. However, those who take action should comprehend neighborhood forces and effects if they are to obtain the desired results. A thorough knowledge of urban land economics is the key to understanding.

REVIEWING YOUR UNDERSTANDING

As Neighborhoods Age

1. Why is age such an important factor in neighborhood change?
2. What are the phases of the neighborhood life cycle? What steps are involved in the rehabilitation phase?
3. Why is rehabilitation significant to the future of American cities?
4. Give examples in your community of deteriorating neighborhoods (not just residential uses) that have recovered, or of neighborhoods deteriorating because of negative factors that can be changed.

CHAPTER SUMMARY

This chapter has discussed the clusters of similar land uses called "neighborhoods." As noted in Chapter Seven, land uses tend to form clusters of similar uses, drawn together by their mutual need for the characteristics of a particular location or place in the pattern of the city.

Because real estate is not movable, its value is influenced by the location of the property as well as its characteristics. Location is the combination of all the influences on land use that are characteristic of a particular place in a community. A neighborhood is simply an area of similar uses and similar locational influences.

Neighborhood boundaries are sometimes set by physical objects (freeways) or political borders (city limits). In other cases, one group of uses will blend into another with no definable boundary. Neighborhood size varies with the use and location.

The study of neighborhoods is important because changes that eventually affect individual values are first visible at the neighborhood level. Investors and homeowners need to interpret neighborhood changes early enough to protect their investments.

Examples of forces that change neighborhoods include physical elements such as age and weather, political factors like school quality and taxation, social factors including group conflicts and group attitudes, and numerous economic influences. Often, the forces behind changes are complex or obscure. Thus the *effects* of these forces usually are the first indication of change.

Condition of properties is a sensitive indication since both age and weather cause deterioration. The rate of turnover of occupants and owners is also a measure of stability. Other barometers of neighborhood stability and change are changes in uses and density of occupancy.

Aging of property is an especially important force because of its constant negative pressure. Neighborhoods and properties start out new, become mature, and decay in a predictable cycle. The length of time of the cycle varies and so does the end result. Some decayed neighborhoods are redeveloped to a new use, either by private or governmental effort. Others become stagnant slums.

Some areas, however, neither change their major use nor slide into blight. Rather, they extend the neighborhood cycle into a new phase of rehabilitation, which repairs and restores the old structures and brings the neighborhood back to its mature, stable stage again. Some American cities have older neighborhoods that have gone through a number of such rehabilitation and decay cycles.

Not every decaying neighborhood can be preserved. However, interest in neighborhood preservation is increasing. The process involves locating those forces that hurt the neighborhood and correcting them. Thus, aging is met by renovation efforts. Economic pressures for land changes can, rightly or wrongly, be blocked by zoning or redirected to limit the impact of change.

IMPORTANT TERMS AND CONCEPTS

Change in use

Deterioration or decay

Forces for change

   Economic

   Physical

   Political

   Social

Neighborhood cycle

Neighborhood obsolescence

Preservation

Rehabilitation cycle

REVIEWING YOUR UNDERSTANDING

1. A cluster of properties of relatively similar land use and value is a:
   a. neighborhood
   b. location
   c. city
   d. block

2. The value of a property at a particular location is created by which force?
   a. political
   b. economic
   c. physical
   d. all of the above

3. A political factor that causes a neighborhood to change is a(n):

    a. earthquake

    b. change in lifestyles

    c. rezoning

    d. new transportation route

4. An economic factor that causes a neighborhood to change is:

    a. an earthquake

    b. change in lifestyles

    c. rezoning

    d. a new transportation route

5. Which of the following establish neighborhood boundaries?

    a. rivers

    b. zoning

    c. private deed restrictions

    d. all of the above

6. An ideal stable residential neighborhood would have:

    a. no turnovers

    b. high turnovers

    c. reasonable turnovers

    d. high percentage of commercial properties

7. All neighborhoods will:

    a. decline

    b. age

    c. stabilize

    d. appreciate

8. High turnover, fallen prices, and deferred maintenance are signs of what phase in the life cycle of a neighborhood?

    a. beginning

    b. stabilization

    c. deterioration

    d. rehabilitation

9. When an attempt is made to save a residential neighborhood from decay, which of the following requires the most reconstruction?

    a. preservation

    b. prevention

    c. rehabilitation

    d. reconciliation

10. A study of changes in city growth patterns, coupled with shifts in neighborhood uses, helps to predict:

   a. changes in values of properties located in the neighborhood
   b. future appreciation rates
   c. good investment opportunities
   d. all of the above

Chapter 9

Housing Markets

Preview

Chapter Nine explores factors that influence residential property values. Section 9.1 discusses the demand for housing and what causes changes in demand. Section 9.2 focuses on the supply of housing, including both new construction and existing structures. Section 9.3 reviews the effects of governmental actions on the market for residential property. When you have finished this chapter you will be able to:

1. List the major forces influencing supply and demand for residential real estate.

2. Locate sources of information about the status of these factors.

3. Discuss how to obtain forecasts of national and local housing market trends.

4. List the major effects of governmental activity in the housing market.

This information will help you to anticipate changes in residential markets in your area.

HOUSING MARKETS

Communities contain many different land uses, but the most common is residential housing. Housing land use includes homes, apartments, hotels, motels, and boarding homes. This chapter concentrates on homes and apartments. In previous chapters, it was noted how the allocation of land in a mixed capitalistic economy occurs mostly in the marketplace. There buyers and sellers interact, and eventually a price is determined and a real estate sale takes place. Government has a powerful influence on the final outcome of a real estate sale and the future use of the property. In this chapter attention is focused on two main topics: (1) How do the laws of supply and demand influence the residential housing market? and (2) What impact does government intervention have on the housing market?

9.1   THE DEMAND FOR HOUSING

Housing demand should be studied from two points of view. The first looks at total demand, or the numbers of housing units needed. The second looks at changes in the composition of housing demand; for example, unit size, age, location, condition, and whether the unit was intended for owner occupancy or for rent. Housing analysis involves both total numbers and detailed preferences.

The demand for housing is influenced by three major factors: (1) population, (2) effective income, and (3) tastes.

POPULATION

The most important influence upon housing demand is population. To put it simply, housing is for people, and their presence or absence affects housing demand. Thus, major growth in community population must be followed by a growth in the number of housing units.

Demography

Sheer numbers of people, however, are not the only influence of population on housing demand. A second major influence is *demog-*

raphy, which is the composition of the population grouped according to age, sex, occupation, income level, and other socioeconomic variables. Demography is important because people of different demographic characteristics have differing housing demands. For example, young children live with their parents. By the time they are 18 or so, some have moved into their own apartments. By age 30, the great majority have moved into a housing unit of their own.

Thus, we can visualize two neighborhoods with the same total populations but with different demography and different housing needs. One neighborhood might contain mostly older, retired people living in apartments. Some might be couples and some single persons. Only a few would have any children living at home. Another neighborhood might be made up of single-family homes occupied by middle-aged, middle-income families. This second neighborhood would have far more children and thus larger families. While the population is the same in both neighborhoods the number of housing units would be less in the second, as a result of the larger average family size. The neighborhoods would also differ in type of housing, demand for schools, shops, traffic volumes, etc.

The Importance of Population Trends

Of all the factors that influence housing demand, population is the most important. Luckily, population information is readily available. Demographic change is especially easy to follow because of the time delay before babies become adults. Researchers can forecast the demography of the next 10 years by adding 10 years to the present age composition of a population and adjusting for births, deaths, and in and out migration. Migration varies greatly, so forecasts will be more reliable in slowly changing areas than in rapidly changing areas.

Each area has its own demographic breakdown, and future changes in each will be different. In some neighborhoods, the kids will grow up and want apartments. In others, the middle-aged couples will grow older, find big homes burdensome, and put their houses up for sale. In another area, the young apartment dwellers may be marrying, having children, and seeking larger dwelling units. For the nation as a whole, the 1980s had a strong housing demand as the "boom babies" of the 1950s became the homebuyers of the 1980s.

However, the 1990s might be different as the fewer "pill babies" of the 1960s and 1970s come of homeowner age. The drop in the number of household formations in the 1990's has led some economists to forecast that the housing market will become a "buyer's" market, in sharp contrast to the "seller's" market of the 1980s.

DIVORCE RATE

The high rate of divorce in the U.S. also influences housing demand. With no increase in population, an increase in the divorce rate will create need for additional housing units. If the divorced person remarries the additional demand is temporary; if the person decides to remain unmarried the demand is permanent. Uncoupling by unmarried people living together can have the same results as a divorce.

In high divorce rate states, such as California, the divorce rate is a major factor contributing to the high demand for housing. The divorce and uncoupling rate is seen by some as an offset for the decline in demand due to fewer household formations as the median age of the population rises. Needless to say, this trend is not well received in some circles!

Sources of Information About Population and Demography Trends

Population and demographic breakdowns are frequently available from county or state planning offices. Their projections range from 10 to 50 years. The longer-range forecasts, however, are less reliable. Good information on population characteristics is compiled every 10 years when the national housing and population censuses are taken. The government tries to estimate and update the information each year. Before attempting to gather this information, be sure to check with the U.S. Department of Housing and Urban Development, local universities, utility companies, planning departments, or private research firms to see if the work has already been done.

INCOME

The second major item influencing housing demand is income. People who lack money cannot afford adequate housing, however great their housing needs. When people have a housing need, and if their income is sufficient to pay the costs of housing, then they create an effective demand for housing. For some people, too many bills to pay or mouths to feed restrict the money available for housing. Thus, when analyzing income as a factor in housing demand, one focuses on that portion of people's total income available for housing use.

Income levels, like population, affect not only total housing demand but also the composition of that demand. Higher incomes often cause people to leave rental units and buy homes or condominiums. People of lower incomes sometimes find they must share housing accommodations with their parents or other relatives. This is called "doubling up." When their income increases, they frequently move out and seek a dwelling of their own. This is a process called "undoubling."

Income Changes

A rise in income can cause a change in the type of unit demanded. Examples include the addition of swimming pools, family rooms, extra bathrooms, and the like. A decline in income, however, leads to more modest housing and perhaps to doubling up. Income levels must also be compared to current housing costs. Thus, in the

1980s housing costs rose more rapidly than income. Although the demand for housing increased during this period, this "affordability" problem kept demand from rising further.

The national trend toward higher incomes is expected to continue. At any particular time, however, some incomes may fall due to a decline in the national or local business cycle. Forecasting income changes in a particular town thus calls for an understanding of the present state of the local business cycle and a forecast of the future cycle, plus a forecast of the long-term trend of area and national incomes.

Availability of Credit

Buying a home is the largest single purchase most people make, and few people have the resources to pay cash for a home. The availability and cost of mortgage credit has an important influence on people's ability to buy, and therefore it has an impact on the demand for housing. For tenants, the cost of mortgage credit affects the landlord's need for rent, which in turn is a factor in setting rent levels. Lower mortgage interest rates have the effect of increasing demand for housing at given levels of income.

A significant increase in housing demand in the past century has occurred because of liberal changes in mortgage credit. Real estate loans have gone from two- to five-year interest only loans, renewed at the lender's discretion, to 30—40-year fully amortized loans. Special loan features, such as below-market adjustable "teaser" rates and equity sharing, plus other innovations have allowed many people to acquire a home they otherwise would not be able to afford. The massive housing boom that followed World War II was aided by the Federal Housing Administration (FHA) and other government programs that liberalized financing standards.

It is clear that future changes in mortgage credit will also affect housing demand. Any U.S. capital shortages in the future will bring hard times to the real estate housing market. Economists closely watch the U.S. savings rate and the rate of foreign investment for signs of shift. If the savings rate rises and/or foreign investment in the U.S. capital market increases, that will spell good news for the housing market. If the opposite occurs, hard times could hit the housing market. Also the size of the U.S. budget deficit has an impact on the availability and cost of mortgage money. If the U.S. government must finance a large deficit, it can "crowd out" the private sector, driving up interest rates. If plentiful, affordable housing is a national goal, society will need to establish capital priorities and reorganize financial institutions so that mortgage credit can remain affordable.

CHANGES IN TASTE

The third major factor influencing housing demand is taste or lifestyle. The most basic need for housing is little more than shelter from animals and the elements. As people seek a better standard of

SPECIAL INTEREST TOPIC

$$$ Affordability Index $$$

The National Association of Realtors® and the California Association of Realtors® have constructed a housing affordability index. The index comprises three basic elements.

1. Determine the median home prices for the area. Median means half of the sale prices were above and half of the sale prices were below.
2. Select the prevailing interest rates on standard home loans. Usually defined as 20% down, 80% conventional home loan, most often using fixed rate loans.
3. Determine the median income level for the area.

How the index is applied:

The median home price is determined, then loan payments are computed using a standard home loan at prevailing interest rates. Then the income needed to qualify for this loan is determined. Finally, the two are put together to complete a percentage. Example: Assume the median-priced home is $200,000. A 80% loan at 10% interest for 30 years equals monthly payments of $1,404.12 × 12 months = approximately $16,849 per year. If current standards require an annual income of $60,000 per year to qualify for this loan payment, the $60,000 is measured against the median income level. In our example, if the median income level for the year is $45,000, the affordability index would be:

$$\frac{\$45,000}{\$60,000} = 75\%.$$

This means that a family earning the median income level of $45,000 only had 75% of the income needed to qualify for the purchase of a median-priced home. This index can be constructed for new homes, existing homes, first-time home buyers and so on. Obviously, the index ratings will vary by regions and cities. A score of 100% means the median income family can afford the median-priced home. A score of more than 100% means good news for the local housing market, while scores below 100% mean that housing tends to be overpriced relative to local income and the housing market may suffer. Current national and local affordability index ratings are published in Realtor® magazines.

---

living, they respond to their own desire or their friends' expectations of what life ought to be. Thus, where people choose to live is not only a function of income and credit, but also personal preference. For example, some people choose to place most of their wealth in their home, while others might choose a modest principal residence, plus a getaway vacation home. Still others decide to spend the minimum on housing and use the extra money for investments, leisure, or hobbies.

Can Consumer Taste and Lifestyles Be Forecasted?

No one can say how long a particular fancy will last or how widespread it will become. The only certainty is change itself. However, real estate investors should constantly monitor the market for change. Students of marketing suggest that taste changes appear first in people who are fashion conscious, then "trickle down" to the general population. Will housing styles be as volatile as clothing fashion? Will the Santa Fe housing motif be like the miniskirt? Are huge houses on small lots in, while condos are out? No one knows for sure, but because of tradition and the long life of homes, changes in housing taste tend to occur slowly. This usually allows builders to adjust their inventory so as not to be stuck with unsold unappealing homes. For existing homes, updating and remodeling are ways to maintain appeal and value.

REVIEWING YOUR UNDERSTANDING

The Demand for Housing

1. What are the three major forces influencing housing demand?
2. How does demography affect housing demand?
3. How does mortgage credit affect housing demand?
4. What do people's tastes have to do with housing demand?

9.2   THE SUPPLY OF RESIDENTIAL HOUSING

It is important to notice that housing differs from many other economic commodities because a very large percentage of the demand is met by the supply of units already in existence. In boom years, new construction has added around 2 percent per year to our national housing stock. Most local areas experience a similar percentage increase. The existing stock is thus 98 percent of all our housing supply in any particular year. In summary, economists consider the supply of real estate housing fixed in the short-run. Therefore, change in supply is viewed as a slow process occurring over a long period of time. The supply of housing must be studied from two viewpoints: (1) the total number of units and (2) the quality or suitability of the units.

EVALUATION OF SUPPLY

The supply of housing at any future time consists of units presently available, minus those units lost due to fires, demolition, and conversions to other uses, and increased by buildings converted to housing and by new construction. The process is illustrated in Table 9.1.

Demolition and Destruction

In a changing community, all land use will eventually become the wrong use of the site at some future time. Changes in the community almost guarantee that this will happen. As a better use comes along, land values rise. The existing building decreases in value as it gets older, and decreases more if the existing use is affected by new buildings with better uses. At a certain point, it becomes economically profitable to tear down the old building and build a new one to reflect the new highest and best use of the land. At this point the old structure has reached the end of its economic life. This economic life

TABLE 9.1   Changes in Housing Stock, Sometown

	21,214	Existing stock, end of previous year
Less	− 137	Demolitions during current year
	21,077	
Less	− 7	Housing units converted to other uses
	21,070	
Plus	+ 4	Other units converted to residences
	21,074	
Plus	+ 38	Added units to existing structures
	21,102	
Plus	+ 393	New construction
	21,505	Existing stock, end of current year

can end *long* before the building has reached the end of its physical life, depending on its location and the rate of change of the community.

Not all buildings are torn down because they have reached the end of their economic lives. Some are destroyed by fire, earthquakes, and other disasters. Some buildings are demolished in order to build public improvements such as highways and schools, or for urban renewal. In many American communities demolition for urban renewal and highway purposes noticeably reduced the existing housing stock.

Thus, in forecasting future housing supply, analysts do not assume that the existing stock will be there forever. Some of the units reach the end of their physical lives. Other units will be torn down at the end of their economic lives for construction of nonresidential properties; the probable rate of demolition for various public purposes must also be taken into account. In some communities, the number of homes demolished to make way for new public improvements exceeds the number demolished because of a loss in economic life. Fortunately, public projects are planned far in advance, and their impact can be anticipated.

Conversion and Its Effects on Supply

In addition to demolition, the housing stock is changed by conversions. Conversions can increase the number of housing units by converting houses or other structures into apartments or flats. On the other hand, some conversions may change a residential unit into an office, medical center, or other nonresidential use, and this reduces the housing supply. One must combine the additions and subtractions to determine what net effect conversions have on the local housing market.

In general, conversion is not a major force in the change of housing supply. Data on past conversions is obtainable from the same building permit sources as demolition and new construction data.

New Construction

New construction varies greatly from year to year and, especially, from area to area. It is also the largest element in the yearly change in housing supply. New construction occurs only when the required resources are available. These are the classic four elements of land, labor, capital, and entrepreneurial skills. Similarly, the costs of obtaining these resources must be in balance with each other and with the housing prices found in the marketplace. Changes in availability of these resources will change their prices and affect the ability to build for a profit.

Past experience demonstrates that shortages in these resources do occur. For example, land shortages can result from environmental restrictions or governmental attitudes toward the zoning of land.

Labor shortages can result from attempts to increase housing construction beyond the limits of the available trained work force. Capital shortages or the so called "credit crunch," consisting of a shrinking money supply and high interest rates, has restricted new housing construction. Shortages of capital also show up as shortages of raw materials, because the raw materials require plants, mines, wells, and the like to produce them. Entrepreneurial shortages are less common in this country because the nature of house construction encourages people in the housing industry to learn development skills. Other countries, however, with different social attitudes have had difficulty in obtaining sufficient people with necessary development skills and knowledge.

Forecasts of new construction thus have to consider the availability of related resources. In fact, the major factor influencing recent variation in new construction (see Table 9.2) has been changes in the cost and availability of capital.

Future Supply Trends

Despite increasing numbers of studies, laws, and programs, many observers say that restrictions on new construction and shortages of key resources are growing very rapidly. Increasing shortages have driven up the cost of land, capital, labor, and many of the raw materials that are produced by others for the construction industry. When costs are going up as they have been, a developer will build only when prices are expected to go up as fast or faster. Some forecast that housing costs will continue to increase faster than buyer incomes, thereby causing a reduction in new housing construction. The renovation and remodeling of the existing housing stock may be a more significant factor to the future housing supply than has been true for the last several decades.

IS THE HOUSING SUITABLE?

For most cities, nearly all the housing supply consists of existing dwelling units. You remember from Chapter Five that two special features of real estate are its long life and fixed location. Thus the suitability of existing housing becomes most important.

TABLE 9.2   New Housing Units Authorized in California (in thousands)

Year	Total	Multiple	Single
1980	144,987	58,355	86,832
1985	263,682	153,873	109,809
1986	302,934	159,921	143,013
1987	248,695	115,406	133,289
1988	252,520	92,001	160,519
1989	237,747	75,096	162,651
1990	164,394	60,219	104,175

Source: California Statistical Abstract 1990, Department of Finance

SPECIAL INTEREST TOPIC

The Savings and Loan Crisis and Its Impact on the Housing Market

Several new federal agencies were created as part of the government bailout of the savings and loan industry. For the real estate market one of the most important new agencies is the Resolution Trust Corporation (RTC). The RTC is responsible for disposing of the assets of failed savings and loan associations. With the number of failed institutions estimated to be 800 to 1,000, the amount of foreclosed real estate that needs to be resold is significant. The first preliminary list of RTC properties, issued in January 1990, had over 30,000 properties with thousands of additional properties still to come. The bulk of the properties are located in Texas and Oklahoma. Only 351 homes from California were on the initial list, whereas 14,328 homes on the list were in Texas. With the small number of California properties, resales there by the RTC should not depress local real estate prices.

The Southwest housing market is another story. As the RTC attempts to resell properties in the Southwest, will the supply so outweigh the demand that all home prices will crash? Will this lead to even more foreclosures as existing owner-occupied values decline below their mortgage loan balances? According to the guidelines issued by Congress, the RTC is to "maximize" profits for the taxpayers, but it is not to "unduly" depress local real estate prices. Is this not a conflict in direction? "Maximize" means to cut losses by selling the homes as soon as possible, eliminating the need for expensive management and maintenance. Will local real estate interests lobby Congress to slow down the resale process? If, as proposed, low income people and the homeless are given preferential rights to the inventory will this have a negative impact on the private rental market? Will the RTC fall victim to politics and be left with unsold inventory, costing the taxpayers billions of unrecovered dollars? The answers to these questions will not be known for some time to come.

What About Condition?

Because of the long life of housing structures, the condition of existing housing is very significant. When only 2 percent of the units are new each year (in a stable community), the average life expectancy of all dwelling units is around 40 years. Few houses are built of materials that will last for 40 years without maintenance. Thus, housing units are vulnerable to deterioration over their lifetimes. The extent to which this has happened is a major question in a review of older housing and older neighborhoods. Real estate economists are particularly interested in this subject. Many older buildings are not receiving adequate maintenance and are gradually deteriorating. When an entire neighborhood suffers, a blight sets in. The deteriorated condition of the area seems to deter people from further maintenance, so that the blighted area gets worse and bigger. This has led to the complete abandonment of whole blocks of buildings in areas of cities like New York, Detroit, and Cleveland. Such abandoned houses effectively reduce the supply of housing units because people refuse to move into the area. This condition, which need not occur, is being carefully studied by urban policy makers. It is a central issue for the 1990s.

What About Features?

Buyers tend to seek "amenities," which are the benefits of ownership or occupancy as perceived by the occupant. These can include physical features such as shelter and warmth, space, age, and condition. Such features can often be measured by objective scales or techniques. Many of the elements of amenity, however, are not so objective. They depend on taste, status, and public opinion. These amenity features are often changeable as well as hard to measure. Forecasting residential markets is thus complicated by the difficulty of forecasting the attitudes of buyers, sellers, renters, and landlords toward amenity features. Buyers and sellers in the past have periodically changed their views on the importance of such amenities as newness, unconventional architecture, and suburban versus central living. Similar future changes are likely and must be considered in reviewing the housing market.

One example of this is the "density of occupancy." The federal government has used one person per room as a housing goal. Some segments of the housing market are seeking lower density, while others are choosing higher densities to free income for other purposes. Over the last 20 years, the trend in new home construction has been to reduce average density, or increase the number of rooms relative to the number of occupants. Some further reduction in density of occupancy is likely in the next few years, but longer-range forecasts are less certain.

As buildings age, it becomes more likely that some aspect of the housing unit will not suit people's changing desires for amenity features. Major changes in the features, design, or equipment of houses occur surprisingly slowly. However, the 40-year lifetime of an average house is long enough that some elements of design become out of date, old-fashioned, unworkable, inefficient, or irreparable. As this happens, the housing unit becomes increasingly obsolete unless corrected by remodeling. Thus, a study of neighborhoods must consider the amount of obsolete features and remodeling rate.

What About Location?

Another unique characteristic of real estate is its fixed location. Because of this, it is possible for changes in the community to make a certain use of the land no longer suitable, i.e., locationally obsolete.

Thus, a building that is nearly new could become so obsolete as to be torn down, causing a fair amount of economic waste. Such waste can be reduced, however, if the unit has the flexibility to be converted to another use.

The problem of fixed location is compounded by the long life of buildings as compared with the rate of change of the community in which they are located. This has been especially true of rapidly growing communities in the western United States. This type of obsolescence, which shortens the economic life of the building, is a noticeable influence on the rate of building demolition in a community. Thus, as stated earlier in this chapter, it is an influence on changes in the supply of housing. As the community's population mix, or demography, changes over the years, the housing supply must meet the demand changes that result.

Suitable for Whom?

In general, the long life of residential real estate means that the building must have sufficient flexibility to meet the changing needs of a long-term occupant or the needs of a series of users. This need for flexibility is a major reason for the slow and cautious rate of change in building design. Only the rich can afford to risk large sums to build a radical design that others may not be willing to buy.

Long life also means that the product can expect to be occupied by people of differing backgrounds and income. Since older units are generally in poorer condition, more obsolete, and less desirable than new ones, their values are generally less than new ones. Thus, housing units are typically occupied by lower-income users as the units get older. Most housing for lower-income occupants comes from this process, which is called *filtering.*

Filtering is a central part of the residential market, given the long life of dwellings and the changing needs and tastes of people. Problems that develop during the filtering process have to do with the condition and obsolescence of the unit. Housing units are clearly capable of periodic renovation and renewal if social and economic circumstances so dictate. The American student of real estate should consider that housing units in many other countries are expected to last hundreds of years. In some European cities it is not unusual to live in a building that is more than 300 years old. These units are given adequate repair and periodic remodeling and provide entirely adequate housing for comparable total costs. The existence of slums, from this view, is primarily a breakdown in the ongoing repair and renovation process that dwelling units must receive as they filter through a series of occupants and owners.

REVIEWING YOUR UNDERSTANDING

The Supply of Housing

1. What are the two central issues of or viewpoints on housing supply?
2. How important is demolition to housing supply?
3. What is the effect of new construction on housing supply and what causes it to vary?

9.3   GOVERNMENTAL HOUSING PROGRAMS

The reason frequently given for governmental interference in the market is to change some unsatisfactory result of the usual working of supply and demand. This could be the result of a lack of adequate knowledge among buyers or perhaps a problem that the market cannot currently solve to acceptable standards (e.g., housing for large poor families). Governmental actions come in the form of housing regulations or outright support.

REGULATING THE HOUSING MARKET

One group of governmental actions is basically restrictive or regulatory. These policies are intended to halt some action that the market would otherwise allow. Zoning and planning are major examples of this type. For example, the zoning ordinance may forbid commercial uses in a residential zone. This regulation follows a belief that someone would put in a commercial use if it were not prohibited and that such a use would have detrimental effects on the residential area.

Others argue that profit motives would cluster similar land uses in the absence of zoning. Each owner, seeking to maximize property values, would only locate next to similar users. Therefore, a commercial building placed in a residential area would not be the highest and best use and should not occur. If by chance it did occur, market forces would soon render the building uneconomical and make it a candidate for demolition and another use.

Subdivision laws are another type of government restriction. Local, state, and federal subdivision laws require complicated and expensive approval procedures. These regulations are government's response to the belief, right or wrong, that some developers would put together an inadequate subdivision, and that buyers would be unaware of the deceit and unable to correct the problem by the market pressures of supply and demand.

The building and housing codes are also regulatory. These codes

SPECIAL INTEREST TOPICS

Rent Controls—Do They Make Economic Sense?

LANDLORD   TENANT

Rent control is a controversial topic with emotions and misconceptions running rampant on both sides of the issue.

From a purely economic point of view rent controls make little sense. The issue has been repeatedly studied by both liberal and conservative economists, and most agree that rent controls do not solve housing problems. Rents are high because demand for apartment housing is high and supply is inadequate. The solution is to either decrease demand for rental units or increase the supply.

Rent controls do neither. Rent controls artificially depress rent levels which in turn stimulates demand instead of reducing it. Rent controls reduce returns and yields on apartment investments, thereby discouraging the construction of new units or the conversion of large homes into apartments. In short, rent controls tend to perpetuate the ill they are supposed to cure!

Condo Conversions

One of the most interesting developments has been the conversion of existing apartment buildings to condominiums. The conversion rate is spurred by:

1. An increase in demand for owner-occupied housing.
2. An increase in profits for apartment owners whose rents have not kept pace with costs and inflation, especially in areas hit by rent controls.
3. An inability to build new housing because of environmental and other controls.

When apartments are converted to condominiums, the supply of housing for purchase increases, while the supply of housing for rent decreases.

Several local governments have enacted ordinances restricting the rate of conversions because of the concern that lower income people will be priced out of the rental market. When condo conversions are restricted, government is essentially declaring that the demand for rental units shall take precedence over the demand for owner-occupied housing—i.e., renters shall have priority over owners.

---

specify *minimum* housing construction standards. This again assumes that some builders would provide inadequate or dangerous construction if not watched and that most buyers are not knowledgeable enough to do the watching. These regulations, in theory, are intended to protect uninformed buyers.

As we discuss further in Chapter Fourteen, "Land-Use Controls," regulatory governmental actions in the real estate market have sharply increased in recent years. No-growth and slow-growth policies by some local governments have restricted the supply of housing. This in turn has driven the price of the existing stock out of the reach of many would-be home buyers. The future will probably see even more. Most industrialized countries have a more restricted housing market than the United States and offer some specific clues to our future changes.

Encouraging Housing Production

The second group of governmental policies attempts to support or encourage housing production. These policies include programs to reduce shortages of land, labor, or capital. Examples are urban renewal for land assembly, organized apprenticeship programs for skilled labor training, and the huge program of federal home loan insurance.

Federal actions in financing have been an especially important (and changing) factor in the residential market. Other actions supporting housing production often seek to correct housing shortages in some parts of the market that are hard to meet. These have included housing for the elderly, the poor, college students, and convalescent hospitals.

Many of these programs have not produced the desired results and have been dropped. Some, like FHA loan insurance, have been so successful in the past that they have encouraged the market to pick up the idea in the form of private loan insurance. When this happens, the need for governmental action is reduced, and the program may be discontinued. In general, despite the changes in the various programs, the overall degree of governmental encouragement of the housing market has been growing. The most obvious examples have been the efforts to meet capital shortages and the subsidies for low-income and elderly housing. Both programs are expected to continue to grow. It is clear, however, that the exact form of governmental action will change from year to year.

It is important to stay abreast of changes in government programs in order to know which are likely to continue to influence housing supply and demand. Remember, many government housing programs fail to achieve their goals and in some cases have been harmful to local real estate values. A real estate analyst should study all existing and proposed government housing programs to estimate what impact they will have on local housing prices.

REVIEWING YOUR UNDERSTANDING

Governmental Housing Programs

1. What are the two types of governmental action in the market?
2. Give examples of each.
3. What are the trends in these governmental actions?

CHAPTER SUMMARY

The residential market is made up predominantly of homes and apartments. This chapter noted the influence of population, income, and taste upon housing demand. However, housing demand really consists of groups of demand for units of differing ages, locations, sizes, features, and so forth. Studio apartments are an example. Housing supply is dominated by the existing stock of housing units but influenced by the changes and trends that develop in new construction. Repair and renovation of older units are especially important factors in light of the long life and fixed location of real estate. The importance of amenities to residential markets was also stressed. Governmental programs were shown either to restrict or to help market behavior. Problems with ineffective or undesirable housing programs were discussed, as was their importance to the residential market. An overriding concern is the lack of affordability in the housing market. The problem is especially acute in high population, high cost areas such as California.

IMPORTANT TERMS AND CONCEPTS

Affordability index

Credit availability

Demand composition

Demography

Doubling up

Economic life

Effective income

Filtering

Governmental market interference

Housing-unit mix

New construction

REVIEWING YOUR UNDERSTANDING

1. Which of the following is considered a demand variable in the housing market?

    a. construction rates

    b. population change

    c. government growth controls

    d. demolition rate

2. If the supply of housing units is fixed, and demand decreases, the price of homes should:

    a. increase

    b. remain the same

    c. decrease

    d. not react

3. The number of real estate listings by brokers has increased and the number of qualified buyers has decreased. This is a(n):

    a. buyer's market

    b. seller's market

    c. balanced market

    d. underbuilt market

4. Which of the following is a supply factor that influences the housing market?

    a. cost of consumer credit

    b. taste and lifestyle

    c. population

    d. no-growth policies by local government

5. The median price of homes is $150,000, the median income is $35,000, the annual loan payment for a standard loan is $13,175, and the annual income needed to qualify for this loan is $42,000. The affordability index is:

    a. 83.3%

    b. 120%

    c. 37.6%

    d. 31.4%

6. When a homeowner trades up to a larger home, this frees his or her smaller home for a first-time home buyer. This process is called:

    a. trading down

    b. exchanging

    c. filtering

    d. leveling

7. The increased migration rate to the Sunbelt and West Coast states, coupled with a high divorce rate in these states, should increase the demand for:

   a. housing
   b. growth controls
   c. jobs
   d. all of the above

8. If housing costs rise beyond the income level of one household unit, two or more households may share a home. This process is called:

   a. cohabitating
   b. equity sharing
   c. time sharing
   d. doubling up

The housing market you are studying is comprised of the following elements: Sewer and water moratoriums have been in place for three years, a large corporation has recently decided to move its headquarters and 500 employees to the city. Construction loan funds are difficult to obtain due to a crisis in the financial markets. A new "slow growth" initiative has qualified for the ballot for the next local election. Citizens are complaining about local traffic congestion. Based on this information alone, answer Questions 9 and 10.

9. In the near future, the greatest increase in values should be in:

   a. unimproved land zoned residential
   b. unimproved land zoned commercial
   c. unimproved land zoned industrial
   d. new homes in a recently completed subdivision

10. In the near future, the value of existing homes should:

   a. increase
   b. decrease
   c. drop sharply
   d. stay the same

Chapter 10

Commercial and Industrial Markets

Preview

This chapter discusses the major influences on the values and uses of commercial and industrial property. Sections 10.1 and 10.2 examine the economic, social, and political forces that affect business real estate. Section 10.3 focuses on commercial properties, and industrial properties are the subject of Section 10.4. Upon completion of this chapter, you will be able to:

1. Explain how economic trends influence the value of business property.

2. List and define the four major forces that determine the selection of commercial sites.

3. Describe the signs of change in commercial real estate markets.

4. Discuss the advantages and disadvantages of foreign investment in U.S. real estate.

10.1 BUSINESS REAL ESTATE

Business real estate includes both commercial and industrial real property. The benefits of ownership for business real estate differ from the benefits of owner-occupied homes. For the homeowner, in addition to appreciation potential, the price paid for the home is influenced by the benefits of ownership, including amenities such as status, security, pride of ownership, school district, and so on. These amenities are not directly related to the home's ability to produce rent. For business properties, these amenities are less important than the direct economic factors that influence the property's ability to generate rent.

The business property road to value is as follows: economic trends influence current business profits. Business profits in turn determine the business owner's ability to pay rent. Rents then help to determine the property's net operating income. Finally, net operating income establishes a business property's market value. Thus, changes in current economic trends usually have a greater near-term impact on business real estate values than on home values. (See Figure 10.1, Road to Value.)

FIGURE 10.1   Road to Value

10.2 MAJOR ECONOMIC CHARACTERISTICS

DEMAND IS TIED TO THE BUSINESS CYCLE

The demand for business real estate is tied to current economic activity. When the economy is booming, sales are up and the need for more commercial and industrial space increases. When business slows down, sales decline and most businesses put expansion plans on hold.

SUPPLY FACTORS

Changes in the supply of business real estate depends upon the rate of new construction, conversions, and demolitions. Because construction takes so long, supply cannot immediately match increases in demand. Business property development projects take years to package. The work needed to meet government requirements is especially time consuming. Also, nogrowth and environment groups frequently challenge major development projects in court or by referendums at the polls. Then, once a project is finally started a "pipeline effect" takes place. Even though a shift in the business cycle reduces the demand for more business square footage, it is difficult to stop a project in mid construction. The business real estate market has a history of building boom, followed by slow construction activity as the excess inventory is worked off.

FINANCING IS CRITICAL

Since business real estate is often expensive, buyers usually borrow money to purchase property. Borrowing is also a standard investment tool when one seeks leverage and income tax advantages. The availability and cost of financing affects the profitability and value of real estate investments. During severe credit crunches, many proposed developments never get off the drawing board for lack of money.

Since the availability of mortgage money is so important, developers cater to the building preferences of lenders. For example, many lenders favor commercial property occupied by national businesses with good credit ratings. As a result, projects aimed for local, smaller tenants may never get built.

Lenders may dictate building design, layout, or wording in leases. In many ways, lenders hold veto power over proposed business buildings. This veto power, and a healthy skepticism, can be a valuable check upon the over enthusiasm of some developers. On the other hand, the savings and loan fiasco and the resulting "crisis" illustrate how some lenders financed many ill-conceived real estate developments.

GOVERNMENT CONTROLS

The development and use of business real estate are subject to government controls, in addition to the restraints that may be imposed by lenders. Governmental land use controls were developed many years ago in response to problems in residential areas, and later were broadened to restrict use in commercial and industrial districts. Real estate economists study government requirements because land use patterns in many areas are dominated more by government controls than by economic forces. Community concern about business property development is more vocal than about any other land use, except for mines, heavy industry, landfills, and power plants.

INCOME TAX IMPACT

Changes in income tax laws have been used to either stimulate or suppress the rate of business real estate development. The Economic Recovery Act of 1981 gave business property owners accelerated depreciation and tax credits to stimulate construction to help the economy recover from a major recession. Then the Tax Reform Act of 1986 reversed the process by eliminating accelerated depreciation, lengthening straightline depreciation, and enacting passive loss rules, all designed to reduce the rate of business property construction. Major tax changes in the 1990s also will have an impact on the supply and demand for business property.

BUYERS AND SELLERS ARE SOPHISTICATED

Contrary to those in the home market, buyers and sellers of business properties are highly knowledgeable about the real estate market. Both buyers and sellers have access to attorneys, accountants, appraisers, and real estate specialists. Frequently the buyer or seller is a financial institution, insurance company, or a real estate syndicate. Sophisticated foreign investors are becoming a powerful force in the U.S. real estate market. These enlightened buyers and sellers frequently insist upon using a well-trained, investment-oriented real estate agent.

USING LEASES

Many business properties are rented out by their investor-owners on long-term leases because the owner wants protection against vacancies and rent losses. The length of the lease and the tenant's credit (or other guarantees against default) are very important to investors. A long-term lease is also important because it is a contract to pay money. Both lenders and investors study the lease carefully. The key elements in the lease are the length of the lease, the rent, the risks, and any special lease insurance or guarantees.

In relying on a long-term lease, one major risk is that the tenant might default. Thus the stability and credit rating of the tenant are important factors. Buyers usually review the lease to be sure that it is binding, but many leases contain loopholes. In case the tenant defaults on the lease, the prudent investor must study what the value of the real estate would be *without* the lease and also determine the strength of the guarantees.

Default is not the lessor's only risk. The problems of leased property change over the years, and people who write leases respond to these changing problems as they arise. Unfortunately, investors can be hurt financially if their lease was written by an inexperienced lease writer or if a lease is signed before a problem becomes apparent.

A major concern to a landlord is the risk that inflation will reduce the purchasing power of the rent money collected on the lease. Therefore, many business leases allow rent increases to match the rate of inflation. In addition, it is common to require the business tenant to pay the landlord's operating expenses, such as property taxes, building insurance, and maintenance. These are called "net leases," with an escalator clause tied to the rate of inflation.

In the past, problems caused by eminent domain takeovers of private property by government agencies have led many attorneys to insert eminent domain clauses in business leases. These clauses spell out the rights of the parties regarding trade fixtures attached by the tenant, loss of business and relocation cost provisions, and other related items. Thus, today's business leases are written with much more concern for the effects changing times will have on people and property values than was true just a decade ago.

REVIEWING YOUR UNDERSTANDING

Business Real Estate

1. How do changes in economic trends influence business property values?
2. What are three types of risk in leased real estate and how can they be reduced?
3. Explain why purchase money financing is important to business real estate.
4. Are land-use controls important in the market for business real estate in your community?

10.3 COMMERCIAL PROPERTY

Commercial property is a broad term that includes various subcategories such as retail, office, lodging, and multiuse buildings that combine both commercial and residential use. Although each subcategory has its own unique economic characteristics, for simplicity this section discusses general principles that apply to most commercial properties.

WHAT ARE THE MAJOR FORCES?

There are four major forces that have an impact on the commercial real estate markets: local community forces, comparative advantage forces, customer convenience forces, and the unique forces of a particular type of business.

Local Community Forces

Local community forces include trends in population, demography, taste, effective income, and purchasing power. These economic trends are important to commercial properties because these properties are used to provide goods and services to the local community.

Increases in local population or income produce demand for more commercial services and goods. This creates demand for more stores, offices, and the like in proportion to the changes in purchasing power and population. Shifts in other social variables such as consumer taste have similar impacts.

Comparative Advantage Forces

Commercial space users want a location where they will have a comparative advantage over their competitors. These advantages are produced by transportation, government controls, combinations of stores, and natural features.

Transportation influences retail locations because customers usually must visit a store to buy from it. The easier to reach (or more accessible) a store is, the better the customers like it. Locations where people already congregate (e.g., at transportation hubs or nodules) are among the most convenient. Offices and warehouses need transportation for customers, suppliers, and shippers.

Government controls also influence commercial locations. Some desirable locations may not be zoned for commercial use. Less desirable locations will then be used because of their commercial zoning. Government controls can also affect the value of a particular location by placing restrictions on lot sizes, yard and parking allowances, building height, setback, and other density items.

A third category of comparative advantage is a favorable *combination of stores*. Simply put, some stores benefit from being near other stores. For example, two dress stores can locate adjacent to one another and have a greater combined sales volume than if they were separated. Favorable combinations also exist for office buildings. Legal offices benefit from proximity to one another and to the courthouse; medical offices seek proximity to a hospital.

Finally, *natural features* form a fourth comparative advantage force. Some sites are more level and draw uses that need level sites.

Climate can play a role if there are noticeable local differences in wind, fog, rain, or snow.

Customer Convenience Forces

The differences in how customers shop for various goods and services influence the location needed. Stores that sell *convenience goods*, like razor blades, hosiery, and everyday groceries must be located close to their customers. Some products (gasoline) should be convenient to the commuter, while others (cafeterias, florists) try for convenience to workers and shoppers. Most convenience stores and offices are oriented to homemakers and their daily purchases and are located near residential areas.

Stores and offices that offer a specialized product or service have a very different relationship to their customer. Specialty businesses find that customers will travel a much greater distance, but they frequently desire to have numerous alternative choices at one location. Thus, similar *shopping goods* stores often benefit from clustering together in favorable combinations.

The type of contact involved in customer relations has changed considerably. Improvements in communication systems and financial procedures have increased the customer transactions that can occur without face-to-face contact. This change is most noticeable with wholesaling. Improved truck transportation and standard product lines now allow wholesalers to be hundreds of miles away from the retailer, instead of a few city blocks.

Effects of the Type of Business

The type of business influences the choice of location. For example, businesses handling inexpensive, bulky products such as sand and gravel need such large amounts of land that location becomes less important than land cost. On the other hand, repair shops for objects of very high value, such as specialized electronic equipment, find that customers will travel long distances to reach them. Service offices such as accountants, appraisers, and consultants may find that they also have flexibility in where they locate. Other offices, such as real estate brokers, locate closer to their customers. In general, the more common a service business is, the more its locations will be scattered through the community. An example is convenience stores.

WHAT ARE THE PATTERNS OF COMMERCIAL LAND USE?

Commercial land use is not scattered uniformly throughout a city. Instead, as noted in Chapter 7, there are four general types of commercial neighborhoods or areas: the central business district, linear strips along main streets, local commercial clusters, and shopping centers. All commercial real estate users are concerned with "linkage" and "accessibility." *Linkage* refers to the interrelationship between one business and others. *Accessibility* is the degree of ease by which a store or business can be reached by employees, customers, and suppliers.

The Central Business District

The central business district (CBD) lies at the center of the community's transportation system, nearly always close to the physical origins of the community. In the smallest town, the CBD may consist of stores at the main crossroads. In a very large metropolis, the CBD is many miles in area, divided into specific commercial neighborhoods.

Commercial uses typically cluster at the major intersection or the frontage of the main streets. In small towns, offices will locate over the stores. As the CBD becomes larger, the offices develop their own location a short distance away from the main intersection. Land-use specialization increases as the CBD grows.

Trends in the Central Business District

Even with advancements in telecommunications, the need to cluster near other businesses (linkage) is still an important issue to certain companies and that is why the downtown business area tends to maintain high land values. In the past several decades the following trends have occurred in central business districts in most major cities.

1. An office building boom has changed the skyline of the city.
2. Major department stores have declined in number and volume of sales. Many have closed and either gone out of business or moved to suburban shopping malls.
3. Movie theaters have closed and moved to the suburbs.
4. Attempts to create downtown malls by closing off streets have failed to produce good results in most cases.
5. Downtown hotels have suffered as more and more business meetings are conducted at airport hotels. In convention cities, like San Francisco and San Diego, downtown hotels are still enjoying a brisk business, but other California cities have experienced a decline in the downtown hotel business.
6. Current attempts to revive the central business district include rapid transit systems from the suburbs to the central city and a push to restore multiuse buildings to make it fashionable to live and work in the downtown area.

Will central business districts return to the bustling round the clock activity of yesteryear? Or will they become strict 8 A.M. to 5 P.M. cities that are abandoned at night? Only time and economics will tell.

Linear Strips

As people travel from the outlying districts to the downtown center, their movement concentrates on particular routes. This can result from the type of transportation system (buses and rapid transit) or from street widths and traffic controls. These avenues of heavy traffic attract commercial uses. Their exposure to the passing traffic can substitute for a desirable downtown location.

Many planners criticize commercial strips because of their poor maintenance, although it is not clear that the linear strip is to blame. Most of the commercial uses occupying linear strips fall in between the convenience-store and the shopping-store categories. These businesses do not need the neighborhood convenience of a grocery store, but neither are they big enough to pay downtown rents. Some are commercial uses with marginal profits, others are easy access stores for those who travel on a particular road.

Local Commercial Clusters

The transportation pattern of the community often produces major crossroads away from the downtown area. These nodes become the focus of a local commercial cluster, similar to a small central business district. Usually these clusters are concentrated just off main streets. There has been a tremendous surge in retail store clusters. They are known as retail "power points" and they are pulling sales from traditional shopping centers.

Shopping Centers

Detached suburban shopping centers date back to the 1920s. The modern central mall shopping center, with surrounding parking, was first built in the 1950s. Shopping centers are traditionally divided into three categories: neighborhood centers, community centers, and regional centers.

Neighborhood centers consist of a supermarket and a few other stores such as a drugstore, service station, and so on. These centers cater to the immediate neighborhood. People do not drive across town to shop at these centers.

Community centers have department stores, banks, variety stores, and some specialty stores, with restaurants clustered nearby. People will drive across town to shop at community centers.

Regional centers are large planned projects containing several major "anchor" department stores. In addition, they include as many as 50 or more national specialty chain stores. Easy freeway access plus acres of free parking have made regional shopping malls a part of the American landscape.

In the larger shopping centers, called super regional, traffic volumes are as great or greater than in central business districts. In addition, these centers have multiple stories, with dental, medical, legal, and accounting, and others. Hotels and restaurants are often nearby, as are apartment complexes. To get better land use, newer regional centers are putting in multilevel parking areas.

These regional centers in turn attract office building developers. In some cases regional centers and the surrounding area become self contained "cities."

INTERESTING CHANGES

Of the many factors that influence commercial property location, three of the more fascinating are changes in transportation, changes in services, and changes in consumer tastes. These changes have had an interesting impact on commercial real estate.

The Automobile City

The late 1820s was the train era for travel, both nationwide and intercity. From the 1920s to the present has been the time of the automobile. The growth of shopping centers and suburban office buildings and the decline of the downtown area reflect the swing

SPECIAL INTEREST TOPIC _____

Shopping Center Trivia

According to the International Council of Shopping Centers, the five states with the largest number of shopping centers are (in ranking order) :

1. California
2. Florida
3. Texas
4. Illinois
5. New York

The five largest shopping malls, as measured by leasable space, in ranking order are:

1. Del Amo Fashion Center, Torrance, California
2. South Coast Plaza/Crystal Court Retail Center, Costa Mesa, California
3. Lakewood Center Mall, Lakewood, California
4. Woodfield Shopping Center, Schaumburg, Illinois
5. Roosevelt Field Mall, Garden City, New York

Special Note: The Mall of America, scheduled to open in Bloomington, Minnesota in 1992-93 should become number 1 or 2.

from streetcars to automobiles. Will the automobile continue to be king? Or will a shift to rapid transit systems, spurred on by air pollution and congestion caused by automobiles, once again change the location sites for commercial real estate users?

The Service Sector Explosion

As the U.S. economy continues its shift from goods to services, the need for office space will continue to grow, while the need for manufacturing plants will decline. This process has been changing the face of American business centers. Office and service center building has expanded rapidly in the last two decades, especially office construction in downtown areas and along suburban freeways. By the early 1990s the supply of office buildings far exceeds the demand, leaving a tremendous amount of unused office space to be worked off. Will the office building market ever balance out to the point where supply and demand are equal?

Shifts in Consumer Taste

Today's consumers are informed and knowledgeable. They seek better prices and a wider selection of goods and services. In the process, consumers have changed the methods used to deliver goods and services. This in turn has created a need for changes in commercial real estate use. Super regional shopping centers, with many stores, provide a wide array of merchandising and services, while clustered local "power points" provide convenience goods and services.

Huge automobile dealerships line freeways, while groups of large free-standing building-supply and discount stores can be found nearby.

Gains in consumer disposable income have increased the purchase of prepared foods and the number of restaurants, especially fast-food places, while it has expanded automobile and airline travel, and reduced rail and bus services. Construction of freeway and airport hotels and motels has increased, while downtown hotels have declined, except for convention centers. These changes are the results of changes in consumer tastes, led by breakthroughs in technology.

IS YOUR LOCAL COMMERCIAL AREA CHANGING?

Real estate is always changing. A reader should be able to determine whether a particular commercial neighborhood is stagnant, stable, or improving.

The Stagnant Commercial Neighborhood

At first glance, the stagnant commercial neighborhood seems all right. Stores and office buildings have been established for years.

Building sales or changes of tenants rarely occur. However, this apparent stability or lack of change is deceptive. Buildings need upkeep and remodeling or they become worn out and obsolete. The condition of properties in stagnant neighborhoods is usually deteriorating.

The lack of change in occupancy is also deceptive. Failure to make needed changes in sizes or types of stores accumulates problems. The lack of new faces and stores in the neighborhood is a sign of stagnation rather than stability.

The Stable Neighborhood

The stable neighborhood lacks these problems. Adequate maintenance and remodeling are occurring. New tenants move in, and new business owners buy out the old. The average age of the persons in business stays relatively constant. The types of businesses and offices in the area slowly change. Occasionally, new buildings may be built, along with additions and remodelings, to existing buildings.

The Rapidly Changing Commercial Neighborhood

Recently built commercial neighborhoods change rapidly. Business people are younger, and there may be failures of new businesses as managers experiment and sort out the location factors in the neighborhood. Sometimes, similar rapid changes strike an older commercial neighborhood. Most often, rapid change is stimulated by a major change in a freeway or transit system, providing better access to the area. First signs often are an increase in property sales as speculators respond to the early clues of the transportation change. Upon completion of the new transportation system, increasing rent levels cause a rapid tenant turnover and an influx of new tenants or businesses.

Another rapid change occurs when the community's population sharply increases, following the establishment of a major manufacturing plant. First come speculators, then construction, and then changes in rent levels, tenants, and types of establishments.

Finally, changes in smaller commercial neighborhoods can result from changes in surrounding residential neighborhoods. This change is visible first in the surrounding residential neighborhood, followed by changes in the number and type of customers on the street, in how much stores sell, and what they sell. In California, this is especially true in neighborhoods that have experienced a large influx of immigrants.

MAKING A SIMPLE MARKET SURVEY

To make a simple commercial market survey means looking for change. Elements of change that are physically closest often have the greatest economic effect. However, occasionally a decision made on a state or national level will be crucial to the local economy. Use the

TABLE 10.2 Elements of a Commercial Market Study

A. The economy of the community
B. Population factors
1. Composition
2. Preferences
C. Institutional Factors
1. Transportation
2. Controls
3. Other
D. Supply characteristics
1. Physical (age, condition, etc.)
2. Occupancy, vacancy, and turnover
3. Economic activity

material presented in Table 10.2 as a framework for conducting a simple commercial market survey.

Community Economics

The economy of the community affects each commercial property. Community economic changes can involve short-term local or national business cycles, or long-term trends of permanent change. It is necessary to understand the national economic picture as well as what is happening to employment in the local community. Contact local planning agencies for forecasts of trends in a community's economic base.

Population Factors

Population changes in the community are related to community economic change. A growth in jobs usually means a growth in community population. Where there is a large nonworking population such as retirees, however, population can increase without employment growth. Changes in demography are important to commercial property because demographic groups vary in income, spending habits, and so forth.

People's tastes also change. Such changes in preference are among the most subtle influences upon commercial property. Sometimes the analyst will find it advisable to "walk the street," asking business people what changes they see in their customers.

Institutional Factors

Transportation change is one of the most dynamic institutional factors. Is the present transportation system adequate? What are the problems and proposed changes? Are these changes likely? How will these changes alter travel patterns? Other institutional factors include controls, with zoning controls as the starting point. Is there local acceptance of the type of community that the master plan and zoning are producing? Are there changes pending? Are pollution problems apparent?

Supply Characteristics

A careful examination of the existing supply of real estate is helpful to a market survey. What are the ages and conditions of buildings? How much and what kind of new construction is there, if any? Is any recent renovation or remodeling visible?

Similarly, information about the local occupants tells much. Is there much vacancy? Has there been much tenant turnover? What are occupants' average ages and length of stay? What is the satisfaction level of occupants with their general business situation, their customers, and location?

Economic data, if available, will sharpen your understanding. Are there sales of commercial properties? Are numbers of sales increasing or decreasing? Are rent levels and values increasing? Are tenants renewing leases? What are the levels of retail sales in the area and how are they changing? If data are available, how are sales volumes changing for the various types of businesses? From this information, the direction of future change in a commercial neighborhood should become apparent. As discussed in Chapter 8, after noting changes, the real estate analyst should try to judge what forces are causing the changes, their strength, and at what pace the changes are occurring. Finally, the analyst tries to estimate what effect the changes will have on commercial real estate needs and investment opportunities.

REVIEWING YOUR UNDERSTANDING

Commercial Property

1. What is meant by linkage? Accessibility?
2. What are four types of commercial neighborhoods? Give an example of each from your city.
3. What are the characteristic differences between stagnant, stable, and rapidly changing commercial neighborhoods?

10.4   INDUSTRIAL PROPERTY

As with commercial property, the demand for industrial property is tied to swings in the business cycle and the availability of mortgage funds. Linkage and accessibility, along with a good shipping system, are important for site selection.

TABLE 10.3 Summary of Location Variables

Land cost	Energy, water, sewage facilities
Transportation cost	Pollution and environmental requirements
Labor cost	Climate
Nearness to materials and markets	Housing cost
Community attitudes	Education facilities
Tax levels	Personal, non-business reasons

THEORY OF INDUSTRIAL LOCATION

A major concept in industrial location is that a business seeks a location that reduces its costs and increases its profits. Obviously, no one location is ideal, so the choice involves compromises. Cost of land is a critical issue. However, land cost is only part of the picture. The availability of skilled labor may also be essential. Transportation costs to move raw materials to the plant and finished goods to market must be considered. Location of markets and raw materials sources thus become issues to consider.

Because of the importance of transportation costs, a plant that uses bulky raw material to make a lightweight, nonbulky finished product would seek to locate near the raw material in order to reduce shipping costs. Processing of tons of ore to recover gold would be the extreme example of this type of location. One should consider what type of raw materials (or inputs) and what type of finished products (or outputs) are involved.

Melvin Greenhut found that for new plants, there were three categories of locational factors, involving either the demand for their products, or its costs, or purely personal elements.[1] *Demand* plants choose locations with easy access to customers. *Cost* plants often choose locations for transportation reasons, especially raw materials transport, or else for particular labor skills.

In addition to demand and cost factors, personal preferences of business owners may dictate industry location. For example, the Boeing family's preference to locate its aircraft factories in Seattle is a personal as well as economic decision. Table 10.3 lists factors companies study when selecting an industrial site.

Others have classified industries as *market oriented, material oriented, labor oriented* or *footloose.* The Los Angeles fashion garment industry, packed within a few block radius, is the classic market-oriented industry. Industries oriented to their raw materials include steel mills, sawmills, and fish processing plants. Labor-oriented industries can locate either for low-cost labor, as do clothing mills of the southeastern United States, or for skills, as do the electronic manufacturing concentrations around the San Jose area.

Footloose industries are considered capable of locating in any of

[1] Melvin Greenhut, *Plant Location in Theory and Practice*, University of North Carolina Press, 1956.

a number of locations depending on personal factors. The number of footloose industries is increasing due to relative declines in the costs of transportation. Many times footloose industries locate midway between suppliers and customers.

THE CHANGING PATTERN OF INDUSTRIAL LOCATIONS

Early industrial communities were mostly in the eastern United States. Many had their origins in port towns such as Norfolk or Baltimore because of the inexpensive water transportation. Often, raw material access was important, especially for coal and timber. Most early manufacturing plants were located downtown for easy worker access and close to waterways or rail lines for raw materials transportation.

Many of these past patterns are no longer true. Raw materials transport is still important, but the orientation has shifted to expanded ports, like Oakland and San Pedro California, and to airports and freeways. Because of its high product-handling cost, the multiple-story plant has been replaced by one-story plants. When combined with the need for automobile parking lots for workers, the one-story plant makes cheap land a necessity. These pressures have led to industrial parks, which are large clusters of industrial uses, often located well away from existing conventional districts. They feature inexpensive land and ample space for isolation from competitive or troublesome land uses. Table 10.4 is a summary of industrial trends.

The industrial market has not suffered the dramatic boom and bust syndrome of the commercial office market. With the price of suburban housing rising so rapidly, some industrial companies in California are having a difficult time attracting employees. Many potential transferees from other states have refused to relocate in California. Those that do often insist on housing subsidies from their employers.

THE INDUSTRIAL MARKET STUDY

For industrial studies, the region's major industries and their economic health are especially important. A city economically dependent upon a large wood products plant, for example, has a different industrial market situation than a city with a large electronics employment base. Thus the state of the particular industry (its past,

TABLE 10.4   Summary of Industrial Trends

1. Development of industrial parks with pleasant settings and employee parking lots.
2. Large, one-story buildings instead of multi-story buildings.
3. Locations near airports, freeways, and major shipping ports.

present, and future prospects) must be part of an industrial market study.

Institutional factors are also important in making industrial market surveys. Are property tax rates reasonable? Are community attitudes receptive to industries of particular types? Is zoning appropriate? Are transportation systems adequate? What are the environmental constraints? Are educational facilities desirable and adequate for the needs of workers involved? Are needed support facilities, such as suppliers and financial, technical, and consulting people, readily available?

Supply characteristics are essential, too. An industrial market survey must examine the age, condition, and vacancy of existing buildings. The rate of new construction and absorption of that construction should be verified. What is the turnover? What is happening to the rate of property sales and prices? Are rents stable or increasing? Are investors happy with their investment experience? Is there land available for additional construction at appropriate locations? Are pollution and noise controls realistic and enforced in a nondiscriminatory manner?

In short, is the community going to be a successful location for a manufacturing operation, or are there factors (reasonable or unreasonable) that block the establishment or expansion of types of manufacturing processes? These factors then become important to the future of industrial land use in the community.

FOREIGN OWNERSHIP OF U.S. REAL ESTATE[2]

In the last decade, major segments of real estate have shifted from being a local business controlled by local developers, lenders, and agents, to a global international business with many foreign investors playing a key role. Foreign investors initially acquired fully-leased commercial properties at excellent locations with triple "A" tenants in major U.S. cities. Foreigners were perceived to be overpaying for the properties and driving up prices in the local real estate market. But now some foreign investors have either purchased or started U.S.-based real estate companies to acquire and manage their properties. Foreign development companies are also beginning to create projects from the ground up rather than depend upon existing buildings. Foreign investors are now considered marketwise and are paying local market prices.

The entire issue of foreign ownership of U.S. businesses and real estate has emotions running high. Here are some of the advantages and disadvantages frequently quoted by persons on both sides of this issue.

[2] This section from Chapter 5, Important Economic Features of Real Estate, is repeated here for emphasis. Information based on the study "The Internationalization of the U.S. Real Estate Industry," Lawrence Bacow, Massachusetts Institute of Technology, 1989. For a copy and price, contact Director of Publications, MIT Center for Real Estate Development, Building W31-310, Cambridge, MA 02139.

Advantages

1. Generates income for U.S. real estate owners who sell. This income is reinvested to stimulate the economy and provide additional employment.
2. Provides tax revenue to the U.S. government from the profits on the sale. This helps cover some of the budget deficit without raising tax rates or cutting government spending programs.
3. Generates commissions and fees for the real estate industry.

Disadvantages

1. Makes the U.S. less self-sufficient and more dependent upon foreigners.
2. Gives the U.S. government less incentive to solve the budget deficit problem by providing a short-run "quick fix" using foreign capital instead of reducing government spending or raising taxes.
3. High prices keep local investors out of the real estate market.

No matter where a person stands on the issue of foreign ownership, it should be pointed out that U.S. citizens have been buying assets of foreign countries for decades. Americans have supported free trade when they were buying into foreign countries; now that the reverse is true, some U.S. citizens are lobbying for restrictions.

REVIEWING YOUR UNDERSTANDING

Industrial Property

1. List five things a company looks for when selecting a site.
2. What are some advantages and disadvantages of foreign ownership of U.S. real estate?
3. What changes in industrial locations have occurred in your community in the past decade?

CHAPTER SUMMARY

Properties in commercial and industrial markets are diverse, but they share some common influences, especially the need for linkage and accessibility. Telecommunications has lessened, but not eliminated, this need. Many properties are leased, so that lease considerations are significant, especially the landlord's security against risks such as default, vacancy, cost increases, inflation, and unforeseen changes.

The availability and costs of financing needed to purchase such properties are also important. The lender's requirements for design, lease language, tenant type, and the like also have significant effect.

Business properties are influenced by public requirements such as nuisance standards, environmental concerns, land-use controls, and others. The number and kinds of controls are increasing, and this crucial subject is discussed further in Chapter 13.

Some influences are especially important to commercial property. These are community economic forces, the forces of comparative advantage, the customer convenience forces, and the effects of the type of business. Because of these influences, commercial land uses occur in four different locations: the central business district (CBD), linear strips, local commercial clusters, and shopping centers. Shopping centers are classified as neighborhood, community, regional, and super regional. Forces that generate changes in commercial locations include transportation changes, the paper and communications explosions, shifts in taste, and increased disposable income.

A particular commercial neighborhood can be either stagnant, stable, or improving. Market surveys are simply careful studies of the neighborhood and all of the above forces that influence it in order to get the best possible description of the current state of affairs.

Special factors in industrial markets determine industrial location. Transportation, labor, materials, community attitudes, and markets are very significant factors. There is a recent trend toward large suburban industrial parks. Industrial market surveys also seek to understand what forces are at work, what changes have occurred, and what current trends are forming. The goal is to develop an image of the community's future employment, population change, and industrial future. This then is used to determine the investment potential for business property. Foreign investment in U.S. real estate has increased dramatically.

IMPORTANT TERMS AND CONCEPTS

Accessibility

Central business district (CBD)

Commercial strips

Comparative advantage

Convenience goods

Footloose

Industrial location theory

Labor oriented

Leasing for security

Linkage

Market oriented

Material oriented

Shopping centers

Shopping goods

REVIEWING YOUR UNDERSTANDING

1. Which of the following is least important for a business property investor?

    a. rent levels

    b. noneconomic amenities

    c. credit rating of the tenant

    d. terms of the lease

2. Nearness to other compatible businesses is called:

    a. accessibility

    b. location

    c. linkage

    d. trading area

3. Which of the following regarding the commercial real estate market is generally untrue?

    a. Demand is tied to swings in the business cycle.

    b. Income tax law changes can influence the rate of construction.

    c. Lenders can have veto power over new projects.

    d. Buyers and sellers are unsophisticated.

4. Once the building of a commercial or industrial project begins, it is difficult to stop even if it becomes apparent that the demand for the project has declined. This is known as the:

    a. gravity effect

    b. pipeline effect

    c. financial effect

    d. continuous effect

5. A thin line of commercial development along a city street is a:

    a. strip development

    b. power point cluster

    c. neighborhood center

    d. community center

6. Small local clusters of trendy retail stores are called:

    a. power point clusters

    b. regional centers

    c. mega centers

    d. super regional centers

7. Changes that have influenced the location of commercial properties include:

    a. the shift from the production of goods to the providing of services

    b. use of the automobile

    c. changes in consumer tastes

    d. all of the above

8. Which of the following is a current trend in the industrial real estate market?

    a. large multiple-story buildings

    b. downtown locations

    c. industrial parks

    d. located near housing developments

9. A market-oriented industry tends to seek a location near its:

    a. raw materials

    b. customers

    c. lenders

    d. employees

10. Which of the following is considered an economic advantage of foreign investment in U.S. real estate?

    a. makes the U.S. more self-sufficient

    b. gives the government more incentive to solve the budget deficit

    c. generates income for property owners and fees for real estate agents

    d. keeps local investors out of the market

Chapter 11

Rural and Recreational Real Estate Markets

Preview

This chapter concludes Part Two, "Understanding Real Estate Markets." It emphasizes rural land uses. Section 11.1 explores agricultural property. Section 11.2 examines rural homes, from farmsteads and retirement homes to second homes and recreation rentals. Section 11.3 studies timber lands and similar resource properties. When you finish this chapter, you will be able to:

1. List and understand the major factors influencing agricultural values and trends.

2. Discuss the important differences between rural homes and urban housing.

3. Understand the special problems and features of resource lands and trends in their uses and values.

11.1   FARM LAND MARKETS

Agriculture is a major land use in the United States, producing a tremendous amount of food and fiber. (See Table 11.1, Top Ten Agricultural States.) The different farming uses such as orchards, irrigated croplands, dry croplands, and irrigated and dry pasture and rangelands vary in value. However, there are common factors at work, determining how farmlands are used and what their value is. This section explores these key factors and discusses major trends.

KEY FACTORS

Soil productivity	Topography
Rainfall	Shape, size, and layout
Growing season	Improvements
Water supplies	Access

TABLE 11.1   Top Ten Agricultural States

Top Ten States by Crop Value

1. California	6. Nebraska
2. Illinois	7. Indiana
3. Iowa	8. Kansas
4. Texas	9. Florida
5. Minnesota	10. Ohio

Top Five Agricultural Counties in California

1. Fresno
2. Kern
3. Tulare
4. San Joaquin
5. Kings

Source: Statistical Abstract of the U.S. 1989, Department of Commerce, and California Statistical Abstract 1988, Department of Finance.

Markets   Urban influences
Community facilities   Crop prices
Permits and quotas   Financing
Competition from other uses

Farmland use is determined by a combination of factors, the main concern being which crops will grow and the estimated yields of each. The more profitable crops will be planted and the less profitable ones eliminated.

Soil Productivity

Formed from the interaction between the underlying rocks, the local climate, and the influences of topography, soils differ in many ways. Some soils (often on hillsides) are only a shallow layer on the rock, while others (in the valleys) are many feet deep. Some are so sandy (many desert soils) that rainfall quickly drains out, while others are so silty that soils stay wet and rot plant roots.

Farm soils are generally placed in one of eight major classes, depending on their productivity or richness. Rural soil mapping is so complete that most established agricultural areas have detailed maps available from the Agricultural Extension Office, County Farm Advisor, or comparable offices. Soil mapping often extends beyond the eight general classes to subcategories and suitability for various crops.

Rainfall

The amount, timing, and nature of available moisture is every bit as important as the soil. In fact, it will have played a large part in developing the soil into its current form. Many marginal agricultural regions are well equipped with everything but natural rainwater, leaving low-value grazing as the only possible land use. Alternatives such as wells, irrigation projects, or cloud seeding can help change marginal soil into productive soil. Most of the U.S. crop land relies upon rainfall, however. As a result, much of the variation in farm production each year results from variations in when, where, and how much rain falls.

Growing Season

The amount of sunlight striking a farm decreases as you move further north or south of the equator. For these areas the summer sunshine is cooler and their growing season is shorter. Frost is also a problem when high winds lower temperatures. These two limits combine to determine the length of the growing season. In some areas, as in Alaska, only one crop can be grown. In others, such as the Imperial Valley, year-round agriculture is practical. However, some crops are attuned to a particular climate and growing season. Oranges, for example, do not thrive in a hot, tropical climate or a cool, temperate climate. They grow best in a narrow subtropical belt that includes Florida and southern California.

Water Supplies

In addition to *rainfall*, other possible sources of water have become more important in recent years. Rainfall runoff in rivers has been used for irrigation in the past. Now, however, its use is subject to complicated water rights that tie up the available water during the drier parts of the year or divert it to storage reservoirs and urban water systems. The use of well water has been increasing for many decades. As more people pump, however, the underground water level recedes. The expense of larger pumps needed to pull water from deeper wells, plus the increasing cost of electricity, have reduced the numbers of new wells. Small irrigation projects of the past were followed by the immense California Water Project of the 1960s, which was developed in part for agricultural irrigation purposes. As irrigation water gets more expensive, salt water and waste water reclamation become more feasible as possible farm water sources. Good water is especially important to agricultural land use in certain areas since some well and groundwater is so salty or full of chemicals (e.g., boron) that it kills plants.

Topography

The slope of the parcel, as well as gullies, rock outcrops, marshes, and the like, affect what the land can produce or how it can be farmed. Crops that are irrigated by flooding, such as rice, must be on level land. Crops that are harvested by big machines, such as wheat, must be on fairly dry land at harvest time. Parcel slope is particularly important because steeper slopes usually have thinner layers of soil and are also much harder to irrigate without causing soil erosion.

Shape, Size, and Layout

All three influence the farm's production. Their effect will depend on the crops involved and the farming technology used. As a result of steep terrain and the use of hand labor, rice in Japan is economically farmed in plots of a few acres, while in California, mechanized rice farms on level terrain require hundreds of acres.

Improvements

This term covers a wide range of physical items. A milking parlor is an expensive and necessary building on a dairy farm. Underground drain tile, to keep fields dry enough, may be an equally necessary improvement for the asparagus farmer. The design and condition of these improvements must be appropriate if they are to have a positive effect on value. Changing crop demands can occasionally make existing improvements obsolete.

Access

Some good farms sell for less than others because of their remoteness. Remoteness can be the distance to markets to sell the farm's products or the distance to shops, stores, and services that farmers need. Isolated farms also have been less popular with farmers' families. In addition to the farmland price pressures caused by encroaching urban sprawl, the close-in farm will often be worth more than the remote one solely because of the time and costs of travel to and from the remote farm. However, there is a market for smaller, isolated farms for people seeking a more self-sufficient life, away from cities.

Markets

Farmers sell many crops through specialized marketing channels. The stockyards and the grain elevator are the most common examples. Some specialty crops are difficult to market except in the places where most of the production is centered. An obscure California valley might thus be an excellent small lettuce-production area, but the extra cost of shipping to the Salinas lettuce markets removes much of the profit. The value of the land for lettuce production is reduced unless increased production will get the needed markets to move locally.

Community Facilities

Rural areas vary just like cities in the amount, variety, and quality of public and private services available, but most rural areas have less of these services. Farmers are as interested as city dwellers in good schools, medical services, and adequate stores. Stories of inadequate rural health care facilities have been highly publicized in the national media.

Permits and Quotas

Governmental permission is needed to grow some crops, including tobacco, fresh milk, cotton, and sugar beets at various times. Forest Service grazing permits allow a ranch to graze its cattle on government land during the summer, sometimes doubling the number of cattle that a ranch can handle. Such permits and quotas can be a very important factor to property value, depending on the amount of production restriction, the ability to hold and sell the permit with the land, and the costs of the permit.

Government price supports and crop payments exert a similar influence. Because of the changes in a support program, farm incomes can change drastically, thereby influencing the value of farm land.

Competition from Other Uses

A particular rural parcel may have limited agricultural value but be of greater utility for other possible rural uses. Many of California's rural recreational subdivisions in the 1960s were located in areas of poor farmland, where low prices made such subdivisions more profitable and thus economically more feasible for the developer. Alternatively, some poorer farmlands have potential value for tree farms that might equal their farmland values. Sand, gravel and other resources may be mined, too, if the competing agricultural uses of the land are not profitable.

Urban Influences

Many states have farming areas close to urban areas. Land values in these locations have usually been influenced much more by speculators who are anticipating future city expansion than by agricultural values and incomes. The nature and expectations of urban expansion, master planning, zoning, utilities, and transportation systems will cause speculative premiums over agricultural values to rise and fall.

Crop Prices

The prices of various farm crops rise and fall with changes in supply and demand. Farmland prices tend to swing with these changes in crop prices. Soaring crop prices in the mid-1970s, coupled with wild inflation, generated record high farmland prices. Then the decline in crop prices in the 1980s, coupled with a drop in inflation, saw farmland prices drop to levels below the balances on existing farm mortgages and loans. The result was a wave of farm foreclosures.

SPECIAL INTEREST TOPIC

Agricultural Foreign Investment Disclosure Act

Although there is no federal law prohibiting foreigners from purchasing U.S. real estate, there has been a concern over recent foreign purchases of U.S. agricultural land. In 1978 Congress passed the Agricultural Foreign Investment Disclosure Act which requires a report be sent to the government within 90 days after the sale of farm or timberland to foreign investors. This law only covers parcels of one acre or more which produces $1,000 or more in output value per year. The purpose of the law is to monitor foreign purchases to see if further action is needed.

SPECIAL INTEREST TOPIC

The Farm Problem

The so called "farm problem" is a classic example of supply exceeding demand, causing a drop in farm product prices and farm income. On the demand side, farm products have an inelastic demand, meaning that a great increase or decrease in price causes only a small change in the amount consumers are willing to buy. If the price of wheat drops by 50%, people do not increase their consumption of wheat by 50%. You will not double your meals if food prices drop by 100%! On the supply side, technological advances in equipment, fertilizers, pesticides, water systems, land management skills, and so on, have greatly expanded the output of farm and ranch products. In short, even with expanding exports to foreign countries, supply has exceeded demand, causing farm produce prices to decline and farm incomes to fall.

The classical economic solution to the farm problem would be to allow enough farmers to fail, thereby reducing supply. This would cause farm products to rise to a point where supply and demand are in balance at a price that would support the remaining farmers at a reasonable income. Why hasn't this happened? The reasons are many, such as: the need to preserve an "American way of life"; farmers have fed a growing nation at great personal cost; farmers sell in a nearly pure competitive market, but must buy goods and services in monopolistic competitive markets, and so on.

Government's Solution—Farm Aid

The major government farm aid programs are:

1. Price supports, where the government guarantees the farmer a certain minimum price for crops. If consumers will not buy up all the output, the government buys the surplus at the support price.

2. Set aside programs, where the government pays the farmer for not planting an allotted number of acres. Sometimes called "soil banking."

3. Increasing demand for farm output by paying for research for new uses for farm products, creating food stamp and other government programs designed to give food to U.S. citizens who cannot afford to pay, and promoting food exports to foreign countries.

The Results to Date

Have government programs solved the "farm problem"? Most economists agree that the answer is no. What is wrong? The farm aid programs to date have focused on keeping farm incomes up, instead of encouraging farmers to leave the farm and seek better paying employment elsewhere. Why should a farmer leave if the government will guarantee loans or grant direct pay to stay! Another problem with government farm aid is that the greatest amount of aid has gone to the large corporate farmer who needs increased personal income the least. The final critique of government farm policy is the tremendous cost these programs have placed on U.S. consumers and taxpayers.

Financing

Farms are usually purchased and also operated with some borrowed capital. Today's fairly rapid changes in the availability and cost of all types of loans affect the profitability of farm operations quite directly. Higher loan interest rates reduce farmland values. The expectation of inflation, while it produces higher loan interest rates, tends to stabilize farmland values as investors seek land investments to hedge against inflation.

Environmentalism

While not a main factor until the 1970s, environmental protection and agricultural pollution controls are now an important factor affecting agricultural operations and thus farmland prices. Early environmental actions focused on broad-span, long-life pesticides such as DDT. Today, all pesticides are under government review. Agricultural burning, such as rice stubble and orchard cuttings, once common in rural areas, is now tightly controlled. Water pollution caused by chemical runoff from irrigation is a major concern. Environmental groups are lobbying heavily to restrict insecticides and other chemicals currently used in farming. If environmental and pollution constraints reduce the volume of crop production, the value of the farmland could be adversely affected. On the other hand, if environmental constraints reduce farm production, assuming demand increases or at least remains the same, the result could be higher market prices for the farmer. If this occurs, the price of farmland could rise or at least hold its present value. Only time will tell!

Labor Relations

As farm operations have become larger and more specialized, they have needed more labor than one farm family could handle. Seasonal labor crews have been necessary to handle key high-labor jobs. The scattered job locations and seasonal work load make it difficult for such crews to bargain effectively over wages and work conditions. In the 1970s unionization, strikes, and jurisdictional fights affected some farm crops. Today, many farmers have successfully turned to mechanization and the use of more constant work crews. All of these changes have affected individual crop costs, profits, and land values.

MAJOR TRENDS

Studies of agriculture over the past century document a huge increase in output per farmer. This increase has involved a sharp rise in average farm sizes, in mechanization, and in the invested capital per farm. However, there have also been big increases in output per acre, in specialization of farmers in one or two crops, and in an increased petrochemical base for agricultural fertilizers and pesticides.

These trends have continued in recent years, but as mentioned before, concerns about agricultural fertilizers and pesticides may slow the rate of output per acre. Crop exports to other nations have grown drastically in recent years, and are expected to increase if world peace opens up foreign markets not currently served by U.S. agricultural products.

The farm crisis era of the 1980s saw a large number of farm foreclosures. Many of these foreclosures were the result of rising farmland values in the 1970s and early 1980s. During these high flying years, farmers and ranchers refinanced their land. These dollars were used for expansion, or in some cases the money was used to purchase luxury goods or to acquire investments. Then when the price of agricultural products dropped and the climate was hit with a drought, farmers and ranchers could not meet their loan payments. The result was a highly publicized wave of farm foreclosures.

Another apparent trend is a growing split between a relatively limited number of efficient big producers and a large body of small, inefficient subsistence farmers. Many of the substance farmers are "part-timers," holding regular jobs and doing farming on the side. Intermediate-size farms appear to be dwindling.

REVIEWING YOUR UNDERSTANDING

Farm Land Markets

1. List at least five factors that influence farm land values.
2. Explain several ways that climate affects these factors.
3. List three current trends in farming operations.

11.2 RURAL HOMES

An increasing number of people are turning to the rural land market for housing rather than farming. The reasons for the rural housing boom are many, but retirement and recreation are two of the more important factors. This section analyzes new rural subdivisions and older homes separately because of differences in marketing and in buyer motivations.

THE NEW SUBDIVISION

Most people have seen a newer rural subdivision or have received promotional mailings from one. Key features in their sales literature generally are the area's recreational facilities. The subdivision often includes some facilities within its boundaries. A lake, lodge, golf course, and tennis courts are common examples.

Rural subdivisions have primarily been marketed as second homesites or retirement areas for weary city dwellers. The subdivisions fall into several categories, generally based on the location of the site. Locations in the ski country have had strong demand, and most subdivisions in this category offer buildings with the land. Condominiums and cluster townhouses are common design features, but project facilities are sometimes limited in favor of maximum development of a nearby or affiliated ski slope. Some coastal beach subdivisions have had similar strong demand and regular building programs. Desert subdivisions have in some cases been successful, but others have been massive failures.

"Buy a Lot at Lost Acres"

Many other rural subdivisions are in remote areas with limited demand prior to the subdivision. This discussion, of course, ignores some subdivisions that are within the daily commuting range of a larger urban area and are essentially suburban. Remote subdivisions have differed from ski condominiums in several ways, the limited preexisting demand being only one. Nearly all such tracts have concentrated on lot sales rather than sales of new buildings. Indeed, even several years after sale, usually less than five percent (and often less than one percent) of the lots have been built upon. Thus the buyer is simply purchasing a site and the potential for future benefits. The seller often provides very generous financing, which makes the purchase easier.

The limited preexisting demand in the area means that such subdivisions must be sold by extensive marketing, often to other areas with more people. The low price for land only, coupled with low down payments, has tended to attract buyers of limited economic means and experience. Their limited resources make second home construction a rather distant possibility. As a result, sales discussions have often emphasized the benefits of land ownership and the profits to be made from the land investment. Unfortunately, this rosy future has not arrived for many past buyers.

From your review of economic principles in Part I, as well as your experiences in the real world, you should be prepared to answer this question: consider a subdivision where 1,000 lots are developed in a remote area, and sold, and only 10 lots are built on in the first four years. If the remaining 990 lots were bought for speculative profit, in hopes of selling for building in five years at higher prices, what will happen to lot resale prices? The laws of supply and demand are hard to evade. In other words, there never was any real permanent demand for the lots; there was only a temporary speculative fever created by an "overactive" sales pitch.

There are examples of recreational subdivision lots that are worth less today than when they were sold 10 or 20 years ago. Moral: not all land values go up—some go down!

"Trends" in Ski Country

The more successful ski and coastal subdivisions differ quite sharply from the examples above because they have enough demand to support immediate housing construction. The success of the initial subdivisions led to a burst of favorable publicity, an increase in demand, and new imitators who often had to pay higher prices for raw land. All of these factors produced rapid increases in values of the original subdivisions, which generated still more favorable publicity.

It is important to stress that the rate of second home and recreational development is tied to movements in the economy and to cost of ownership. When the economy is booming, many people optimistically spend their discretionary income. The second home and recreational property market is tied to the swings in this discretionary income.

Another issue influencing the market for second homes and recreational properties is price. Prices in many of these markets have risen rapidly. This results from high demand and increased building cost, because of escalating land prices, expensive building components, and added cost to meet environmental requirements.

As costs of projects rise, many families find that their use of a second home is too infrequent to justifying owning it. They then try to rent it out when they are not occupying it. Experience with this growing supply of rentable buildings has led to sophisticated rural property-management firms, and the concept of *time-sharing*, or ownership of a unit during a specified time block (e.g., the month of May). Unfortunately, some poorly conceived time-share projects, plus the growing volume of renters, the increasing occupancy ratios, and turnover of strangers have tended to reduce sharply the rural features that were original attractions of the projects. As owner usage declines, the space can be filled with renters, but only as long as renters are interested.

An Overview

The key factors of the newer rural subdivisions are their orientation to recreational attractions and their limited market. Even in the stronger markets, rising prices have reduced user's demand and led to attempts to support ownership cost by part-time rentals. Investment motives have been a factor in a surprising number of purchases, often openly stated in land subdivisions, but more subtly in those with houses and condominiums. The strength of *use* demand, as contrasted with *investment* demand, will have an impact on future property values.

THE OLDER HOME

Older rural homes, as well as single rural lots or homesites, have entirely different market factors than the newer recreational subdivisions. Many recreational subdivision buyers are not aware of these differences and of the numerous buying choices they have.

The Local Marketplace

One of the major differences between new rural developments and older rural homes is that the older rural home is generally sold on a local market, through the local newspaper, brokers, or word of mouth. This does not mean only local people are the buyers, for many newcomers look for housing using local information. However, this local market contrasts sharply with the mass-advertising urban market to which the new recreational subdivisions are sold. Historically, small-town prices have been much lower than comparable locations in larger cities, since population pressure forces land and home prices up in larger cities. When recreational properties are sold on the urban market, their prices seem bargains in comparison to urban prices and tend to get bid up to urban levels. Rural markets, meanwhile, continue on their own way, at their own price levels.

Local influences in each local rural market determine the price level. Some towns and rural areas are declining in population as logging mills close or the number of farmers decline. Then prices tend to be low or declining. Other rural areas gain new employment, and their population gains and prices move higher. This is especially true in rural areas on the edge of urban growth.

On the Other Hand, . . .

The older rural home, while often quite inexpensive by urban standards, is not always a bargain. Some factors taken for granted in the city become major problems in the country. For example, city sewer mains and treatment plants are not common in the country, while septic tanks are. Problems with sewers backing up, polluted wells, and saturated septic tank drain fields are all too common.

Water availability is also a problem. The polluted well is one aspect, the dry well another. Legal quarrels over water rights are occasionally a problem: some residents have good water, others have water that is so salty or contaminated by agricultural chemicals as to be undrinkable or fatal to plants. Not all sites have water, but the only way to find out is to drill, which costs money.

Buyers of older rural properties may have trouble finding boundaries, obliging them to pay for a survey or risk later problems. They may also encounter problems with the condition of their dwellings. Older rural homes were occasionally built without building permits or code inspector supervision, or they have had substantial owner alterations of varying quality. Even when new, heating, wiring, and plumbing systems usually do not meet the standards expected of most urban homes. Deferred maintenance of roofs, chimneys, windows, and sills is common. Foundations may be far more casual, or even nonexistent, and damage from wood-destroying organisms (termites, fungus, and beetles) may be extensive.

Thus the buyers of an older rural home must anticipate more problems, ask more questions, and look far more carefully than they would for an urban home purchase. The benefits of lower prices are there, but lower prices can be offset by high repair expense if the buyer is not wary. Even with today's higher standards of seller and broker disclosure requirements, urban buyers of older rural homes need to be careful.

Who Buys What?

Buyers of such older rural homes are often quite different from buyers of recreational subdivision homes. Many are older, either retired or nearing it, and seeking a less expensive or more peaceful retirement home than their former urban location. Others are young families with children, unable to afford the prices in recreational subdivisions, but eager to obtain a rural recreational second home. These contrast with the couples without children or well-to-do middle-aged families that buy many newer recreation subdivision homes. However, all these groups can occasionally be enticed into buying the recreation subdivision lot because of the lure of supposed profits on resale.

A final factor in the market for older rural homes is the relatively small job base in the area. This is particularly noticeable in areas dependent upon one industry, such as logging, tourism, food processing, or a mine or other mineral operation. All too often, that industry will reach the end of its economic profitability and close or move its local operation. When it does, the local area will go into a severe economic depression because of the loss of jobs. People will leave town looking for work, and real estate prices will fall. In time, they may return and prices may rise, but some towns never recover and become stagnant or even ghost towns, abandoned and worthless. The rural town with one major employer is thus a special risk, and the buyer should be wary.

11.3   TIMBER AND OTHER RESOURCE LANDS

There are a number of different resources on rural lands and often on urban lands as well. These include timber, water power, oil, coal, gravel or rock, geothermal power, salt ponds, and numerous ores, either strip-mined or underground, including iron, uranium, copper, salt, diatomaceous earth, and many others. Their location and marketing factors differ in many ways, making this subject far too complex for full coverage here. But this section will examine a series of related factors and trends that influence most resource lands. Each individual resource then brings its own market, processing, and locational characteristics to mix with these factors and produce resource land prices and trends.

KEY FACTORS

The most important fact about all resource lands is that *the demand for the resource*, and thus for the land, is usually not connected to the local economy or real estate market. Rather, the demand and supply of the resource in nationwide or regional resource markets will dominate. This is opposite, of course, to the usual land market. The map of coal fields in Figure 11.1 illustrates that the resource need not be located where it is used.

A second major factor is *transportation*. Most resource commodities are relatively bulky, low-valued materials, and their transportation cost per dollar of value is higher than most other transported goods. Most resource commodities also require some processing at a timber sawmill or smelter, reduction plant, or crushing mill, which usually reduces the bulk considerably and increases the commodity's value per pound. The location of these processing plants, their trans-

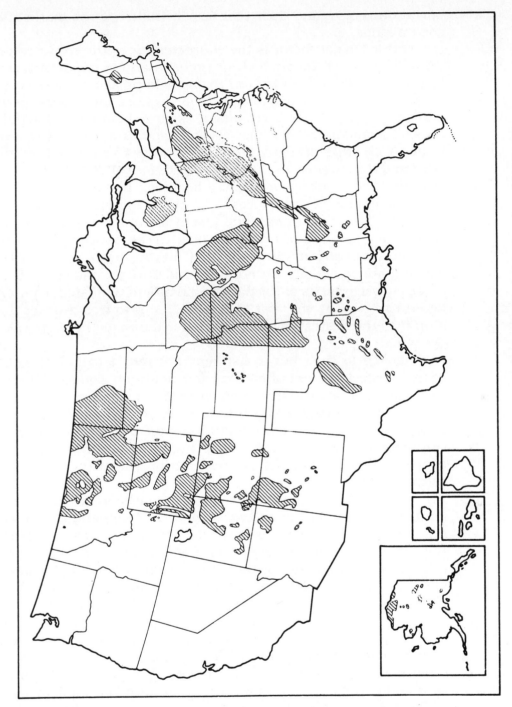

FIGURE 11.1   Coal Fields. *Source: Economic Research Service, Our Land and Water Resources.* Washington D.C., Government Printing Office, 1974.

portation access, and their cost heavily influence the market for resource lands.

A third major factor is the *characteristic of the resource parcel* itself. The size of the ore body or timber stand is important, since a larger collection of the resource in one holding allows more potential revenue to cover the original costs for exploration, roads, permits, and the possible huge development expense before the first sale occurs. The land parcel size may also be important, either to provide a buffer from other property owners who might be injured by the operation if it were close to them or as space for various support, maintenance, and resource-processing facilities. Parcel topography and shape may also be influences, as well as the exact nature of the resource. This could cover the chemical composition of ores, the species composition of timber stands, the thickness of ore bodies, the amount of dirt on top of the ore ("overburden"), the density and age of timber stands, the amount of underbrush, and so forth. All of these characteristics of the parcel, and others not listed, combine to determine what it will cost to prepare the resource, extract it, and ship it to the nearest market. The lower the cost, the more valuable the land.

Related to this, but a distinctly different fourth factor, is the limiting effect of *environmental* and *pollution controls*. They will vary for different resources and in different political jurisdictions. Their effect is primarily to increase the cost of producing the resource or to require the product to assume directly the full costs of resource development, rather than imposing a portion of costs on people, animals, or lands downstream or downwind from the resource lands.

Finally, the fifth key factor found in markets for these resource lands is the presence of *special income and property tax laws* and *title laws and procedures*. That is, resource lands are generally treated as a special category by many government agencies, often in a favorable or preferential way. Income tax treatment includes depletion allowances for underground resources and capital gains treatment for timber sales. Special property tax treatment in California is primarily for timberlands, which have both potential for agricultural preserve taxation by contract and also constitutional restrictions on taxation of immature timber. California and many other states give preferential treatment for agricultural land in exchange for the land owner's promise to keep the land in farming and ranching.

MAJOR TRENDS

As with the other land uses surveyed, there are clear trends in resource land markets. The extent and importance of these trends will vary from location to location.

One of the longest established trends is the slow-paced, gradual depletion of the richer resource concentrations and eventual development of what originally would have been inferior quality resources. Some firms today, in fact, are successfully mining waste dumps of older mines and oil wells. In part this is a result of higher resource prices, but sometimes new processing techniques allow low-cost utilization of minerals that once were too expensive to process.

A second long-term trend is the general increase in resource market prices. While some, like oil prices, have had ups and downs over the last 20 years, most have gone up. In recent years, nearly all resource goods have increased in price as a result of supply cost increases, growing scarcity of quality resource concentrations, and rising demand. The increase in market price for processed resources often leads back to an increase in resource land prices, as, for example, western timberlands.

More recently, the search for lower quality resources has emphasized research in exploration techniques. The concepts and tools now in use are increasingly complex and expensive to own and operate. As a result, the small prospector on a burro is not a major source of today's resource discoveries. Instead, it may be equipment on an airplane, a helicopter, or a space satellite, owned or controlled by corporations able to fund this type of study.

Finally, the rapid increase in environmental and pollution control costs directly paid by the resource developer are a major recent trend. Many new resource programs are more influenced by this than by any other factor. For some resource users, adequate pollution control instruments cost too much relative to current resource market prices. New technology, lower costs, higher prices, or some combination of these three, will be necessary for continued resource production at lower pollution levels.

All of these major trends are interrelated to the key factors initially covered. As before, different resources are being influenced by these trends at different rates, as are different areas of the country. The interplay of factors will determine what happens to resource land values in each region and category.

REVIEWING YOUR UNDERSTANDING

Timber and Other Resource Lands

1. List five key factors influencing resource land use.
2. Give two examples of each, and explain their effect on resource land use or value.
3. List four recent trends in resource land use.

CHAPTER SUMMARY

This chapter has emphasized important influences upon the markets for rural land uses, stressing agricultural property, rural homes, and resource properties.

Key factors in determining uses and values of farmland include soil productivity, rainfall, length of growing season, water supplies, topography, parcel size, shape and layout, and farm improvements. Others include access, markets, community facilities, permits and quotas, competition from other rural uses, urban influences, crop prices, financing, environmentalism, and labor relations.

Major trends include increases in output per farmer, average farm size, specialization, and export orientation. More recently, factors include increases in farm foreclosures, natural as opposed to chemical fertilizers, and increasing environmental requirements.

The rural homes market is really two markets—new recreational subdivisions and older rural homes. Each market attracts a different type of purchaser, and each has its own advantages and liabilities. Investors in new subdivisions may pay a premium and must beware of buying into areas for which there is little or no resale demand. Buyers of old homes must carefully inspect their prospective properties for problems and investigate the economic strength of the area they are considering.

Investors in rural lands for resource purposes should examine a series of key factors that relate to the cost of processing the resource. Recent trends in technology and the continued depletion of our resource stocks have made attractive the exploration and further exploitation of old resource areas.

IMPORTANT TERMS AND CONCEPTS

Crop markets   Resource processing plants

Environmentalism   Soil productivity

Local market   Topography

Permits and quotas   Transportation

Pollution controls   Water

Recreational subdivision

REVIEWING YOUR UNDERSTANDING

1. The U.S. "farm problem" is caused by:
   a. demand exceeding supply
   b. supply exceeding demand
   c. technology occurring more slowly in agriculture than in other industries
   d. worldwide hunger

2. A technique used by the government to reduce the supply of farm products is:
   a. favorable tax breaks for farmers
   b. price supports
   c. soil banking
   d. guaranteed farm loans

3. Which of the following would *not* have an impact on the price of farmland?
   a. soil productivity
   b. direction of urban growth patterns
   c. access
   d. all have impact

4. Which of the following is a demand, as opposed to a supply, factor that influences the value of farmland?
   a. increased output per acre
   b. better pesticides
   c. government quotas on crop output
   d. low interest rate farm loans

5. A rural residential homesite subdivision is considered misplaced if after several years:
   a. no building occurs
   b. the resale market for lots is active
   c. extensive building occurs
   d. commercial stores are constructed

6. The demand for recreational real estate is increased by all of the following, *except* an:
   a. upswing in the business cycle
   b. increase in the cost of building
   c. improved transportation access
   d. increase in discretionary income

7. Purchase of the use of real estate for a particular two-week period is called:

   a. condominium
   b. equity-sharing
   c. time-sharing
   d. periodic tenancy

8. Which of the following is typical of older rural homes?

   a. easier to finance than urban homes
   b. rarely suffer from deferred maintenance
   c. private water and sewer systems
   d. prices always rise in future years

9. The value of timber and other resource land is tied to the demand for the resource itself. The market price of the resource is determined primarily by:

   a. supply and demand forces in the national and international market
   b. supply and demand forces in the local market
   c. government decree
   d. the health of the local economy

10. All of the following are trends in resource real estate markets, *except*:

   a. gradual depletion of resources
   b. less concern for environmental issues
   c. resource land prices shift with the market price of the resource
   d. improvements in resource extraction technology

Chapter 12

The Economics of Real Property Taxation

Preview

In an effort to raise needed revenue, governments levy various taxes on real estate. This chapter examines the impact that real property taxes have on private real estate activity. Section 12.1 reviews the principles of taxation with emphasis on what influences the selection of a particular type of tax. Section 12.2 outlines the effect of real property taxes on real estate values. Section 12.3 deals with the problems of real property tax reform. When you have completed this chapter you will be able to:

1. List two basic taxing philosophies in the United States.
2. Describe why the property tax is used by your local government.
3. Discuss why many economists feel that the real property tax is regressive and a burden on lower income persons.
4. Give three examples of how real property taxes can influence land usage.
5. Discuss current and proposed real property tax reforms.

12.1   THE PRINCIPLES OF TAXATION

Why must the government collect taxes? What is the philosophy behind taxation? Why doesn't the government just print more money? Who bears the burden of taxes? This section answers these questions, thereby laying the foundation for understanding what impact property taxes have on real estate activity.

TAXES CAN BE USED TO REDISTRIBUTE WEALTH

The government levies taxes to generate revenue. The tax revenue is used to buy resources, which the government then redistributes in the form of governmental goods and services.

The taxing process can be viewed as follows: a tax on consumers or business reduces their spendable income. With less spendable income, consumers and business buy less, causing a drop in demand. This drop in consumer and business demand releases resources—unsold resources are left on the seller's shelf. The government then uses tax money to acquire these released resources. In short, a tax diverts some resources from the private sector (consumers and business) to the government sector. Once acquired, the government redistributes these resources according to the guidelines established by elected officials.

In addition to taxing, the government can obtain revenue by borrowing, charging fees and issuing fines, and by printing money. Fees, fines, and borrowing operate somewhat like taxes in that spending in the private sector is reduced, thereby releasing resources for governmental use. However, printing money is an entirely different matter. Printing money does not reduce spending, it stimulates spending. During periods of prosperity and full employment, printing money can cause excessive spending and bring on massive inflation. Thus the government is reluctant to print money as its only source of revenue. Given all the alternatives—taxes, fines and fees, or printing money, taxation has become the major method for generating government revenue. However, it should be noted that in recent years, the U.S. government has borrowed heavily to raise money to fund government spending.

THE THEORY OF TAXATION

In *The Wealth of Nations*, Adam Smith stated that a tax should be:

1. Equitable, *meaning that the tax burden should be spread equally among all citizens.*
2. Certain, *meaning that every taxpayer should know how much tax is owed, when it is due, and for what it is being used.*
3. Economical, *meaning that the cost of collecting the tax should be small in relation to the amount of taxes collected. In other words, it is uneconomical to institute a tax that costs $1,000 to administer, but only brings in $2,000 in tax revenue.*

TWO PHILOSOPHICAL PRINCIPLES

There are two major alternative philosophies regarding taxation. The first is that taxes should be based on a person's ability to pay. In other words, the rich should pay a higher percentage of their income for taxes than do the poor. The federal income tax is an example of a tax based on the ability-to-pay philosophy.

The second major philosophy is that taxes should be paid according to the benefits received from the government. A bridge toll is an example of a benefits-received tax. If a person uses the bridge, he or she pays the toll. If the bridge is not used, the toll is not paid. This is a so-called "user" tax.

Both of these philosophies have their problems: does taxing based on ability to pay stifle incentive? Does it encourage people to seek tax "loopholes"? Or worse yet, does it provide an excuse for illegal tax evasion? On the other hand, if taxation is based on the benefits-received or "user" philosophy, will only the middle- and upper-income citizens receive government services? Will the poor, who may need the government's help the most, be denied this help because they cannot afford to pay? Would this increase conflicts between the rich and the poor?

MAJOR TAXES AND EXPENDITURES

Each level of government—federal, state, and local—uses several different types of taxation in an effort to generate revenue. Table 12.1 shows the major tax and the largest single expenditure for each level of government in the United States.

The major source of revenue for the federal government is the personal income tax. The largest federal expenditure is for income security, while the second largest expense is for national defense. Income security refers to various federal programs to assist the un-

TABLE 12.1 Major Tax and Expenditure by Each Level of Government

Government Level	Major Tax	Largest Expenditure
Federal government	Personal income tax	Income security
State governments	Sales tax	Education and welfare
Local governments	Property tax	Education

employed, disabled, people on welfare programs, the homeless, and so on.

For most state governments, the major source of tax revenue is the sales tax, and the largest expenditures are for education and welfare. Those states without a sales tax, such as Oregon, usually use a strong state income tax as a substitute. Some states, such as California, use a combination of a sales tax and a state income tax. In California, the state sales tax and state income tax produce almost the same revenue.

When it comes to local government the property tax is by far the largest single source of tax revenue. Even with an increasing amount of local income and sales taxes, the property tax is still the main source of tax revenue for local governments. The major expenditure by local government is for education, followed by public safety.

IS THE TAX PROGRESSIVE, PROPORTIONAL, OR REGRESSIVE?

One way of evaluating a tax is to determine how the cost of taxes relates to the taxpayer's ability to pay. To help analyze the burden of a tax, economists describe taxes as progressive, proportional, or regressive.

A *progressive tax* increases in rate as the value of a taxable item increases. Thus, if taxable value increases from $1,000 to $2,000, the tax rate will also increase from perhaps 5 percent to 15 percent. A *proportional tax* retains the same rate as the value of the item being taxed increases. If the value of the taxable item increases from $1,000 to $2,000, the tax rate remains the same (5 percent at $1,000, and still 5 percent at $2,000). A *regressive tax* declines in rate as the value of the item being taxed increases. If the value of the taxable item increases from $1,000 to $2,000, the tax decreases, perhaps from 5 percent to 2 percent.

When evaluating a tax based on a taxpayer's ability to pay, economists frequently modify the definition of "progressive," "proportional," and "regressive" by substituting the word "income" for the phrase "value of the item being taxed." Thus, a progressive tax in this sense means that when income increases, the percentage of the tax also increases. A proportional tax means that when a taxpayer's income increases, the percentage of tax remains the same. A regressive tax means that when the income of the taxpayer increases, the percentage paid in taxes decreases.

SPECIAL INTEREST TOPIC

Are State Lotteries a Form of Regressive Taxation?

During the 1980s, state governments were looking for additional sources of revenue and many turned to state-operated lotteries. Groups opposed to lotteries warned that the source of this revenue would be those citizens least able to pay. Since people who buy lottery tickets tend to come from low-income backgrounds. The money spent on lottery tickets would be better spent on food, health, clothing, and other essentials of life.

Groups in favor of a lottery argue that lotteries would raise money for education and other programs that benefit everyone, including low-income people. The alternative would be to cut education and other programs because people would refuse to vote in the required tax increases to maintain these programs. However, people would vote for a lottery and some of the lottery revenue would be targeted for education and other needed programs.

What have been the results? When presented to the people for a vote, in almost every case the state lottery law passed. Did the prediction come true that the lottery would be primarily used by low-income people? According to a recent study by the National Bureau of Economic Research in Cambridge, Massachusetts, approximately 50% of all money spent on lottery tickets comes from 5% of the lottery players. This group bets approximately $1,100 annually and its profile is middle-aged and/or minority, with a blue-collar background.

Win $20 Million (and Get a Lot Less!)

If you beat the odds and win a $20 million lottery, how much do you really get?

Most state lotteries are exempt from state, but not federal, income tax. Thus the after-tax proceeds are not paid up front, but rather in 20 equal annual installments.

Example:

$20 million less 33% for federal income taxes leaves a balance of approximately $13,400,000, which divided by 20 years equals $670,000 per year. $670,000 per year discounted for the time value of money, say 7%, for the next 20 years equals a present value of $7,097,990, and this is the value of your prize. Not shabby, but not $20,000,000!

EVALUATING MAJOR TAXES—WHO BEARS THE BURDEN?

The personal income tax is somewhat progressive in that the tax rate rises as taxable income increases. This reflects the ability-to-pay philosophy. However, it should be noted that higher income individuals tend to make use of tax experts and tax loopholes to reduce their tax bite. So in the real world, the progressiveness of the income tax is not as steep as the tax charts indicate.

The sales tax appears to be proportional in that the tax rate remains the same as the value of taxable items increases. But if one plots the amount of taxes paid against the income level of persons paying the sales tax, the *impact* of the sales tax turns out to be regressive. The poor end up paying a higher percentage of their income for sales taxes than do the wealthy. Lower income individuals spend a greater percentage of their income on items that are subject to the sales tax than do wealthier individuals. When you are poor, you must spend all your income to live. Wealthy people do not spend all their income on taxable living expenses. They save a certain portion (savings are not subject to the sales tax) and spend some on non-taxable services. Assuming a sales tax rate of 6 percent, Table 12.2 illustrates a hypothetical example of the regressiveness of a sales tax when compared with income.

In an attempt to make the impact less regressive, many states have exempted food, rent, and utilities from the sales tax. Poor people tend to spend a major portion of their income in these areas, and by providing exemptions, low-income people gain some relief from the regressive nature of the sales tax.

TABLE 12.2   Example of the Regressive Impact of a Sales Tax

Income	Amount Spent	Tax Rate	Sales Tax	Percent of Income
$ 10,000	$10,000	6%	$ 600	6%
$100,000	$30,000	6%	$1,800	1.8%

REVIEWING YOUR UNDERSTANDING

The Principles of Taxation

1. In addition to taxes, name three other sources of government revenue.

2. How does taxing according to ability to pay differ from taxing based on benefits received?

3. Describe the differences between progressive, proportional, and regressive taxes. What are some problems associated with a progressive tax? With a regressive tax?

12.2 EVALUATING THE PROPERTY TAX

Use of the property tax in the United States dates from the founding colonists, who brought to this country Britain's concept of taxing land. After the U.S. Constitution was written, the new federal government used excise, sales, and other forms of taxation, leaving the property tax for state and local governments. By 1900, state governments for the most part had also abandoned the property tax in favor of other forms of taxation. This left local government as the sole collector of the property tax. This tradition has continued; property taxes are still the major source of revenue for city and county governments. This section examines what impact real property taxes have on real estate values.

LOCAL GOVERNMENT AND THE PROPERTY TAX

Why have local governments held on so firmly to the property tax? With so many people complaining about high real estate taxes, why do local governments continue to use this tax?

First, if the property tax is discontinued, a new tax would be needed to take its place. The levying of any new tax runs into massive political and administrative problems. So, for better or worse, there is a tendency to stick with the existing tax system. Second, a tax on real estate has certain advantages that other taxes do not have. Real estate is visible and immobile—real estate cannot be hidden from the tax collector. Also, unlike the income tax or the sales tax, property tax revenue does not fluctuate widely with short-term swings in the business cycle. People tend to pay their property taxes because the penalty for not paying is loss of the property, and for most people, this is too high a price to pay.

Local governments like the property tax because it provides a stable source of revenue. This in turn makes establishing annual local and county budgets an easier task.

SPECIAL INTEREST TOPIC

The Dilemma of the City

TAX PAYERS

TAX USERS

Taxpayers Are Decreasing While Tax Users Are Increasing

When city congestion drove upper- and middle-income people to the suburbs, their places were often taken by poor rural people seeking jobs. When the jobs failed to materialize, the poor went on welfare and drew upon other government services. Many major cities now have a dilemma: taxpayers are decreasing while tax users are increasing.

How can this problem be solved? Should the city raise taxes to generate the needed revenue? Or would a tax increase just drive out additional taxpayers? Should the federal government increase its subsidies to the cities? Will suburban and rural people resent paying taxes to support cities where they do not reside?

WHO REALLY PAYS THE PROPERTY TAX: OWNERS, TENANTS, OR CONSUMERS?

Who actually pays the tax? The property taxes paid on owner-occupied homes are usually nonshiftable—the owner pays. There are no tenants or customers to whom the tax can be passed. However, the situation for rental and business-owned property is entirely different. In the long run, property taxes are one of the costs of doing business and are shifted to customers—be they apartment tenants or business clients.

What about tax increases? Are they immediately shifted to consumers? If market conditions allow, landlords usually shift property tax increases to tenants in the form of higher rents. It must be recognized that this shift will occur only if there is a "landlord's market"—a strong tenant demand and a limited rental supply. When this exists, property tax increases are easily shifted to tenants. On the other hand, in a "soft" rental market with many vacancies, property tax increases tend to be absorbed by the landlord for fear that higher rents would cause a loss of tenants.

What if the tenants are businesses? If landlords can shift property tax increases to business tenants, do these businesses then shift the taxes to their customers in the form of higher prices? Do businesses that own their property shift the tax to their customers? The answer depends on the condition of the market in which the tenant-business operates. If the market is highly competitive, business can shift the tax to customers only to the extent that other business competitors pay the same taxes. If Business A pays a tax of $10, and competitor Business B pays $5, then in order to remain competitive, Business A must absorb the difference. If both Business A and Business B pay the same tax, they both can shift the full tax on to customers.

When discussing who pays increases in property taxes, it must be realized that some properties are rented on long-term leases, which may control whether the tenant or the landlord absorbs the tax increase. Also, in some areas, governmental rent controls determine who shall pay the increase in taxes.

PROPERTY TAXES AND CAPITALIZED REAL ESTATE VALUES

It was stated earlier that an increase in real property taxes that cannot be shifted to others (e.g., tax increases on owner-occupied homes) can reduce the value of real estate. How much value will the property lose? Will the loss be equal to or greater than the tax increase? The answers to these questions depend on how the tax monies are spent. If the government uses the increased revenue from property taxes for expenditures that benefit the taxpayer's home, such as street improvements, outdoor lighting, or neighborhood cleanup, the taxpayer's property values may remain stable or even increase. However, if the tax increases are spent in such a way that the taxpayer receives no benefits, the taxpayer's property will lose sales value. The amount of the maximum loss would be the capitalized value of the tax increase. Table 12.3 illustrates this concept.

TABLE 12.3 Capitalized Loss Due to Property Tax Increase

	Before	*After*	*Change*
Taxes	$1,000/yr.	$1,100/yr.	$100 tax increase
Net Income	$10,000	$9,900	$100 reduction
Capitalization Rate	10%	10%	none
Value Estimate	$100,000	$99,000	$1,000 loss

$$\frac{\text{Net Income}}{\text{Capitalization Rate}} = \text{Value Estimate}$$

SPECIAL INTEREST TOPIC _____

How the Budget Process Works

Local government expense budgets are established, then sources of revenue are estimated and subtracted from the budget. The remaining expenses must be cut or paid by increased taxes. Participants in the tax procedure are:

> The *Board of Supervisors* or *City Council* members, who set the budget.
>
> The *auditor*, who maintains the tax rolls.
>
> The *assessor*, who appraises the property.
>
> The *tax collector*, who is responsible for actually collecting the tax.

When there is a property tax increase, the loss in real estate value is not the amount of the annual tax increase, but rather the loss is the tax increase, capitalized over a number of years. Of course, this applies only if (1) the tax increase does not benefit the taxpayer's property, and (2) the tax increase is not shifted onto others in the form of higher rents or prices.

IS THE REAL PROPERTY TAX REGRESSIVE?

Do poor people spend a higher percentage of their income on real property taxes than do wealthy persons? If so, the property tax is regressive. If real estate taxes tend to take the same percentage of income regardless of how much is earned, the property tax is proportional, not regressive.

Real property taxes are levied at so much per tax rate value. Thus, higher-valued properties are charged the same tax rate as lower-valued properties. But studies reveal that when one plots the dollar amount of real estate taxes paid against the income levels of the taxpayer, the real property tax is regressive. Lower-income persons spend a higher percentage of their income on property taxes than do wealthy persons.[1]

REASONS FOR REGRESSIVENESS

Economists usually note two reasons for the regressiveness of the property tax. One deals with the tax assessment procedure; the other looks at the percentage of consumer income spent on housing. First, assessors may assess high-priced properties more conservatively than low-priced properties because (1) there are more low-

---

[1] D. Netzer, *Economics of the Property Tax*, Washington D.C., Brookings Institute, 1966, pp. 46–56.

priced properties, (2) they tend to be alike, and (3) they are bought and sold frequently. This gives the tax assessor plenty of current market information for assessment purposes. On the other hand, high-priced properties are not as common, they are exchanged less frequently, and therefore the tax assessor has less information to work with. In addition, wealthy property owners are usually able to hire experts to challenge the assessor's value estimates. Not wanting to face the dilemma of a show-cause proceeding, the assessor tends to assess the expensive property at a lower value. In essence, the assessment process is regressive, and this in turn makes the tax regressive. However, property tax "revolts," such as California's Proposition 13, have tended to even out the tax assessment process and defuse a portion of this argument.

The other main reason given for the regressiveness of the real property tax is that lower-income people must spend a higher percentage of their income on housing than do wealthy individuals. Although people do "trade up" to better housing as income levels increase, it appears that spending on housing does not increase as fast as gains in personal income.[2] If their income doubles, people usually will not double the price they will pay for a home. Therefore, as income rises, housing costs (and property taxes paid) become a smaller percentage of income. This is a classic example of regressiveness.

REAL PROPERTY TAXES AND LAND USAGE

Although the primary purpose of the property tax is to generate revenue for local government, it is also possible for government to influence land use by manipulating the property tax. Some examples of how real property taxes can influence land use are given below.

1. By exempting religious, educational, and charitable institutions from taxation, the government is, in effect, using taxes as an incentive to create more of these institutions.

2. Assessing rural land based on its suburban residential potential can force up property taxes to the point that rural owners must sell to developers. On the other hand, a low preferential tax treatment of rural property may create an incentive to keep the land rural, thereby maintaining open green space.

3. Taxing resources such as timber and minerals at full value may force quick exploitation tactics, while special tax concessions during growing periods may encourage resource redevelopment and conservation.

4. Some communities have used artificially low property tax rates to attract industries and other new businesses to occupy city-owned industrial parks. Other cities may pursue a "no-growth"

---

[2] Ibid., p. 57.

philosophy by raising taxes in an effort to discourage commercial development.

5. High property taxes during economic depressions can cause private ownership to be converted to government ownership as property owners default on their tax payments. Many cities and counties acquired large land holdings during the major depression of the 1930s.

6. Higher property taxes can cause more intensified land use as property owners rent spare rooms and garages, plow more acres, use more fertilizer, and so on, in an effort to offset tax increases with higher incomes.

These are but a few of the many ways in which government can direct land use via changes in property taxation.

It should be stressed that any special concession to one type of property shifts the tax burden to the nonexempt property. In your community, who pays for church exemptions? Veteran's exemptions? Rural property exemptions? New business exemptions? Homeowner's exemptions?

REVIEWING YOUR UNDERSTANDING

Evaluating the Property Tax

1. What are some reasons local officials give for continued use of the real property tax? How much of your local government's revenue comes from property taxes? What is your largest local expenditure?

2. What is meant by "shifting" the property tax? When is it difficult to shift the tax?

3. How does an increase in real property taxes affect real estate values? How does it affect land use?

4. When people state, "Real property taxes are regressive," what do they mean by "regressive?"

12.3   REAL PROPERTY TAX REFORM

Real property taxes are despised by property owners and tenants, labeled as regressive by economists, attacked by politicians up for election, and lobbied against by real estate trade organizations. Why does such an unloved tax still exist? If everybody hates it, why hasn't it been eliminated? This section examines real property tax reform.

POLITICAL REALITIES

In spite of all its faults, the property tax, as mentioned earlier, does have a strong feature—it produces a constant, predictable source of revenue that does not fluctuate widely with short-term movements in the business cycle. Some local governments have experimented with other forms of taxation, namely sales and income tax, but have run into numerous political problems. Citizens resent new taxes. They approve the removal of existing taxes but fight the introduction of a new, substitute tax. So it appears that until an acceptable substitute tax is devised, the property tax will remain.

CURRENT REFORMS

If people are stuck with the real property tax, can it be modified to remove some of its inequities? Most criticism of the property tax concentrates on its regressiveness. Thus, many reform proposals are aimed at aligning property taxes more closely with one's ability to pay. Several reforms are currently underway that can help to reduce the regressive features of the real property tax.

Exemptions for Low-Income Persons

Some communities have provided property exemptions for low-income people, especially for the older, retired property owner. This exemption reduces the tax bite for people with low or fixed incomes, thereby shifting the property tax burden to those with higher incomes.

Exemptions for Homeowners

Some states have enacted laws exempting from taxation a flat dollar amount of the value of owner-occupied residential property. For example, California homeowners are allowed a $7,000 exemption, which works as follows:

Appraised value	$200,000
Less: homeowner's exemption	− 7,000
Assessed value for property tax purposes	$193,000

This gives some degree of relief to homeowners, who are usually unable to shift the property tax on to others.

Upgrading the Professional Skills of the Assessor's Office

Many states are attempting to establish uniform assessment procedures to correct certain inequities in local assessors' offices.

THEORIES AND THEORETICIANS

Library of Congress

Henry George and the Single Tax

Henry George (1839–1897) was a reformist concerned about economic inequities. As a newspaperman in the San Francisco area, he wrote emotional articles about the problems of rising land values and profiteering. George outlined his philosophy in a book entitled *Progress and Poverty*, published in 1880.

Henry George believed that land was a free commodity, like air and sunlight, and thus it belonged to all the people. However, he did believe in other forms of private property ownership. Therefore, George proposed that all rents for land were unearned surplus and should be taxed away and given to the government to help eliminate poverty. He envisioned that if landowners were charged 100 percent taxes on land value, they would still develop the land because profits made from improvements upon the land would not be taxed. George concluded that if all land were taxed as surplus value, enough revenue would be generated so that no other form of taxation would be required.

His book was an instant success, and Henry George became famous. He moved to New York where, in 1886, he came close to being elected mayor of New York. He died in 1897 while campaigning once again for the mayor's office.

Although the single tax has never been used in the United States, Henry George had a tremendous impact on the whole idea of equity and taxing according to the ability to pay. Some current reform proposals regarding higher taxation on land and less on improvements have their roots in Henry George's philosophy.

Statewide assessment rates, mandatory review procedures, and professional appraisal training are a few of the reforms. In most areas, the assessor is an elected official, and some reformers advocate changing this to a civil service appointment to try to remove the possibility of political favoritism from the assessment procedure.

Placing a Limit on Property Taxes

The so-called "taxpayers revolt" began on June 6, 1978, when the voters of California passed Proposition 13, the Jarvis–Gann Initiative. Proposition 13 limits real property taxes to one percent of the "full cash value" of the real property, plus an additional amount for local assessment bonds.

Beginning with a retroactive cutoff date of March 1975, property taxes can only be increased by two percent per year. The real estate can only be reassessed to full cash market value upon sale or other specified transfer of title. The effect is to limit property tax increases to two percent per year measured from the time a property owner acquires title. Thus, two homeowners, side by side with identical valued homes could have vastly different property tax bills depending upon how long each has owned the home. Several states have followed California's lead and enacted their own versions of Proposition 13.

Groups opposed to this property tax limitation concept have challenged the constitutionality of these laws on grounds of unequal taxation. Some groups attack the concept based on the observation that owners of commercial and industrial properties get a better break than do homeowners. This argument points out that homes are bought and sold more often than commercial and industrial properties. Therefore, homes are reassessed and taxed at the new market price more often than business properties and this shifts more property tax burden from business property owners to homeowners.

POSSIBLE FUTURE REFORMS

Other reform possibilities include increasing the tax burden assigned to land and reducing the tax rate on improvements. If land is taxed at a higher rate than improvements, there would be an incentive to bring vacant land into use. Also, an incentive would exist for property owners to improve their properties without the fear of a large increase in assessed value. However, there may be some practical problems in implementing this proposal. For example, it may be opposed by groups who wish to keep land as open space.

Another reform proposal states that inefficient, overlapping community services should be combined into larger regional units to gain economies of scale. For example, instead of having individual city schools, water, sewer, road construction, and utility departments, there would be a combined regional system, thereby reducing overhead. However, others object that combinations such as this would isolate government from the control of local citizens.

Still another reform proposal would limit the amount of property tax revenue that can be spent on education and welfare, the two major expenditures of local government. This proposal would, in effect, shift the tax burden for education and welfare from local to state government. Those in favor of this proposal believe that property owners pay a disproportionate share of the cost for educational and welfare programs.

California's Proposition 13 has in effect done exactly that. By limiting local property tax revenue, the state of California has needed to increase its share of the cost for local education and welfare. This has started a controversy of "local versus state" control over schools and welfare programs. Critics of Proposition 13 point out that "he or she who pays (the state) gets to call the local shots." These same critics also point out that property tax limitation proposals merely substitute one regressive tax (property tax) for another regressive tax (state sales tax or lottery).

OTHER TAXES AFFECTING REAL ESTATE

People tend to forget that in addition to the property tax, there are many other taxes that affect real estate. Major examples include:

Special assessments	Transfer taxes
Inheritance taxes	Severance taxes on natural
Gift taxes	resources
Income taxes	

All of these taxes are controversial in their own right. Currently, the issue of a real estate transfer tax is being hotly debated in many areas of the United States. In an effort to raise additional revenue, local governments are looking at the possibility of a tax on the sales price whenever real estate is sold.

REVIEWING YOUR UNDERSTANDING

Real Property Tax Reform

1. List four types of real property tax reforms.
2. List two types of real property tax exemptions. Who pays for these exemptions?
3. What was Henry George's idea?

CHAPTER SUMMARY

When government levies a tax, resources are diverted from the private sector to government for redistribution according to the decisions of elected officials. Taxes are based on either the ability to pay or on the benefits received. Any tax can be analyzed to determine who bears the greatest burden relative to their ability to pay. A progressive tax, like the federal income tax, places a heavier burden on the wealthy. A regressive tax, like the sales tax and property tax, places a greater burden on the poor.

The property tax is used primarily by local governments, and in most cases constitutes the single largest source of total revenue received by cities and counties. The greatest criticism of the property tax is its regressiveness—the heaviest burden is placed on lower-income individuals. In spite of all its shortcomings, the property tax persists because it does have one saving grace. It generates a constant, steady, and predictable source of revenue that does not fluctuate widely with short-term movements in the business cycle. Unlike federal and state governments, which depend on fluctuating income and sales taxes, local government can accurately predict how much property tax revenue it will receive and can budget accordingly.

Property taxes can reduce real estate income flows. If the taxes are not spent in a manner that enhances real estate, property values decline. The loss in value is the capitalized amount of the property tax. Real property taxes can be used by local government to influence land usage. Preferential tax treatment will encourage certain kinds of development, while abnormally high taxes can discourage other development.

A number of property tax reforms are under consideration, including low-income exemptions, homeowner's exemptions, and upgrading the skills of tax assessment officials. However, reform does not mean replacement. In the immediate future, it appears that the property tax will still remain as the primary source of revenue for local governments.

IMPORTANT TERMS AND CONCEPTS

Ability to pay

Benefits received

Homeowner's exemption

Personal income tax

Progressive taxation

Property tax and land usage

Proportional taxation

Real property tax

Regressive taxation

Sales tax

Single tax theory

REVIEWING YOUR UNDERSTANDING

1. All of the following sources of government revenue reduce private demand, *except*:

    a. taxes

    b. borrowing

    c. user fees

    d. printing money

2. Two major taxing philosophies are (1) ability to pay, and (2):

    a. redistribution

    b. regressive

    c. benefits received

    d. better distribution

3. As the taxpayer's income increases, the tax rate increases faster. This is an example of a:

    a. progressive tax

    b. proportional tax

    c. regressive tax

    d. reverse tax

4. Which of the following property owners is least able to shift a property tax increase to others?

    a. homeowner

    b. apartment landlord

    c. retail store owner

    d. office building owner

5. When measured against the income of the taxpayer, all of the following are considered by most economists to be regressive, *except*:

    a. property tax

    b. income tax

    c. sales tax

    d. lottery tickets

6. If the prevailing capitalization rate for real property is 10 percent, an increase in real estate taxes of $500 that cannot be shifted and is not beneficial to the subject property will cause a loss in value of approximately:

    a. $500

    b. $5,000

    c. $50,000

    d. $500,000

7. Taxes are used by governments to:

    a. raise revenue

    b. redistribute income

    c. encourage or discourage a private activity

    d. do all of the above

8. A charge levied by government to a developer for the cost to upgrade a city road to accommodate the increased traffic caused by the proposed development is a(n):

    a. ability-to-pay charge

    b. benefits-received charge

    c. progressive charge

    d. proportional charge

9. The main advantage of a property tax for local government is that it:

    a. is popular with voters

    b. swings quickly with changes in the local business cycle

    c. places a greater burden on the wealthy, as opposed to the modest landowner

    d. is easier to predict revenue than other taxes

10. Regarding property tax limitations, such as California's Proposition 13, which of the following is true?

    a. the tax is evenly spread across all homeowners

    b. homeowners seem to get a better break than business property owners

    c. tax expenditure decisions have shifted from local to state government.

    d. all economists agree that the limitations are beneficial

Chapter 13

Land-Use Controls

Preview

Land-use controls are controversial: some people feel that land is a commodity to be bought and sold like any other product. They consider any type of land-use control an infringement on free enterprise. At the other extreme are those who believe land is a resource that belongs to all the people, the use of which should be completely controlled by public agencies. Somewhere in the middle is the view that land is both a commodity and a resource that should be privately owned but used constructively to benefit society.

Section 13.1 outlines the major forms of private and public land-use controls. Section 13.2 summarizes the principles of urban land-use planning. Section 13.3 examines recent land-use trends, noting nationwide emphasis upon the environment, coastal zoning, and pollution regulations. When you have completed this chapter you will be able to:

1. List two reasons for the current controversy over land-use controls.

2. List two forms of private land-use controls and two forms of public land-use controls.

3. Describe the three major steps in creating a comprehensive plan for a community.

4. Describe recent trends in land-use controls.

13.1   TYPES OF LAND-USE CONTROLS

The current debate over public land-use control has its roots in two economic concepts: (1) the supply of land at the right location is now scarce, and (2) many people view land as a resource, not just as a commodity.

In the frontier days, land was plentiful and inexpensive, and there was little concern over its use. Wastefulness was tolerated because of the seemingly inexhaustible supply. Land was treated as a commodity to be bought, sold, and speculated on, much like agricultural products.

With the settling of the West and the massive increase in urban population, land-use controls were deemed necessary to protect neighbors from each other and to protect and preserve the land. However, controls meant surrendering a degree of individual freedom and conflicted with the deep-rooted traditions of free enterprise and private property rights.

Today the land-use controversy centers around this question: to what extent can private land be controlled without destroying the principles of private property rights? There is no "right" answer to this question. Each person must make a decision based on his or her own interpretation of the issues. This section outlines private and public land-use controls.

PRIVATE LAND-USE CONTROLS

Private land-use controls refer to nongovernment regulation of land. Two major private controls are (1) economic highest and best use, and (2) private deed constructions.

Economic Highest and Best Use

In a pure capitalistic economy, the basic control over land use is market allocation: the interaction of supply and demand will eventually determine the highest and best use of land. *Highest and best use is defined as that legal use that will produce the greatest net income attributable to the land at a specific location.* In theory, if the market is left alone, competitive bidding would eventually determine what is the most profitable use of the land. Once this use has been established, it will continue until a more profitable use comes along. The private market controls land use through the maximization of private profit.

In a pure capitalistic system, land control using the concept of economic highest and best use can work. But our capitalistic system is mixed, not pure, and the goal of private profit may not correspond with social goals. Under mixed capitalism, if private interests differ from social interests, private interests must frequently be modified to support social goals. In today's real estate market, the economic concept of highest and best use exerts a powerful influence on land use, but it is not the only one. Other private and public tools are used to modify land use in spite of profit considerations.

Private Deed Restrictions

Private land use can be controlled by the placing of restrictions in deeds. Private deed restrictions are commonly referred to as "covenants, conditions, and restrictions," or C, C, and R's for short. The law of real property allows owners to limit the use of land by contract as long as the contract restrictions are not contrary to public policy. Although there are technical differences between a covenant, a condition, and a restriction, the basic concept is the same—they attempt to maintain property values by preventing surrounding land from being used in a manner that would be adverse to nearby properties. The importance of compatible nearby uses was stressed in Chapter 8.

Private deed restrictions are usually created in one of three ways:

SPECIAL INTEREST TOPIC _____

Property Rights

Historically, the word *property* does not refer to the thing owned but rather to the right or interest that the owner has in the item possessed.

Basic property rights are:

    The right to possess
    The right to use
    The right to encumber
    The right to dispose
    The right to exclude others

The current controversy over land-use controls centers around the extent to which these private property rights should be amended to promote the public welfare.

(1) Existing property owners get together and agree to create restrictions mutually beneficial to all parties; (2) an owner of a large parcel of land sells off a portion or portions and inserts restrictions in the deed to protect his or her remaining parcels from adverse uses by the new neighbor(s); (3) a land developer creates blanket tract restrictions for a new subdivision.

Recent inroads made by public controls have somewhat diminished the use of private deed restrictions. However, many questions not usually controlled by zoning or by codes can be handled by private restrictions. Examples include architectural uniformity, landscaping standards, light and air easements, maintenance agreements, and homeowner association controls.

PUBLIC LAND-USE CONTROLS

Industrialization and urban crowding have created a need for public controls to maintain order and promote social harmony. One way to maintain order is to control the use of the land. Government can use one or all of the following powers to control land use: (1) police power, (2) the power of eminent domain, (3) government spending power, and (4) the power of taxation. Taxation was discussed in Chapter 12, so this section discusses only police power, eminent domain, and government spending.

POLICE POWER

Police power refers to the constitutional right of government to regulate private activity to promote the general health, welfare, and safety of society. Police power has often been used in the United States to direct land use. Some major examples of police power include zoning ordinances, building and health codes, set-back requirements, pollution abatement, and rent controls. Of the many police power enactments, zoning and subdivision regulations emerge as the most influential methods for controlling land use.

Zoning

Zoning refers to the division of land into designated use districts. In its simplest form, zoning districts are divided into residential use, commercial use, industrial use, and rural use. Each use in turn can have several subclasses. For example, residential can be broken down into single-family, multifamily, and mobile home zones. Commercial zones are usually divided into retail, office, and wholesale space. Industrial zones are divided into light industry and heavy industry, and rural zones into agricultural, resource, or recreational uses.

Zoning as a land control tool was not common in the United States until the 1920s. Prior to this time there was some doubt about the constitutionality of zoning, although early zoning laws can be

SPECIAL INTEREST TOPIC

Conflicts Between Police Power and Eminent Domain

POLICE
POWER

EMINENT
DOMAIN

Police power allows government to regulate private land without the payment of compensation, while eminent domain converts private property to public ownership and requires the payment of compensation. The question might be asked, How far can the government limit or interfere with the private use of land without taking the land for public use, which involves eminent domain and the payment of compensation? There is no clear answer. The line of distinction between the police power and eminent domain is fuzzy. Various courts have moved back and forth depending on the circumstances in each case.

---

traced to colonial times. But in the 1926 landmark case *Euclid* v. *Amber Realty Company*, the Supreme Court held that zoning was a reasonable exercise of government police power. Since this decision, every state has passed legislation allowing individual cities and counties to enact zoning ordinances.

Early zoning ordinances were aimed at safety and nuisance control. The idea was to use zoning to protect individual property values by prohibiting offensive use of surrounding land. The use of zoning has gradually been expanded, and now it is used to "promote the general welfare" of the entire community.

Subdivision Regulations

Another important use of police power is subdivision regulation. Poorly conceived subdivisions, with inadequate streets and facilities, can become a burden to taxpayers in later years when expensive redevelopment is needed to correct earlier oversights. Proponents of subdivision controls believe that the origin of slums and urban blight can be traced to inadequate regulations. Opponents disagree, noting that today's slums are the result of government ordinances that prevent land from rising to its economic highest and best use.

Today, subdivision regulations are used in most areas of the United States. Real estate developers are frequently required to provide water, sewer, paved streets, sidewalks, street lights, and school and park sites as a condition of being allowed to subdivide. The idea is to plan for the future at the inception and to require the purchaser of the subdivided lot, not the community as a whole, to pay the expense of added community facilities. Like all public controls, subdivision regulations are controversial in that they require the surrender of some individual rights in an attempt to promote the general welfare.

EMINENT DOMAIN

Police power allows government to regulate private land without the payment of compensation. The power of eminent domain is different in that it allows the government to acquire title to private land in exchange for the payment of just compensation. Eminent domain is used for a variety of government land-use projects such as highways, public housing, and urban renewal.

All levels of government may exercise power of eminent domain regardless of how unwilling the property owner may be. The main issue in most eminent domain cases is the amount of compensation. The courts have ruled that the property's fair market value is the proper basis for determining compensation. In addition, most federal and some state agencies must also pay for moving and other miscellaneous expenses incurred by those being displaced.

GOVERNMENT SPENDING AS AN INFLUENCE ON LAND USE

Through its enormous spending power, the government can influence the use of land. The courts have held that the government can spend money for almost any purpose as long as it is for the benefit of the public. Government funds have been used to finance many types of real estate-oriented developments such as roads, dams, canals, and power facilities. In addition, governmental subsidies such as aid to farmers and FHA and VA (Veterans' Administration) mortgage guarantees can also influence land use. The spending power of the government is so great that it can direct some land use without the necessity of eminent domain, police power, or taxation.

REVIEWING YOUR UNDERSTANDING

Types of Land-Use Controls

1. List two economic concepts that are at the root of the current land-use controversy.
2. List two private land-use controls and give one example of each.
3. List two public tools for controlling land use. Give two examples of each.
4. How does the power of eminent domain differ from the police power?

13.2   PRINCIPLES OF URBAN PLANNING

Since the early 1900s, the United States has shifted from a rural to an urban nation. In 1900, approximately 40 percent of the United States population lived in urban areas. By 1990, this percentage had increased to over 70 percent. Some states have even greater concentrations of population; over 90 percent of Californians live in urban areas.

Most cities and suburbs were unprepared to handle this massive increase in urban growth. The result has been overcrowding, slums, property tax problems, traffic congestion, and many other urban ills. Out of this confusion has risen the cry for better urban planning. This section describes the principles of urban planning.

DEFINITION OF URBAN PLANNING

The dictionary defines *planning* as "thinking out acts and purposes beforehand." When applied to urban areas, planning can be defined as anticipating and achieving community goals in light of social, economic, and physical needs. Urban planning requires that a community analyze its assets and liabilities, establish its goals, and then attempt to achieve these goals using land-use control as a primary tool.

The word *planning* causes apprehension among some people. They fear planning will mean loss of economic and political freedom, while others who support the concept of urban planning believe that directing a community's growth presents no threat to personal freedom.

CREATION AND IMPLEMENTATION OF URBAN PLANNING

The establishment of a community plan requires three major steps: (1) resource analysis, (2) formulation of community goals, and (3) implementation of the plan.

Resource Analysis

The first step in urban planning is to recognize the individual character of the community. What are its strong points? What are its weaknesses? To accomplish this, several substudies will be required, including an economic base study, a population trend study, a survey of existing land use, a city facilities study, and an analysis of the community's financial resources. Once a resource inventory has been taken, the next step is to formulate community goals in light of its resources.

Formulation of Community Goals

The formulation of community goals is the most difficult phase of urban planning because of the conflict between various special-interest groups, each trying to secure its own definitions of the community goal. However, citizen input should be encouraged. A community plan must be based on the desires of community residents as a whole, not on the desires of staff planners alone.

Once the goals are established, a comprehensive plan to achieve these objectives must be formulated. The plan is frequently referred to as the *general plan* or the *master plan*, and it should encompass all social, economic, and physical aspects of the desired growth. The plan should be long range but provide for short-range flexibility as the need for modification arises. Under no circumstances must the master plan be viewed as an inflexible, permanent fixture that will never require modification. A community's attitudes and resources can change, and the master plan must be modified to recognize these changes.

Implementation of the Plan

The final step in urban planning is to implement the community plan. The implementation phase requires local government to use police power, eminent domain, taxation, and control over government spending to enact the plan. These powers have been discussed earlier, but it should again be stressed that the two most powerful tools for implementing a community plan are zoning and subdivision regulations.

Zoning can be used to separate incompatible land uses, promote health and safety standards, preserve property values, and minimize the cost of public improvements, while subdivision regulations can be used to chart the quality and quantity of future land division.

SPECIAL INTEREST TOPIC

Summary of Planning Terms

Planning commission—An appointed body of citizens charged with the responsibility of advising the elected board of supervisors or city council members in matters of land use.

Planning department—City or county staff employees who lend professional and technical assistance to elected officials.

Zone—An area defined on a map by a boundary line within which the land-use regulations are the same.

Rezoning—The process of changing land-use regulations on property from one zone to another.

Variance—A deviation from the zoning regulations for a particular parcel.

Condition—A requirement imposed by the government in connection with the approval of a permit or a division of property.

Development plans—Plans showing the details of the proposed development. Normally includes plot plan, architectural renderings, and statistical information relative to acreage, building area, units, and parking.

Subdivision—A division of property into five or more parcels.

Lot split—A division of property into two, three, or four parcels.

Architectural review—Certain zoning areas where a special citizen group approves or rejects the proposal based on its architectural compatibility with the surrounding area.

Appeal—The right to request review of a negative planning commission decision. The appellate process goes from the planning commission to the board of supervisors or city council to the courts.

When these two tools are used in conjunction with other public controls, the master plan has the best chance of being implemented.

If the master plan has been well conceived, and if it represents a consensus of the community, the implementation should proceed

THEORIES AND THEORETICIANS
Early American Planners

Library of Congress

William Penn (1644–1718)

Systematic land planning in the United States began with William Penn in 1682. Penn, an English Quaker and founder of the Commonwealth of Pennsylvania, began in 1682 to plan and design the city of Philadelphia. Using a checkerboard grid, he mapped out the city and a surrounding system of agricultural villages to help feed the city inhabitants. As a land promoter, Penn traveled throughout Europe selling land in an attempt to populate his colony. Penn died in 1718, deeply in debt.

THEORIES AND THEORETICIANS

Early American Planners

National Archives

Pierre Charles L'Enfant (1754–1825)

L'Enfant was a French-born engineer and architect who fought for the colonies during the Revolutionary War. In 1791, L'Enfant was commissioned by George Washington to design a new federal city in the District of Columbia. Avoiding the grid street plan, L'Enfant designed a city of radiating streets with wide avenues and numerous parks. Two years later, a dispute with Congress led to L'Enfant's dismissal. Numerous disputes over compensation followed, and L'Enfant died in poverty in 1825, never seeing his dream city completed. However, many of his key ideas can be seen in the city today.

with a minimum of friction. On the other hand, if the community plan fails to represent citizen input, or if public agencies misuse the tools of implementation, the plan will meet with failure.

THE NEED FOR REGIONAL PLANNING

Historically, planning has been a local matter. Each community developed its own plans within the confines of its own territorial limits. In the process, each community attempted to optimize its own social and economic well-being, frequently at the expense of surrounding areas. For example, the placing of a smelly industrial plant on the border of one city has a spillover effect on the neighboring community downwind.

The growth of multicity metropolitan areas has underscored the need for more efficient planning on a regional basis. Water and sewage systems, rapid transit, highway traffic patterns, airports, and pollution controls are some examples. Any attempt by individual cities to attack these problems can result in inefficient small-scale operations and needless duplication.

From an economic point of view, what might be needed is a regional government with the power to tax and administer regional programs. However, from a political point of view, there is a widespread popular resistance to the creation of another layer of government. Moreover, local government officials are reluctant to surrender some of their power. What usually occurs is a compromise—a regional commission or district created to solve a single problem. Metropolitan rapid transit districts, regional park commissions, regional water quality control boards, and so on are some examples.

Regional planning is easiest to implement when the regional organization is given the power to tax and receive direct federal and state aid. If the regional commission depends wholly on annual grants from the treasury of individual cities within the geographic area, political in-fighting between cities tends to dilute the implementation of regional planning.

There seems to be a movement toward more planning on a regional basis. The impact of this planning will depend on the willingness to forgo some local control in favor of a regional commission. In some cases, local communities have little choice because national and state legislation may require regional controls. But regional planning will work best, required or not, if it can be proven to local citizens that the result will be better coordination and perhaps a savings of tax dollars. If the evidence is to the contrary, regional planning will meet tremendous resistance.

REVIEWING YOUR UNDERSTANDING

Principles of Urban Planning

1. What is the purpose of urban planning?
2. List three major steps needed to establish a community plan.
3. What are the two most powerful tools for implementing a community plan?
4. Why is regional planning being used?

13.3 RECENT TRENDS IN LAND-USE CONTROLS

As stated earlier, land-use controls are controversial. At the core of the controversy is the recognition that usable land is a scarce resource that needs some public controls. But how much control is needed? There are those who feel that recent land-use controls are too stringent, while others feel that more controls are needed.

Some of the more recent and controversial land-use controls include: (1) control over premature subdividing, (2) pollution and environmental regulations, (3) "slow growth" or "no growth" policies, (4) the creation of new towns, (5) state and federal intervention in land-use controls, and (6) inclusionary zoning. Many of these are interrelated and are a by-product of the environmental movement.

PREVENTING PREMATURE SUBDIVIDING

Public control over the subdividing of land has existed for decades. However, there has recently been a concerted effort to control what is known as premature subdivision. A subdivision is "premature" when home construction fails to take place after the subdivision lots are sold. Frequently, the developer has already dedicated the streets, sewers, and other off-site facilities to the local government. Local government then finds itself in the position of having to maintain the unused facilities. The lack of home construction fails to generate the needed tax revenue, and the local government is put in a financial bind. For small, rural governments, this situation can be especially painful.

To prevent premature subdivision, some planning agencies require would-be developers to show the likelihood of home construction as one of the conditions for obtaining a subdivision permit. This requirement, along with the difficulty in meeting environmental regulations, has caused subdivision activity to decline in many rural areas.

POLLUTION AND ENVIRONMENTAL REGULATIONS

Beginning in the 1960s and continuing today, there has been a tremendous amount of federal legislation dealing with pollution and environmental issues, including water and air quality, waste disposal, resource recovery, endangered species, coastal preservation, and environmental impact report requirements just to name a few. State efforts at pollution and environmental protection have produced similar laws.

Much of this legislation seeks to regulate land use to minimize environmental damage. Before a construction project is approved, the developer must show what impact the proposed project will have on the environment. The permit-issuing agency then decides, after first consulting with experts, whether to issue the permit.

Like other controls, pollution and environmental regulations increase the cost of land development in terms of both time and money. The contents of an environmental impact report will be discussed in more detail in Chapter 15, *Required Government Reports*.

"SLOW GROWTH" AND "NO GROWTH" POLICIES

For many years, communities and local business groups spent large sums of money advertising the amenities of their area in an attempt to attract industry and people. Their goal was more growth. However, increased congestion and pollution have led some communities to reverse their positions. They are adopting "slow growth" or "no growth" policies.

Communities can discourage growth by making it difficult to establish a home or by preventing the establishment of businesses that will create jobs. Land-use controls can be an effective tool in discouraging unwanted growth. For example, a community can keep additional people out by converting all vacant land to public parks. Or it can allow only the affluent to move into a community by creating expensive residential zones. Another common slow growth tool is to allow a limited number of building permits each year. Builders competing for permits are required to submit proposals that are "beneficial" to the community. A community can prevent business expansion by creating tough pollution standards, levying excessive taxes, or by preventing the construction of new transportation facilities.

A case can be made for slow or no growth policies by stressing the need to preserve open space, to avoid pollution, to maintain the community's way of life, and to keep from straining community fiscal budgets. However, equally good cases can be made against no growth policies by pointing out that they discriminate against lower-income persons who are attempting to improve their status. A no growth policy can freeze low-income people at their present level by reducing economic opportunities, which in turn can prevent upward social mobility.

On a national basis, the only effective no growth policy is a decrease in the rate of population growth. However, on a state or local basis, no growth can be achieved by shifting the population burden to another state or community. This naturally leads to infighting and dissension among states and communities. Several court cases are currently attempting to resolve the no growth question by delineating the right of the government to control growth and the rights of individuals to live and work where they please. Once this question is resolved, the answer will have significant impact on local real estate activity.

THE CREATION OF NEW TOWNS

Among planners a debate exists about whether urban density can best be solved by (1) creating new towns in rural areas, (2) shifting people to existing smaller cities, or (3) leaving the countryside as it is and redeveloping the major cities to accommodate more people.

Planners who favor the creation of new towns feel that, in the long run, it is more economical to build entire new cities to handle population increases instead of attempting to redevelop existing major cities. The new cities would be self-contained so that people could live, work, and shop with a minimum of commuting. Columbia, Maryland, and Reston, Virginia, are two examples of such new cities.

Others feel that instead of building entire new cities, the government should encourage the growth of existing small towns. Greatest emphasis would be placed on enlarging towns in economically depressed areas where such action would help fight chronic unemployment. A key proposal is to use government contracts or subsidies to entice industries to relocate in the depressed regions.

Some planners are critical both of the new town concept and the idea of encouraging growth in existing smaller towns. They believe that the problems of urban America will not evaporate with the development of new towns. They also feel that it is improper to destroy existing rural areas by importing population from major cities. Instead, this group believes that the best solution is to redesign existing metropolitan areas to allow for living with a higher density. The planners note that by European standards our major cities are underpopulated and that through good design we can increase the number of people per acre without an increase in their feelings of being crowded. This can be accomplished by converting our existing horizontal parking, residential areas, and shopping centers to high-rise buildings. This would instantly generate more space without expanding the city limits. However, planners who favor new towns or the expansion of existing smaller cities rebut by stating that given the opportunity, people prefer low as opposed to high-density living.

Although planners disagree on the best solution for urban congestion, most do agree that any solution is going to require massive government assistance, in at least two forms: land assemblage, using the government's power of eminent domain; and financial assistance to build initial off-site improvements such as streets, sewers, water plants, and other basic facilities. However, the building of new towns or reconstruction of existing cities need not be a total government project. After the initial planning, land acquisition, and off-site development financing have taken place, the project can be turned over to private enterprise for completion. The combination of urban dwellers seeking better surroundings and profit-motivated business persons willing to provide these surroundings, could produce the economic setting needed to help defeat urban congestion.

STATE AND FEDERAL INTERVENTION IN LAND-USE CONTROLS

In the past, land-use controls were essentially a local matter. Cities and counties enacted land controls to achieve their own individual goals. However, recent urban pressures have increased the amount of land regulations at the state and federal level. There is a feeling that some problems are too large for a single city to handle, or that self-interest causes some communities to seek a solution that has a detrimental effect on a neighboring community.

Metropolitan problems have led to the creation of regional commissions charged with overseeing the activities of all regions within the state. An example of a regional-state relationship is the California Coastal Zone Conservation Act of 1972. This act recognized that the coast of California "belongs to all the people and that it has a delicately balanced ecosystem that should be permanently protected." The act requires local regions and communities to incorporate coastal planning into their general plan. Each local entity is charged with controlling coastal development within its area, but the state commission has the power to reverse the decisions of the local planners if not consistent with state guidelines.

On a still higher level, there is considerable discussion whether a comprehensive national land-use policy should be enacted by the federal government. The proposal would require each state to adopt a statewide environmental, recreational, and industrial land-use plan. The federal plan would require the establishment of industrial, conservation, and recreational sanctuaries. Federal grant-in-aid funds would be available to assist states in creating and maintaining the plan. To assure adoption, the federal government would use its power to withdraw federal aid and expenditures from any state that fails to comply with the regulations. This threatened loss of federal funds would assure state compliance.

People in favor of more state and federal land-use controls believe that an overall master plan for land use is needed. They note that communities have master plans for development within local boundaries, and that state and national governments should likewise have a master plan for land within their boundaries.

Opposition to state and national land-use controls comes from individuals who feel that the power of land regulation should be limited to local government. They fear that planning on a state or federal level will not be sensitive to local needs. Who is correct? Like most land-use controls, the correct answer depends on one's value judgment. However, the current trend is toward more regional, state, and federal control over land use.

INCLUSIONARY ZONING

Inclusionary zoning is a type of regulation that requires a developer of new residential housing to set aside a designated number of units for low and moderate-income people. If the project is an apartment complex, the developer must rent a percentage of the units to low-income people at below market rents. If the project offers houses for sale, a certain percentage must be sold at below-market prices. To assure that the units will remain available to low-income families after the initial sale, restrictions are inserted in the deed.

If a developer refuses to provide units per the inclusionary ordinance, either the building permit is denied, or in some cases an in lieu fee is paid to the government entity. To entice builders to cooperate, many inclusionary zoning ordinances provide for density bonuses, where the builder is allowed to construct more units per acre.

As is commonly stated "there is no such thing as a free lunch." Inclusionary zoning does incur a cost. The price of other units in the development are increased to offset the losses the builder incurs on the below market priced units. In essence, the buyers of regular units subsidize the buyers of the below market priced units. Thus the burden for providing affordable housing units is shifted from the government sector to the private sector. Inclusionary zoning laws are highly controversial and the issue is constantly under legal challenge.

LAND-USE CONTROLS AND THE REAL ESTATE INDUSTRY

The trend seems to be set—more and more public control over private land use. Instead of being just a vehicle for the production of profit, land will more than likely also be viewed as a resource to be used to achieve social as well as economic well-being. As this newer attitude toward land use emerges, the real estate industry must participate in the decision-making process to present its views. Both property owners and the real estate industry must see that land-use regulations consider the views of all the citizens, not just those of a select few. The key is to eliminate the undesirable aspects of poor land management while maintaining the good qualities of private real estate ownership. This is a difficult task that will require cooperation and compromise from preservationists, conservationists, environmentalists, private real estate interests, government, and all other groups who are interested in real estate use.

REVIEWING YOUR UNDERSTANDING

Recent Trends in Land-Use Controls

1. List two examples of recent pollution and environmental regulations that have influenced land use in your area. Are they local, regional, state, or federal land-use controls?

2. Some economists believe that no growth policies are discriminatory against lower-income people. What reasons do they give?

3. In the past, land-use controls were essentially a local matter. Why have recent land-use regulations come from state governments?

CHAPTER SUMMARY

The current debate over public land-use controls has its roots in two economic concepts: (1) the supply of land at the right location is scarce, and (2) the public is viewing land as a resource, not just a commodity. Land-use controls can be divided into two broad categories: private controls and public controls. Private land-use controls include economic highest and best use and private deed restrictions. Public land-use controls include the use of government police power, eminent domain, government spending patterns, and taxation. Increased urban density has created a need for land planning. Planning can be defined as "anticipating and achieving community goals in light of the community's social, economic, and physical needs."

The establishment of a community plan requires three major steps: (1) resources analysis, (2) formulation of community goals, and (3) implementation of the plan. Zoning and subdivision regulations are the two most powerful tools for implementing a community's master plan. With the growth of multicity metropolitan areas, some planning has shifted from the local community to regional commissions.

Recent trends in land-use controls include the prevention of premature subdivisions, pollution and environmental regulations, slow growth or no growth policies, the debate over the creation of new towns, and state and federal intervention. The trend seems to be more public control over private land uses. This has caused a polarization of the issue. There are those who feel present land controls are too stringent and are a threat to our economic system. Others feel that more controls are needed. Proper land-use control is a difficult issue that will require cooperation and compromise between all interested groups.

IMPORTANT TERMS AND CONCEPTS

Economic highest and best use

Eminent domain

Environmental controls

General or master plan

Inclusionary zoning

No growth policy

Police power

Private deed restrictions

Property rights

Regional planning

Resource versus commodity

Slow growth policy

Subdivision regulations

Urban planning

Zoning

REVIEWING YOUR UNDERSTANDING

1. The land-use controversy is a debate on whether land should be viewed as a resource or:

   a. a commodity

   b. an asset

   c. an investment

   d. a possession

2. Critics of government use of land-use controls feel that it infringes on:

   a. zoning

   b. property rights

   c. eminent domain

   d. equal protection

3. A real estate example of government use of police power is:

   a. zoning

   b. property rights

   c. eminent domain

   d. equal protection

4. A real estate example of private land use control is:

   a. zoning

   b. eminent domain

   c. deed restrictions

   d. inclusionary exceptions

5. The creation of a community general plan requires resource analysis, formation of goals, and:
    a. federal guidelines
    b. urban analysis
    c. health codes
    d. implementation

6. A wrench is to a mechanic as _____ is to a planner.
    a. money
    b. escheat
    c. zoning
    d. a public hearing

7. Which of the following is true?
    a. land-use controls reduce the cost of building homes
    b. environmental regulations reduce the cost of building homes
    c. the ability to obtain building permits for homes is speedy
    d. government controls have probably increased the quality of homes

8. Slow growth policies that limit the number of annual home building permits:
    a. are examples of supply and demand in balance
    b. tend to decrease local home prices
    c. tend to increase local home prices
    d. do not distort real estate market forces

9. A type of land-use control that requires a builder to set aside a certain number of units for low- to moderate-income people as a condition for obtaining a building permit is:
    a. inclusionary zoning
    b. fair housing law
    c. affordable domain
    d. equal housing rights

10. Which of the following is a trend in land use controls?
    a. more state and regional control as opposed to local control
    b. more environmental regulations
    c. more shifting of costs from government to subdivision buyers
    d. all of the above are trends

Chapter 14

Real Estate Development

Preview

This chapter outlines the principles of real estate development. Section 14.1 focuses on real estate construction activity, with special emphasis on the economic characteristics of the home-building industry. Section 14.2 deals with the development and building process and features flowcharts that illustrate the steps in real estate development. When you have completed this chapter you will be able to:

1. List three categories of real estate construction.

2. List five economic characteristics of the home-building industry.

3. Differentiate between land development and construction.

4. Describe the six major phases of land development and construction.

14.1   REAL ESTATE CONSTRUCTION

Real estate construction is a major contributor to the economic expansion of the United States. Each year, new construction generates billions of dollars in income and directly or indirectly employs several millions of workers. This section outlines the various categories of real estate construction and then concentrates on the economic characteristics of the home-building industry.

CONSTRUCTION ACTIVITY

Real estate construction activity can be divided into three main categories: residential, nonresidential, and public works.

Residential construction includes single-family dwellings, condominiums, and multifamily apartments. The volume of residential construction is closely tied to movements in the mortgage money market, employment, and personal income. When people are working and mortgage credit is available at reasonable interest rates, residential construction tends to accelerate. During periods of high unemployment or tight mortgage credit, residential construction usually declines.

Nonresidential construction consists of retail and office buildings, industrial plants, and institutional buildings such as schools and libraries. Nonresidential construction activity usually parallels changes in the business cycle. When real GNP is growing and the economy is experiencing prosperity, nonresidential construction increases. When there is a downturn in economic activity, nonresidential construction slowly tapers off.

Public works construction refers to the building of streets, sewer systems, highways, bridges, and public projects other than buildings. Many public works projects are financed by federal grants supplemented by local matching funds. During periods of economic prosperity, tax revenues for local and state governments increase, thereby stimulating public works construction. In economic downturns local tax revenues decline, but at the same time government attempts to fight a recession by increasing its spending. In short, the changes in public works construction normally do not fluctuate as widely as do changes in residential and nonresidential construction.

SPECIAL INTEREST TOPIC
Mobile Homes

Skyrocketing construction costs have priced many people out of the conventional housing market. Older people living on fixed incomes and others who own large homes may wish to reduce expenses by selling their existing homes and moving into less expensive quarters. For these people and many others, the answer has been mobile home living.

The chart below shows mobile homes as a percentage of new single family dwellings for selected years.*

1980	1985	1987	1988	1989
23.2%	26.5%	20.7%	20.1%	19.3%

As can be seen, mobile homes account for a significant number of all new, single-family home sales in the United States. Mobile home dealers could probably increase their sales even more if a sufficient number of mobile home sites could be located. In many areas, mobile homes are allowed to be placed only in poor locations. This discrimination can be traced back to the transit "trailer" type camps of the 1930s. However, today's mobile homes are not trailers, nor are they very "mobile." Studies have shown that four out of five mobile homes are placed on land sites and never moved. In fact, it is becoming more difficult to distinguish some mobile homes from conventional homes. Some mobile units come with wood shingle siding, step-down living rooms, two baths, and three bedrooms. They can be purchased using FHA, VA, or conventional financing.

* Source: U.S. Department of Commerce.

Table 14.1 shows the value of new construction by categories as a percentage of total construction for select years. These figures show the relative importance of each construction category.

TABLE 14.1 Value of New Construction by Categories as a Percentage of Total New Construction

	1987	*1988*	*1989*
Residential construction	47.5%	46.9%	45.5%
Nonresidential construction	30.5%	30.6%	31.5%
Public works construction	22.1%	22.5%	22.8%
Totals (slight variations due to rounding off)	100 %	100 %	100 %

Source: U.S. Department of Commerce.

CHARACTERISTICS OF THE HOME BUILDING INDUSTRY

The home building industry is noted for its booms and busts. Periods of high rates of construction are followed by hefty declines in buying. Why does each new residential construction fluctuate? Why isn't the rate of new homes built steady and predictable? The answer lies in the economic characteristics of the home building industry, a list of which follows.

SPECIAL INTEREST TOPIC

The Price of New Homes Sets a Ceiling on the Price of Existing Homes

Whenever the demand for homes is strong, prices for existing properties tend to rise. What stops them from rising dramatically, however, is that they get close to the cost of building a new home. Buyers refuse to pay so much for an older home when the same money can purchase a new home. Thus the cost of new homes sets a ceiling on existing home prices. The long-term price trend for older homes will follow along just under the cost trends for new construction.

1. The industry is comprised of many small, independent builders and a few hundred large, corporate companies. This means that most home building is a local operation that cannot generate enough production to gain savings from large-scale building.

2. It is relatively easy to enter into the home-building industry—a skilled construction worker can usually start a small company with a limited amount of capital. This ease of entry, coupled with inadequate capital backing, generates a high failure rate in the home-building industry.

3. As a result of long physical and economic life, residential homes last for many years. In any given year, the supply of new homes rarely adds more than two percent to the total supply of homes in the United States. In short, a home does not wear out rapidly and thus the replacement demand is low. A home builder, unlike an automobile manufacturer, cannot count on a replacement market to bolster activity.

4. Home construction is heavily influenced by the actions of government. The government can stimulate housing construction with special programs such as the FHA. Or the government can retard housing construction through environmental controls or burdensome real property taxation.

5. The home-building industry depends on liberal mortgage credit terms so prospective home buyers can finance the purchase of new homes.

From the preceding list, it is apparent that home building is a fragmented industry, comprised of many local builders who depend on the whims of others for their survival. But in spite of these handicaps the home-building industry is making some innovative progress in construction technology, building design, and cost controls. The standardization of parts, the creation of better tools, and the prefabrication of building components have helped to streamline the construction process. The rate of innovation in the future will require a positive attitude from lenders, government, construction workers, and home buyers alike.

14.2   THE DEVELOPMENT AND BUILDING PROCESS

The creation of a new real estate project needs managerial talent to plan, coordinate, and control the factors of production (land, labor, and capital). This managerial skill is provided by developer-investors, contractors, and architects, all of whom are instrumental in the creation of a successful real estate development. This section outlines the development and construction process.

LAND DEVELOPMENT AND CONSTRUCTION

The production of urban real estate can be broken down into two major categories: *land development* and *construction*. Land development refers to subdividing and preparing the land for building, while construction refers to the actual erection of buildings and improvements. However, before private land development and construction begin, at least four things should be thoroughly investigated: adequate market, government approval, adequate financing, and a reasonable profit margin.

Market Analysis

Prior to undertaking a real estate project, a developer should conduct an in-depth market analysis. The purpose of a market analysis is to determine whether a user's market exists for the proposed project. Market analysis techniques vary according to whether the study is for residential, commercial, industrial, or rural purposes. But regardless of the nature of the proposed project, certain questions need to be answered: What is the present and future demand for this type of real estate? Is the proposed site a good location? Are buyers ready to purchase? If not now, when? What is the current and future supply? Are there other sellers? What does the competition plan to do in the future? Is now the right time for this project? These questions form the heart of a market analysis and should be answered before any firm commitments are made. The time to be concerned with sales potential is *before* the project begins, not after!

Government Approval

A real estate project is not possible unless proper government permits can be obtained. Government regulations, such as zoning, building codes, density maximums, environmental reports, and utility requirements, are an essential part of any real estate development. A developer must be familiar with government requirements and must assess the likelihood of obtaining government approval. *The key factor is the time needed to obtain approval.* Long delays because of government "red tape" can cause a project to fail due to missed sales and increased cost for land, labor, materials, and capital. A careful review of the time needed and the penalties for delays is essential. Government reports and their time delays will be discussed in greater detail in the next chapter.

Financing

Real estate developers and investors rarely pay cash for their projects; they are strong believers in the principle of leverage (using a minimum amount of equity funds and a maximum amount of borrowed funds to control a large investment). The funds needed for land acquisition can come from several sources. The seller can carry back a purchase money deed of trust, the developer can form a syndicate and raise the needed capital for selling ownership shares, or the funds may be borrowed from a financial institution or a private party.

After land acquisition, the funds for construction usually come from traditional lenders—banks, savings and loan associations, insurance companies, and mortgage companies. In addition to traditional sources, construction funds are occasionally available from pension funds, trusts, and endowment funds. The importance of financing cannot be overemphasized. Without adequate funding, a real estate project, as developers put it, cannot "fly."

Adequate financing depends on two main variables: (1) the market potential of the project, and (2) the condition of the money market. If a developer can prove to lenders that a strong market exists for the proposed project, and if lenders have funds available at reasonable interest rates, chances are the project will be funded. On the other hand, if the money market is tight and the supply of funds limited, a developer may find it impossible to borrow the needed capital regardless of the market potential for the project. The project will have to be shelved because of the lack of mortgage credit.

Profit Potential

After analyzing the market, estimating the cost and likelihood of government approval, and projecting the cost of financing, private developers can estimate the profit potential. If the profit return is too low relative to the costs and risks, the proposal is rejected as unfeasible. On the other hand, if the profit potential appears reasonable, the project commences.

Figure 14.1 summarizes the four studies that should be conducted before real estate development and construction takes place.

WHEN THIS PROCESS IS IGNORED, OVERBUILDING CAN OCCUR

The four steps listed above are what should be done before ground is broken for a new project. However, during the 1980s a tremendous amount of overbuilding occurred in the commercial real estate market in most cities across the United States. This created an excess supply of commercial office buildings and retail floor space. The reasons frequently given for this overbuilding include: economic slowdown, income tax incentives, easy money from unregulated banks and savings and loans, tax base hungry local governments, anticipated foreign investment, and so on. Most of this overbuilding, and the resultant foreclosures, could have been prevented if realistic market studies had been conducted before the projects were developed. But rather, what occurred was analysis based on gut feelings, hopes, prayers, and a false sense of perpetual increases in real estate values!

STEPS IN CONSTRUCTION

Land development and construction take place in steps or phases. Figure 14.2 summarizes the major steps in land development and construction.

The *planning phase* encompasses market analysis, government approval procedures, financing, and profit analysis.

Land procurement refers to the purchase of the property. In some cases the purchase is just the acquisition of a single parcel. In other cases, however, land procurement may require the painstaking assemblage of several smaller parcels under different ownership in order to create one larger parcel.

The *land preparation phase* is concerned with the clearing of land and the installation of off-site improvements such as utilities, streets, and gutters to make way for on-site construction.

The *construction phase* begins as soon as land preparation permits access. In construction, timing is a critical factor. Building is done in phases, frequently by different subcontractors. Blending each phase to eliminate delays is one of the most difficult aspects of construction. Delays between construction phases can occur because of adverse weather, labor strikes, material shortages, and improperly

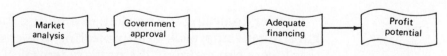

FIGURE 14.1

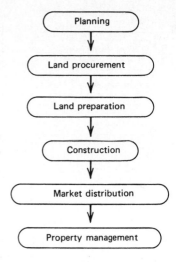

FIGURE 14.2

estimated time requirements for various construction activities. Delays cost money as interest accrues on construction loans and labor is paid for standby time.

The *market distribution phase* is concerned with the selling and transfer of property. Frequently, the sale takes place before construction begins. These are called "build to suit" projects. If the project is built on speculation, ideally the property is sold before construction is completed. In other cases the property is not sold until final construction is completed. However, the actual legal transfer of title usually does not occur until the property is completed and ready for occupancy.

The *property management phase* refers to the maintenance and servicing of the development after construction. If the property is owner occupied, the service and upkeep rests with the owner. If the project is tenant occupied, frequently a professional property manager is hired to supervise the servicing of the property. Property management involves two major activities—physical upkeep and record keeping. Physical upkeep refers to maintenance and repairs, while record keeping involves rent collection, ledger accounts, and the preparation of income and expense sheets for tax purposes.

Figure 14.3 is an expanded version of the construction process, outlining the individuals and institutions that are involved in each phase of construction.

THE COST OF CONSTRUCTION DELAYS AND IMPACT FEES

The old saying, "time is money," is especially true in real estate development. Many real estate developers work on relatively thin profit margins and any unforeseen delay can quickly erode profits. Construction delays can be caused by required government reports, mismanagement by developers, labor strikes, adverse weather, changes in the mortgage money market, and so on.

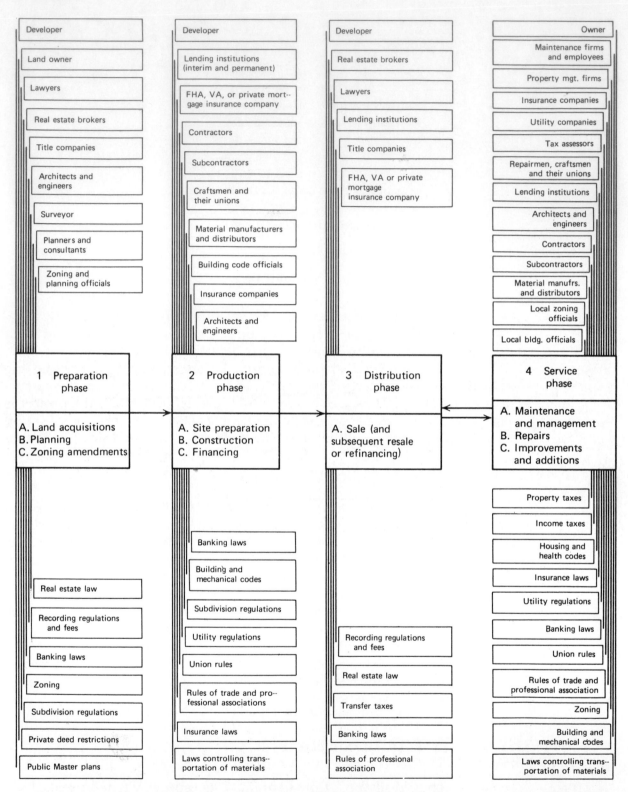

FIGURE 14.3.   The Housing Process—Major Participants and Influences. *Source:* The President's Committee on Urban Housing, *A Decent Home.* Washington, D.C., Government Printing Office, December 1968, p. 115.

Studies and reports by various universities and building trade associations state that somewhere between twenty and forty percent of the price of a new home, depending upon the location, can be directly attributed to government regulations. These high regulation costs are especially prevalent in California, where local governments have been sharply increasing fees (called impact fees) charged to developers for the right to obtain a building permit, in an attempt to make up for lost property tax revenue due to the passage of Proposition 13.

Not only are developers asked to pay for direct costs such as new streets, water, and sewer hookups for the project, they have been required to pay for schools, parks, and other community facilities that are not directly related to the project. Developers recoup their impact fees by raising prices for the new property buyers. This can be viewed as a way for local government to indirectly raise money from property owners to make up for tax revenue lost by not being able to increase property taxes sufficiently to pay for these facilities as a government entity.

REVIEWING YOUR UNDERSTANDING

The Development and Building Process

1. What is the difference between land development and construction?
2. List four things that should be considered before beginning a real estate project.
3. List six major steps in land development and construction.

CHAPTER SUMMARY

Real estate construction activity can be classified as residential, nonresidential, and public works. The real estate development process flows in a series of phases or steps: planning, land procurement, land preparation, construction, market distribution, and property management.

The home-building industry is highly fragmented, consisting of numerous small builders, plus a few large corporate builders. Erratic home-building activity can be traced to the unpredictable nature of lenders, buyers, builders, labor unions, and government. Government impact fees have increased the cost of property ownership as developers pass these costs on in the form of higher prices.

IMPORTANT TERMS AND CONCEPTS

Economic characteristics of the home-building industry

Impact Fees

Land development versus construction

Residential, nonresidential, public works construction

Steps in the construction process

REVIEWING YOUR UNDERSTANDING

1. The three main categories of real estate construction are residential, nonresidential, and:
   a. mobile homes
   b. office buildings
   c. public works
   d. farms

2. The largest percentage of construction takes place in which sector?
   a. residential
   b. nonresidential
   c. public works
   d. farms

3. Fluctuation in the rate of new home construction is caused by:
   a. government actions
   b. availability of mortgage credit
   c. phases of the business cycle
   d. all of the above

4. Mobile homes comprise approximately what percent of new single family home sales in the United States?
   a. 0–5
   b. 10–15
   c. 20–30
   d. 40–50

5. Regarding the prices of existing homes:
   a. prices are usually higher than new comparable homes
   b. prices are usually lower than new comparable homes
   c. prices are usually the same as new comparable homes
   d. prices are set by government actions

6. In terms of the factors of production—land, labor, capital, and entrepreneurship—the developer is the entrepreneur and therefore should earn:

    a. rent

    b. wages

    c. interest

    d. profit

7. Subdividing is considered:

    a. construction

    b. land development

    c. building

    d. assemblage

8. The first step in the real estate development process is to:

    a. do a market analysis

    b. obtain government approval

    c. line up the financing

    d. compute the return on investment

9. Impact fees are paid by developers to government as a condition for issuing a building permit. In the final analysis the cost for these fees is ultimately paid by:

    a. developers

    b. lenders

    c. taxpayers

    d. buyers

10. Real estate development takes place in a series of phases. The first phase is:

    a. planning

    b. procurement

    c. construction

    d. property management

Chapter 15

Required Government Reports

Preview

This chapter briefly describes the reports that real estate developers must prepare to obtain government building permits. Section 15.1 discusses the types of reports required by federal, state, and local government agencies. Section 15.2 examines both the costs and the benefits of government reports. When you have completed this chapter you will be able to:

1. Explain the reasons given for requiring government reports before private real estate may be developed.

2. List the types of reports required by federal, state, and local government agencies.

3. Describe both the costs and the benefits to real estate developers, property owners, and society of requiring government reports.

15.1   TYPES OF REQUIRED GOVERNMENT REPORTS

Government agencies need reports to see that proposed real estate projects conform to land-use laws. Reports and investigations provide the basis for government agencies to approve, deny, or modify real estate development. This section summarizes major legislation to which real estate developers must comply in order to obtain governmental approval for their projects.

FEDERAL LEGISLATION

Although there are many federal laws and agencies that regulate the use of real estate, the two most important agencies are the United States Department of Housing and Urban Development (HUD), and the Environmental Protection Agency (EPA).

The United States Department of Housing and Urban Development (HUD)

HUD is an umbrella department that oversees the activities of several federal agencies that control real estate development. Some of the more important agencies are listed below.

1. The Federal Housing Administration, *which federally insures real estate loans made by approved lenders.*

2. The Public Housing Administration, *which helps to fund and administer low-rent housing projects.*

3. The Community Facilities Administration, *which provides funds to cities, counties, and colleges to construct buildings and public works projects.*

4. The Urban Renewal Administration, *which provides financial assistance to local governments for slum clearance and rehabilitation.*

5. The Office of Interstate Land Sales Registration, *which regulates the interstate sales of subdivided land.*

This is only a partial list of HUD's activities, but it is obvious that many real estate projects fall under the jurisdiction of one or more of these agencies. When this occurs, HUD requires extensive reports to see that its regulations are being followed. Some typical report topics include relocation plans for persons being displaced by the proposed project, a statement of fair employment practices, equal housing opportunities questionnaires, environmental impact statements, a complete economic base analysis, and a detailed market analysis.

Environmental Protection Agency (EPA)

The EPA was created in 1970 and, along with the Council on Environmental Quality, is responsible for seeing that federal pollution standards are enforced. Some of the federal environmental legislation acts of special interest to real estate users are given below.

1. National Environmental Policy Act (NEPA), *which requires the preparation of environmental impact statements on all federally assisted real estate projects.*

2. Federal Water Pollution Acts, *which regulate real estate development along waterways and underground water channels. These acts have been used to halt real estate construction until adequate antipollution protection devices are developed. They require the preparation of an extensive report outlining the water pollution impact before a developer is allowed to grade the land or erect a building.*

3. Clean Air Acts, *which control real estate development that could add to air pollution. These acts have been used to deny building permits for industrial and commercial real estate projects on the grounds that additional development will aggravate air pollution. They require a complete report regarding air pollution standards before construction is allowed to proceed.*

Other federal acts that influence real estate development include the Noise Control Act, the National Coastal Zone Management Act, and the Flood Disaster Protection Act. All of these acts require the submission of reports before real estate development is allowed.

STATE LEGISLATION

In addition to federal reports, real estate developers must comply with state laws that also require reports. State regulations of special interest to real estate include: state housing and construction codes, state sanitation and health codes, subdivision requirements, statewide zoning controls, and state environmental regulations.

State Housing and Construction Codes

Most states have passed minimum construction codes that require all new construction to meet state standards. As a condition for receiving a building permit, a developer must submit a plot map and building plans with detailed specifications. After a complete examination of the plans, making revisions where necessary, the state agency usually approves them.

State Health and Sanitation Codes

State health departments regulate statewide health measures. Drainage, plumbing, sewage disposal, hazardous waste materials, and water supply all come under the jurisdiction of health and sanitation codes. Each health officer has the authority to halt any proposed development that fails to meet state standards. As a condition for obtaining a building permit, a developer must submit a report showing that the proposed project meets all health requirements.

Subdivision Regulations

Subdivision regulation is one of the main tools used by state governments for controlling real estate development. Although subdivision laws are not new, amendments and changes are constantly being added by legislators.

State agencies require comprehensive subdivision reports to ensure that a developer is complying with all subdivision laws. A typical subdivision report must outline title holdings, flood and drainage conditions, water and sewage handling, land filling, roads and access, utility hookup, complete plans for all off-site and on-site improvements, environmental impact, financing, proposed market techniques, and many other technical items.

Statewide Zoning Controls

Historically, zoning has been a local matter. Cities and counties enacted zoning ordinances to achieve their own individual goals. However, as urban pressures create problems that overlap city and county boundaries, state governments have been enacting statewide zoning. Much of the recent legislation has been environmentally oriented, and states have assumed control over areas considered to have regional importance, such as coastlines, lake and river frontage, agricultural land, and desert areas. Statewide zoning also occurs in high hazard areas such as flood plains, earthquake faults, and landslide areas. Here again, real estate developers submit reports showing that their proposed project conforms to state zoning laws.

State Environmental Regulations

Since the late 1960s, state legislatures have been enacting environmental laws similar in nature to the federal legislation. Individual states have created special environmental agencies to ensure that the environmental impact of a real estate project is studied before a building permit is granted.

15.2   COSTS VERSUS BENEFITS

As mentioned in Chapter 14, "There is no such thing as a free lunch." Any use of resources, whether it be land, labor, or capital, incurs a cost that someone must pay. This section studies required government reports by comparing their costs with the benefits received.

DEFINING "COSTS" AND "BENEFITS"

To simplify their analysis, economists break costs and benefits into the following categories: private costs, social costs, private benefits, and social benefits.

Private costs are those expenses paid by a particular individual or business firm. They are the actual out-of-pocket money expenditures of that individual or business.

Social costs are the expenses paid by society as a whole, rather than by an individual or business. For example, if a business constructs a $20 million factory, this is a private cost. But if the factory then pollutes the air, the pollution becomes a social cost paid by all, not just the factory owner or its customers.

Private benefits are rewards that are enjoyed by a particular individual or business, and not by society as a whole. Private benefits are frequently stated in terms of money profits.

Social benefits are rewards that accrue to all of society, not just to an individual or business. For example, if a real estate developer builds a successful shopping center, the developer may reap private profit. In addition, if the project stimulates local business and increases employment and income, this could create a social benefit—a reward shared by all of society, not just the real estate developer.

ANALYZING THE COSTS

The cost of required government reports can be broken down into private and social costs. *Private costs include preparation costs, holding costs, inflation costs, and overhead costs.* The cost of preparing government reports varies with the size and scope of the proposed project. But the consulting fees charged by attorneys, engineers, appraisers, economists, and environmental researchers can run hundreds or thousands of dollars per day, and when all the required reports are completed, the cost can be quite high.

The cost for holding unused land includes expenses for property taxes, interest on land loans, minimum maintenance, and opportunity costs. Opportunity costs refer to the potential earnings that the money tied up in unimproved land could have earned if invested elsewhere.

Inflation costs refer to the increase in material prices and wages that occurs during construction delays. The longer construction is delayed, the greater the likelihood that inflation will drive up the cost of construction.

Overhead costs are the costs that continue whether a developer is working or not. Overhead costs include rent on the developer's building, bank payments on equipment, minimum maintenance, fixed salaries for office workers, and so on.

Preparation, holding, inflation, and overhead costs are all private costs that are either absorbed by the developer or, as in most cases, passed on to the developer's customers in the form of higher real estate prices.

What are the social costs of required government reports? Does society also pay a price for construction denials or delays? Yes, society as a whole may bear some costs such as a loss of jobs and income. Another social cost might be an increase in consumer prices because of the cost-push inflation sparked by inflated construction prices.

ANALYZING THE BENEFITS

The benefits gained by requiring government reports on real estate projects can be broken down into social benefits and private benefits. *Social benefits include less environmental damage, better land planning, and the fostering of social integration.* Many of the recent land-use regulations have been aimed at protecting the environment. By requiring environmental reports, society benefits by knowing that potential environmental damage will be studied before a real estate project is approved.

Another social benefit frequently cited is better land-use planning. By requiring reports, the government can see that private land is not used to harm surrounding landowners.

Still another benefit from government regulation is that it can be used to promote social integration. By requiring real estate developers to submit reports on social goals, such as minority employment in construction trades, equal housing opportunities, and relocation assistance to persons being displaced by the real estate project, disadvantaged persons are given a chance to become a part of the social mainstream.

Are there any private benefits that real estate developers or their customers gain from requiring detailed reports? Yes, in the long run the private costs paid by requiring government reports may be offset by private benefits such as higher real estate values. For example, it is possible that by requiring a careful study of the environment, a completed real estate project may be so harmonious in its surroundings that its value rises rapidly. This enhances the image of the real estate developer and generates profitable resale potential for the existing owners of the real estate projects.

THE TREND

As you can see, there are certain costs associated with government laws and reports and there are certain benefits. Do the costs outweigh the benefits? Or do the benefits outweigh the costs? Obviously, there are no easy answers. Each case must be analyzed independently, but the trend appears to be set—more and more government reports will be required before a real estate project will be approved.

If this is the case, can the costs be reduced without sacrificing the benefits? The answer is a resounding *YES*. One area that real estate economists, conservationists, and developers agree on is that the duplication of work required by the various levels of government must be eliminated. In many cases, a real estate developer must prepare four or five different forms of the same report to conform to separate, overlapping guidelines of different government agencies. What is needed is a simpler review system, where approval or denial is relayed more rapidly, thus saving both private and social costs.

REVIEWING YOUR UNDERSTANDING

Costs Versus Benefits

1. What is the difference between a social cost and a private cost, and between a social benefit and a private benefit?
2. Define the following: preparation cost, holding cost, inflation cost, and overhead cost.
3. List three social benefits that result from government regulations of private real estate.

CHAPTER SUMMARY

Legislators pass land-use laws and then create government agencies to enforce these laws. As an enforcement tool, government agencies require real estate developers to submit reports verifying that public regulations are being met.

The cost of requiring government reports includes private costs such as preparation cost, holding cost, inflation cost, and overhead cost. Society also bears some costs, such as higher prices and loss of employment and income. The social benefits derived from requiring government reports in private real estate activities include less environmental damage, better land-use planning, and the fostering of social goals. Private benefits may include an increase in real estate values.

The trend seems to indicate that more government reports will be required in the future. The key is to streamline the reporting system so that both private and social costs can be reduced without sacrificing the benefits.

IMPORTANT TERMS AND CONCEPTS

Environment   Social benefits
Private benefits   Social costs
Private costs

REVIEWING YOUR UNDERSTANDING

1. The stated purpose of requiring government reports before a developer is issued a building permit is to:

    a. see that the project conforms to land-use laws

    b. allow environmentalists to delay or stop the development

    c. satisfy the lender's requirements for loan approval

    d. issue opinions as to the profitability of the project

2. Which law requires an environmental impact report on all major federal public works projects?

    a. Clean Air Act

    b. Hazardous Waste Materials Act

    c. National Environmental Policy Act

    d. Federal Projects Act

3. The "environment" includes:

    a. economic and social impact

    b. economic and biological impact

    c. economic, social, and biological impact

    d. economic, social, biological and physical impact

4. Instead of a full environmental impact report, a small project with little if any impact on the environment can be approved using a:

    a. negative declaration

    b. payment of a waiver fee

    c. federal district attorney

    d. small claims court order

5. The final approval for the actual design and layout of a housing subdivision rests with the:

    a. federal government

    b. state government

    c. local government

    d. developer

6. The pollution of the air by an unregulated factory is what type of cost?

    a. private

    b. social

    c. customer

    d. environmental

7. The profits generated by owning a real estate building is what type of benefit?

    a. private

    b. social

    c. community

    d. environmental

8. The costs incurred due to the delays of required government reports include:

    a. holding costs

    b. inflation costs

    c. overhead costs

    d. all of the above

9. The benefits of requiring government approval before a real estate project can be built include:

    a. higher property values

    b. reduced social costs

    c. less environmental damage

    d. all of the above.

10. Economists, real estate developers, and environmentalists tend to agree that:

    a. the duplication of work by various government agencies is wasteful

    b. real estate is a commodity to be bought and sold like corn

    c. environmental concerns will decrease as time goes on

    d. in the future government will have a smaller voice in real estate development projects

Chapter   16

Summary of Real Estate Investment Principles

Preview

This chapter looks at the economics of individual properties. Section 16.1 discusses basic investment principles. Section 16.2 demonstrates real estate cash flow analysis. Section 16.3 shows how cash flows are used to estimate offering prices and computer rates of return. When you have finished this chapter you will be able to:

1. Define investment and list the five essential elements to consider when selecting an investment.

2. Complete a first-year real estate cash flow analysis.

3. Explain how real estate offering prices are determined.

4. Discuss how real estate returns are calculated.

16.1   BASIC INVESTMENT PRINCIPLES

Investing is defined in a variety of ways, such as placing money for profitable purposes or extending capital in exchange for perceived profits. Another definition for investing, favored by many economists, is this: *investing* is defined as giving up present consumption in exchange for future benefits. This definition focuses on the idea that investing is the opposite of consumption.

In one way or another, most people generate money. Money can only be used in two ways: (1) spent, or (2) invested. Every dollar spent is a dollar that cannot be invested. Every dollar invested is a dollar that cannot be spent. Therefore, one must decide how much money to use for present consumption and how much to invest. Any money not used for consumption is automatically invested. Whether the investment is in the form of savings, stocks, gold, real estate, or idle cash, for better or worse, these are all forms of investments!

Obviously, some people invest very little. This may be due to the fact that they may need every dollar to subsist, or, if more affluent, they simply choose to consume now and not worry about the future. On the other hand, some people are active investors, who give up some current consumption to build a nest egg for the future. This section concentrates on real estate as an investment.

THE KEY INVESTMENT FACTORS

The five major *economic* characteristics of an investment are return, management, taxability, liquidity, and risk.

Return

Most investments involve an initial capital outlay, which if successful is followed by the recovery of benefits over a period of time. This recovery of benefits is the *return*, or economic reason for making the investment. Return can be in money, as from building rents, or in less tangible benefits (amenities), such as occupancy of a home. The returns can also vary in their timing; returns can arrive now or later, and can come as one payment, a series, or as irregular payments. Common patterns include:

1. A series of payments over a period of time;
2. A series of payments plus a large single end-payment;
3. A large single payment only.

Higher returns increase the value of the investment. However, a return two years from now or at some other distant time is worth less than a return today. Thus, in comparing investments, the amount of returns and the timing of their payment are all-important.

Management

Different investments require different types and amounts of *management*: the supervision needed to oversee the investment. A savings account needs almost no management, while an apartment building calls for a considerable amount. Various investments should be compared on the basis of the amount and skill of management time each requires. Since "time is money," an investment that requires more management should produce a higher return to pay for the time and effort.

Taxability

Investments differ in how their earnings are *taxed*. Some investments, like certain municipal bonds, are effectively free of taxes. Others, like corporate income dividends, are subject to corporate income tax and then to personal income tax. The investor is interested in the return received *after* taxes, so the taxability of the investment is important in evaluating investment alternatives. Taxability of real estate investments is so important (and complex) that Chapter 17 is devoted to it.

Liquidity

Liquidity refers to the ease and speed of with which an investment can be converted into cash. Investments differ in their liquidity. Blue chip stocks on the New York Stock Exchange are highly liquid—you can sell them on any business day and receive your money in a day or so. Savings can be withdrawn in cash on the spot from a bank and therefore are very liquid. However, other investments, such as a loan to a new business, are illiquid—you might need to wait years to recoup your money.

Real estate is considered an illiquid investment. It is difficult to quickly convert real estate equity to cash. To convert real estate equity to cash there are two choices: (1) sell the property, or (2) borrow against the property. Both of these take time and also cost money, in the form of seller closing costs or borrower loan fees. Therefore it is

frequently stated that one should only invest in real estate after seeing that liquidity needs have been met with other forms of investment.

Risk

Investments vary in the amount of risk. *Risk* is defined as the
danger of loss in value of the investment. The categories are financial, interest rate, purchasing power, social change, and legal
change.

In many investments, *financial risk*—the loss of investment or
earnings through failure to make payments when due—is the greatest hazard. The financial risk of each investment varies, depending
on the stability of the investment, the reliability (or uncertainty) of
our estimate of stability, and the margin or allowance that the investment has before little problems become big ones! Financial risk
is particularly important to real estate investments because of the
large total investment, its slow return or turnover, and the usually
high use of borrowed funds.

Interest rate risk refers to the possible loss in value of an investment as a result of increases in market interest rates. This risk is
usually associated with the market for corporate or government
bonds. The basic rule is as follows: a decrease in market interest rate
will increase the resale prices of existing bonds; or the opposite: an
increase in market interest rates will decrease the resale prices of
existing bonds.

For example, assume that an investor bought a new $10,000,
30-year bond, paying 10% interest in 1991 for the face amount of
$10,000. Therefore the annual income is scheduled to be $10,000 $\times$
10% = $1,000 per year. Suppose the investor needs money and at-
tempts to sell the bond in 1996 and finds that market interest rates
have risen to 20% on this type of bond. This means that a buyer of
this bond will only pay the investor $5,000 for the $10,000 bond!
Why? If the existing bond pays interest at $1,000 per year ($10,000
$\times$ 10%), to earn 20% the new buyer will invest $5,000 $\times$ 20% to
generate the $1,000 interest paid on the existing bond. Thus, the
market value of the bond has dropped from $10,000 to $5,000 due to
changes in market interest rates.

Are there interest-rate risks for real estate investments? Yes, the
wide swings of market interest rates have produced real estate risks.
For example, assume that an investor purchased a leased warehouse
for cash in 1990 on the basis of an 8 percent return. The investor
attempts to sell the warehouse in 1995 and discovers that buyers
now demand a 10 percent return because of changes in market interest rates. This situation will reduce the selling price of the warehouse 20 percent below the investor's purchase price. This is a
dramatic example of how a change in market interest rates can reduce the value of an otherwise secure investment.

Purchasing-power risk refers to the possibility of loss due to
inflation. The investor can receive the same dollars from the invest-

ment, but with inflation the dollars purchase less. Investments that pay a fixed dollar return, such as savings bonds, are vulnerable to purchasing power risk. Investments such as common stocks or real estate can provide protection from inflation and purchasing power risk *if* the net earnings increase with inflation. Since inflation eats away at investment dollars, many investors insist upon a higher rate of return to make up the difference. Thus the fear of continued inflation leads to a demand for higher rates of return.

Risk of social change arises because every investment is vulnerable to social changes that can influence supply or demand and in turn can affect the earnings of an investment. Real estate investments are especially vulnerable because real estate is tied to a fixed location. For real estate investments, social-change risk can be hidden by inflation. For instance, some downtown commercial properties have gained little in value in recent years. The decline in purchasing power due to inflation actually means that they have decreased in real value by substantial amounts. What caused the decline? It was the result of social changes in how and where we live and shop.

Risk of legal change means that new laws may have an impact on an investment's ability to produce income. Legal change had not been a recognized major risk until the mid-1960s, but since then changes in laws regarding taxes, pollution, zoning, and landlord-tenant relations have had a significant impact.

Other Risk Variables: Visibility and Specialization

Visibility means that the investment or the building or the co-owners are visible, or likely to be noticed, which affects the risk of social or legal change. A building occupied by a controversial tenant is more visible than one occupied by minor tenants. The lease of an office building to the city is more visible than a lease to an insurance sales office. An investment with a city council member as a partner is more visible than one with someone less well known. Visibility can also help an investment, as when a central corner location gets office tenants or when having a big-name tenant gets loans and buyers.

Specialization refers to the degree of uniqueness of a building. Often this means the cost of converting the building to other uses. A highly specialized building, such as a medical office building or a fast-food franchise restaurant, is more expensive to convert to other uses than a standard building and is therefore riskier.

THE INVESTMENT DECISION

Each investor approaches an investment decision in his or her own manner. Some are careful and analytic, while others plunge in. The economic approach to decision making should consist of balancing the characteristics and risks of investments against the requirements or needs of the investor. In this fashion an investor can describe an investment in terms of returns, risks, liquidity, and so on, to see if it meets his or her needs.

The next section describes how to calculate the owner's cash flow on an income-producing property. Before you proceed, answer the review questions to test your understanding of the material in this section.

REVIEWING YOUR UNDERSTANDING

1. Define *investing*.
2. List and describe the five economic characteristics that affect an investment.
3. How would you rank real estate, high or low, in terms of these five economic characteristics?

16.2   REAL ESTATE CASH FLOW ANALYSIS

It should be stressed that real estate is an investment that normally produces a slow recovery of profit and initial investment over a period of many years. The process of forecasting the amount of money received each year, including the year of resale, is called *cash flow analysis*.

The cash flow analysis for each year can be viewed as a series of steps. These steps are outlined in cash flow forms. Cash flow forms vary in steps and terminology, but a typical example is shown in Figure 16.1.

THE STEPS IN ANNUAL CASH FLOW ANALYSIS

To illustrate the steps in a first year cash flow analysis, look at the following case study:

Case Study

A 20 unit apartment, with an asking price $1,700,000, requires $500,000 cash down, plus a new loan of $1,200,000. Each unit rents for $800 per month; other income is $300 per month; and the vacancy/credit loss factor is 5%. Annual verified expenses are $43,100 and the annual fixed debt service for the $1,200,000 loan is $126,370.

The first year's interest deduction on the loan totals $119,700, and the annual estimated depreciation for income tax purposes is $38,760. The potential investor is in a combined federal and state

FIGURE 16.1

First Year Cash Flow Analysis

1. Gross Schedule Income ($800 × 20 units × 12 mos.)	$192,000
2. + Other Income ($300 × 12 mos.)	+3,600
3. Total Gross Income	$195,600
4. −Vacancy/Credit Loss (5%)	−9,780
5. Gross Operating Income	$185,820
6. −Annual Operating Expenses	−43,100
7. Net Operating Income	$142,720
8. −Annual Debt Service	−126,370
9. Before Tax Cash Flow	$ 16,350

Tax Benefit Analysis

10. Net Operating Income	$142,720
11. −Interest (Loan 1)	−119,700
12. −Interest (Loan 2)	0
13. −Cost Recovery (Depreciation)	−38,760
14. Real Estate Taxable Income	$ 0
15. Estimated Allowable Loss (If Loss)	$<15,740>
16. × Tax Bracket (× Line 14 or 15)	×.38
17. Taxes Saved or Paid	$ 5,981

Net Spendable Income

18. Before Tax Cash Flow (Line 9)	$ 16,350
19. +/−Taxes Saved or Paid (Line 17)	+5,981
20. Net Spendable Income (After Tax Cash Flow)	$ 22,331

income tax bracket at the marginal rate of 38%. According to the investor's accountant, all passive losses can be used each year. No passive losses will be carried forward to reduce gain in the year of resale.

Based on this information, a cash flow analysis is presented in Figure 16.1.

BEFORE TAX CASH FLOW

The first series of steps in cash flow analysis computes what is commonly called Before Tax Cash Flow. It is also known as the Economic Cash Flow. (See Figure 16.1.)

Total Gross Income

The first figure is *Gross Scheduled Income*, and it is defined as the maximum amount of rents if 100% occupied at either current rents or market rents. Current rents refer to lease or contracted rents, while market rents refer to what the space or units would rent for if new tenants were sought. Whether current or market rents are being used should be noted by the analyst on the form. In the case

study, the current rents are also the market rents, therefore, $800 ×
20 units × 12 months = $192,000 Gross Scheduled Income.

Next, Other Income, if any, is added. *Other Income* refers to
items other than rent, such as vending machine income, storage or
parking space income, and so on. In the case study, the Other Income is $300 per month. Thus, $300 × 12 months = $3,600 Other
Income. The combination of Gross Scheduled Income ($192,000)
and Other Income ($3,600) equals *Total Gross Income* of $195,600.

Vacancy/Credit Loss

Then a dollar amount for Vacancy and Credit Loss (uncollected
rents), estimated as a percentage based on experiences in the market, is subtracted from the Total Gross Income to arrive at *Gross
Operating Income*. In the case study a 5% Vacancy/Credit loss factor
results in $195,600 × 5% = $9,780, which is subtracted from
$195,600 to equal $185,820 Gross Operating Income.

Annual Operating Expenses

The next item deals with the property's operating expense estimate. In some properties, like leased commercial and industrial
buildings, it is common for the tenants to pay operating expenses
under what is known as a *net lease*. In other properties, the owner
pays these operating expenses. The expense analysis usually starts
with an examination of the property's past expenses as shown by
property management records or the owner's income tax statements.
It is important to note that operating expenses do not include loan
payments or depreciation write-off. Operating expenses are the actual cost incurred to run the property, such as property tax and
insurance, maintenance, repairs, management fees, utilities, and
supplies. Loan payments are a financial cost to an owner who chooses
to borrow rather than pay cash. Loan payments are not a charge to
operate a property. Depreciation is a non-cash income tax deduction
that is not related to the property's physical operation. Depreciation
is a mere paper write-off for tax purposes and therefore is not an
actual out-of-pocket expense. Loan payments and depreciation are
dealt with in cash flow analysis, but not as operating expenses.

Once past expenses have been verified, the expenses must be
adjusted to reflect current information and the management policies
of the new investor. When the adjustments have been made, they can
be compared to expense data for other comparable properties to determine reasonableness. In some cases, funds will be set aside as
reserves for replacement of major repairable items, such as new roof
or carpets. This will be reflected in the operating expense deduction.

Net Operating Income

In the case study, annual operating expenses were given as
$43,100 and are subtracted from the Gross Operating Income of
$185,820 to give a Net Operating Income of $142,720. Net Operating

Income is a key figure in cash flow analysis. First, it is the amount of money the property is estimated to produce to help cover the Annual Debt Service (loan payments for the year). Second, as shown later, the Net Operating Income is used by investors and appraisers to determine the price or value of the property.

Annual Debt Service

The *Annual Debt Service* is simply the monthly loan payments, if any, times 12 months. Obviously, the size of the annual debt service is a function of the amount of cash down payment and the size and terms of the mortgage(s). In the case study, the $1,200,000 loan, based on a certain interest rate and term, was estimated to produce a monthly loan payment of $10,530.83, which when multiplied by 12 months produced an annual debt service of $126,370.

Before Tax Cash Flow

In the case study, Net Operating Income of $142,720 less the Annual Debt Service of $126,370 = $16,350 positive Before Tax Cash Flow. If the Annual Debt Service is ever larger than the Net Operating Income, the property will produce a negative Before Tax Cash Flow.

Before Tax Cash Flow is what the investor is estimated to keep after covering all costs, including loan payments, but before the payment of income taxes, if any, on the collected rents. In some circles this is known as the "Economic" Cash Flow.

TAX BENEFIT ANALYSIS

In addition to Economic Cash Flow, there are income tax aspects to owning and operating rental real estate. The income tax aspects could be positive and add to Before Tax Cash Flow, they could be negative and reduce the Before Tax Cash Flow. A tax benefit analysis computes the positive or negative impact income taxes have on cash flow.

Taxable Income or Loss for the Year

To compute the taxable income or loss for the rental year, the Net Operating Income is listed, then the allowable interest deductions on the mortgage(s) are subtracted. It should be noted that only the interest portion of the loan payments, not the principal, is deductible for tax purposes.

The interest portion is computed using a financial calculator or amortization tables. In our case study the deductible interest is given as $119,700. There is no second loan, so the next step is to deduct the depreciation write-off, which is called Cost Recovery. (The depreciation rules will be explained in the next chapter on income taxes.) The figure of $38,760 given in the case study is subtracted as indicated. Thus, Net Operating Income $142,720, less $119,700 interest, less $38,760 depreciation = ($15,740) tax loss for the year.

Note that after deducting interest and depreciation from the Net Operating Income you could have income left over, which would be taxable income. However, in the case study, the interest and depreciation deductions exceeded the Net Operating Income, thereby generating a tax loss for the year. The loss of $15,740 is a paper loss, not a real out-of-pocket loss! How is this so? The depreciation deduction of $38,760 was a non-cash deduction for income tax purposes and this deduction created the ($15,740) loss at no current out-of-pocket expense to the potential investor.

Taxes Saved or Paid for the Year

If an investor has a taxable income or taxable loss for the year, a set of rules called the passive income and loss rules apply. The passive rules will be discussed in the next chapter on income tax. Assuming here that the ability to use the income or loss applies for the current year, a real estate investor calculates the taxes saved or paid by multiplying the taxable income or loss by the marginal tax bracket for the year.

In the case study the investor's marginal tax bracket is 38%, therefore the ($15,740) usable tax loss × 38% = a positive $5,981 tax savings. How can a loss turn into a positive tax savings? First, remember the loss is paper, not real! Then this paper tax loss of ($15,740) is used dollar for dollar to offset other income the investor has outside of the property. When $15,740 of other outside income is offset by the paper loss generated from the property, an investor would save $5,981 in taxes he or she otherwise would need to pay on that outside income. This $5,981, in the form of tax savings, increases the investor's spending power.

NET SPENDABLE INCOME

Net Spendable Income, also known as After Tax Cash Flow, is the Before Tax Cash Flow, plus or minus the taxes saved or paid. This is the so-called first year "net bottom line." In the case study, the Before Tax Cash Flow is $16,350, while the taxes saved is $5,981. Therefore, $16,350 + $5,981 = $22,331 Net Spendable Income.

MULTI-YEAR ANALYSIS

The cash flow steps given in Figure 16.1 reflect the first year estimate. Although many small investment properties are purchased just using a one-year analysis, investors in larger properties insist upon a multi-year analysis, where the cash flow is projected for each year of the investor's estimated holding period. Typical multi-year analysis periods are for five, 10, 15, or 20 years.

Given a set of assumptions regarding future rent, vacancy, expense, loan payment, and tax aspect changes, the real estate analyst estimates a cash flow forecast for each subsequent year of the investor's projected holding period. The result is a Net Spendable Income estimate for each future year. Net spendable income is also known as after tax cash flow. In some situations multi year analysis is completed using before tax, instead of after tax cash flow.

Net Sale Proceeds

When the Net Spendable Income has been estimated for each year of the investor's project holding period, the cash flow analysis is still not complete. One step remains: calculation of the Net Sale Proceeds.

Net Sale Proceeds, often called the reversion by appraisers, is the amount of money the investor is estimated to net, after escrow and income taxes, when the property is sold at the end of the holding period. In some situations, sales proceeds are calculated omitting the income tax aspects. If this is the case, the result is called net from escrow or net from sale, excluding income tax aspects.

To calculate the Net Sale Proceeds the analyst estimates what the property can be sold for at the end of the investor's holding period five, 10, 15, or 20 years later. This is done using an annual compound appreciation rate or a capitalization of net income approach based on the last holding year's Net Operating Income (capitalization of Net Operating Income will be discussed in the next section of this chapter). Once the resale price is estimated, seller closing cost, old loan balances, and capital gain taxes are subtracted to produce the Net Sale Proceeds.

Referring to the previous case study, if the original price of the 20-unit apartment property is $1,700,000 and the annual appreciation rate is estimated to be 6%, the projected resale price in five years would be approximately $2,275,000 ($1,700,000 × 1.06, repeated five times). Then the seller's closing cost for the sale of a $2,275,000 property is estimated, say at 8%. The result would be a seller closing cost of $182,000 ($2,275,000 × 8%).

Next, the outstanding balance, after five years, on the original loan of $1,200,000 would be estimated using a financial calculator or remaining loan balance table. In our case study assume the remaining loan balance on the original loan amount of $1,200,000 after five years is down to $1,158,900. The next step would be to estimate what the capital gain tax would be on the profit when the property is resold for $2,275,000. This involves a series of substeps illustrated in the next chapter on income taxes. Let us assume that the capital gain tax came to an estimated $250,000. Then the net sale proceeds would be computed as follows:

$$
\begin{array}{rl}
\$ & 2,275,000 \text{ estimated resale price} \\
- & 182,000 \text{ seller closing cost (8\%)} \\
- & 1,158,000 \text{ outstanding balance on loan} \\
- & 250,000 \text{ capital gain tax on resale profit} \\
\hline
\$ & 685,000 \text{ Net Sale Proceeds (net to seller upon resale)}
\end{array}
$$

SUMMING UP CASH FLOW ANALYSIS

Cash flow analysis consists of three major steps:

1. Estimate the first year's Net Spendable Income (After Tax Cash Flow).

2. Using a set of assumptions, estimate each subsequent year's Net Spendable Income for the length of the investor's holding period.

3. Estimate the net sale proceeds when the investor sells the property at the end of the holding period.

When these three steps are completed, the analyst has all the cash flow numbers—the amount of investment it takes to get into the property and the property's net bottom line estimates for each year of ownership, plus the Net Sale Proceeds in the year of sale. The next section discusses the various methods used to arrive at offering price, and several techniques used to compute rates of return once these cash flow numbers are generated. Before moving on, review your understanding of cash flow analysis.

REVIEWING YOUR UNDERSTANDING

1. Recite the steps to arrive at Before Tax Cash Flow.

2. Under the concept of tax benefit analysis, starting with Net Operating Income, list the steps to arrive at taxes saved or paid for the year.

3. If Before Tax Cash Flow is a negative ($1,000), while taxes saved is a positive $3,000, what is Net Spendable Income?

16.3   ESTIMATING PRICE AND RATES OF RETURN

Once an investor decides to seriously consider making an offer on a particular property, the three key economic issues are: (1) the offering price, (2) the amount of the cash investment, and (3) the rate of return on the cash investment.

THE OFFERING PRICE

Most investors make an offer to buy contingent upon the approval of an appraisal made by a qualified appraiser. The issue here is not how appraisers arrive at value. That is the subject of a course in real estate appraisal. The issue is: what rules of thumb do investors use to arrive at an initial offering price? Investors' rules of thumb are as many and varied as are investors, but three common techniques are: Gross Rent Multiplier, Capitalization Rate, and price per square foot.

Gross Rent Multiplier

The formula for gross rent multiplier is:

$$\frac{\text{Asking Price}}{\text{Gross Scheduled Income}} = \text{Gross Rent Multiplier}$$

The investment property's asking price is divided by its Gross Scheduled Income to arrive at the property's Gross Rent Multiplier. In other words, "How many times does the potential rent go into the asking price?" Referring to the current case study, the asking price for the 20-unit apartment property is $1,700,000, while the Gross Scheduled Income from Figure 16.1 is $192,000. Therefore the Gross Rent Multiplier is:

$$\frac{\text{Asking Price } \$1,700,000}{\text{Gross Scheduled Income } \$192,000} = 8.85 \text{ Gross Rent Multiplier}$$

The 8.85 Gross Rent Multiplier itself is meaningless, until it can be compared to the market Gross Rent Multiplier for comparable properties. Investors and their real estate agents are usually aware of prevailing Gross Rent Multipliers and apply the following rule of thumb:

The lower the property's multiplier below the market multiplier, the better the asking price. The higher the property's multiplier above the market multiplier, the worse the asking price.

If the prevailing market multiplier for comparable 20-unit apartments is 10, the 8.85 Gross Rent Multiplier of the case study indicates a good buy. If the prevailing market multiplier is 7, then the case study's asking price of $1,700,000 seems too high. If in fact the market multiplier is 7, an investor would compute the maximum offering price as follows:

Gross Scheduled Income ×
Market Multiplier = Maximum Offering Price
Thus, $192,000 × 7 = $1,344,000 offering price.

The Gross Rent Multiplier approach, because it uses gross income instead of net income, ignores the impact that vacancies and expenses have on price. It is possible that two properties could have the same gross income, but because of various factors could have very different Net Operating Incomes. Due to this shortcoming, the Gross Rent Multiplier is most often used for apartments and other residential properties. It is rarely used for commercial and industrial prop-

The typical procedure for the developer is to present the proposed real estate project to an environmental review board. The review board then decides if the proposed project will have a significant impact on the environment. If the answer is negative, the developer then proceeds with the project. If the review board feels that the project will have a significant impact, the developer must then prepare and submit a comprehensive environmental impact report.

For report purposes, the "environment" is defined as all social, economic, biological, and physical surroundings. Thus, a typical environmental impact report contains a detailed analysis of how the proposed real estate project will affect each of these four areas. The report also requires that the developer outline the steps to be taken to counteract any environmental damage that might result from the real estate project.

Once the environmental impact project is completed, it is submitted to the environmental review board for a decision. The general public is usually invited to make comments on the report before a final decision is rendered by the review board. All environmental review board decisions, either for or against the proposed project, can be challenged in the courts.

LOCAL LEGISLATION

In addition to meeting federal and state requirements, developers must also conform with local real estate codes. City and county governments must have local planning, public works, building, and sanitation agencies that require the submission of reports before a local building permit is issued. Typically, local reports are needed in the following areas: construction details, lot design, street and other off-site facilities, property tax impact, zoning and architectural conformity, environmental impact, and other areas.

Who pays the cost of these government reports? What is the trade-off between costs and benefits? Is it worth the "red tape"? These topics will be covered in the next section, but before you proceed, check your understanding by answering the following questions.

REVIEWING YOUR UNDERSTANDING

Types of Required Government Reports

1. What is the reason for having government regulatory agencies?
2. Why does the EPA wish to regulate real estate development?
3. In addition to housing codes, list four other state codes or regulations that require the preparation of a report.

erties. Investors in commercial and industrial real estate generally prefer the Net Operating Income approach called the Capitalization Rate.

Capitalization Rate

To arrive at an offering price using the Capitalization Rate approach, the following formula is used:

$$\frac{\text{Net Operating Income}}{\text{Asking Price}} = \text{Capitalization Rate (Cap Rate)}$$

Notice in the formula that the property's Net Operating Income, not its gross income, is used, and it is divided by the asking price. The answer is expressed as a percentage. In essence the question is "What percent of the asking price is the net operating income?" Assuming an investor were to pay all cash and therefore have no loan payments, the Cap Rate would be the first-year before tax rate of return if the investor paid the full asking price. In essence the investor is asking "If I paid cash for the property, does the net income produce an adequate rate of return for my money?"

Using the 20-unit apartment case study in Figure 16.1, the Net Operating Income is $142,720, and the asking price is $1,700,000. Therefore the Capitalization Rate is:

$$\frac{\text{Net Operating Income } \$142,720}{\text{Asking Price } \$1,700,000} = 8.4\% \text{ Capitalization Rate}$$

The 8.4% Capitalization Rate is meaningless until the prevailing market Capitalization Rate for comparable properties is known. Most investors and their agents and consultants know the prevailing Cap Rates in the market for comparable properties. Once the market Cap Rate is identified the following rule of thumb is usually applied:

> The higher the property's Cap Rate above the market Cap Rate, the better the asking price. The lower the property's Cap Rate below the market Cap Rate the worse (or too high) the asking price.

If the prevailing market Capitalization Rate is 7.5%, while the property's Capitalization Rate at the asking price is 8.4%, this would indicate that the asking price is below market, and on the surface appears to be a good buy. If on the other hand the prevailing market Capitalization Rate is 9.5%, the case study's rate of 8.4% is too low, meaning the asking price of $1,700,000 appears to be too high. If in fact the market Cap Rate is 9.5%, the investor then figures the maximum offering price for the property as follows:

$$\frac{\text{Net Operating Income } \$142,720}{\text{Market Capitalization Rate } 9.5\%} = \$1,502,316 \text{ Maximum Price}$$

This Capitalization Rate technique is preferred by many investors because it closely parallels a more sophisticated capitalization approach used by appraisers to arrive at the market value of an income property.

Price per Square Foot

As a backup to the Gross Rent Multiplier and Capitalization Rate approach to determine an offering price, many investors use the price per square foot technique. Here the offering price is divided by the square footage of the building to calculate the price per square foot. Then the price per square foot is compared to the price per square foot of other, similar properties to see if the price per square foot is in the market range.

AMOUNT OF THE CASH INVESTMENT

As noted above, one of the major economic issues is the amount of cash needed to acquire the real estate investment. Obviously, the amount of cash required varies with the terms and conditions of the sale, as well as the current requirements of real estate lenders. Some investors prefer to pay all cash, while some investors attempt to buy without putting any personal money down. There are numerous seminars, some questionable, on how to buy real estate with no money down. For the most part, these seminars only apply to small residential rental properties.

In most cases investors are required to put 20 to 30% cash down, with lenders willing to finance the difference if the borrower and property meet certain standards. The terms of the financing will depend upon four major items: (1) the current state of the real estate market, (2) the current state of the financial markets, (3) the current state of the occupancy and cash flow of the property, and (4) the credit rating and financial strength of the investor. Once these issues are settled, the amount of cash invested for computing rates of return is considered to be the cash down payment, plus all buyer's closing costs.

COMPUTING RATES OF RETURN

Formulas for computing rates of return on cash invested can be broken down into two general categories: (1) rates of return for the first year, and (2) rates of return for the entire holding period.

Rates of Return for the First Year

The two common calculations to arrive at the first-year rate of return are the before tax cash on cash rate and the after tax cash on cash rate. The first year before tax cash on cash rate formula is:

$$\frac{\text{First Year Before Tax Cash Flow}}{\text{Cash Invested}} = \text{First Year Before Tax Cash}$$

Referring to the 20-unit apartment case study shown as Figure 16.1, the Before Tax Cash Flow is $16,350 and the cash invested is $500,000; thus:

$$\frac{\$16,350 \text{ Before Tax Cash Flow}}{\$500,000 \text{ Cash Invested}} = 3.27\% \text{ Before Tax Rate}$$

The before tax cash rate ignores any impact income taxes may have on the rate of return. The before tax cash rate is also called the "economic" cash on cash rate.

Another common first-year calculation is the after tax cash on cash rate. This formula is as follows:

$$\frac{\text{First Year Net Spendable Income}}{\text{Cash Invested}} = \text{First Year After Tax Rate}$$

Referring to the 20-unit apartment case study, the Net Spendable Income is $22,331, the cash invested is still $500,000; therefore the after tax rate is:

$$\frac{\text{Net Spendable Income } \$22,331}{\text{Cash Invested } \$500,000} = 4.47\% \text{ After Tax Rate}$$

In both of these examples, the first-year rates are low.

Occasionally, some people will factor in the first year's principal payments on the loan and the first year's estimated appreciation to compute a first-year rate of return. This is the so-called "equity yield rate for the year." More sophisticated real estate analysts reject this concept by pointing out that a rate of return should be on a cash-equivalent basis. They note that principal payments and appreciation are only on "paper" until the property is refinanced or sold. They are not received as cash each year. They also point out that when a property is refinanced or sold, closing costs greatly reduce the actual cash received. Therefore, any equity yield computed prior to liquidating the investment will be overstated and can be a form of misrepresentation.

Multi-Year Rates of Return

There are basically two types of multi-year rates of return calculations used by real estate investors. They are the: (1) Internal Rate of Return (IRR), and (2) Financial Management Rate of Return (FMRR). Both of these rates recognize the time value of money and use a discount system that reduces the future cash flows to a present value.

Multi-year rates are preferred over first-year rates because they reflect performance over a period of years, as opposed to a single year, and they recognize the time value of money. Simply put, the time value of money states that a dollar today is worth more than a dollar tomorrow. The idea is that the faster you get your money, the quicker you can put it to work to earn even more money. Conversely, the longer you wait to receive your dollar the less the dollar is worth due to the missed opportunities because your money was not reinvested to earn even more money.

Real estate investments are influenced by the time value of money. Investors place cash up front as down payment (present-valued dollars) and over time receive back annual cash flows, plus net sale proceeds upon resale (future-valued dollars). Therefore the concept of discounted cash flow analysis to adjust for the time value of money is appropriate when computing rates of return for real estate investments.

Internal Rate of Return (IRR)

The Internal Rate of Return (IRR) is defined as that discount rate that reduces the future cash flows to just equal the amount of money invested. The calculation is done on a financial calculator or a computer. The steps are as follows:

1. Once the IRR program is ready to run, the analyst enters the initial cash invested and the after tax cash flows for each year in the order received, including the Net Sale Proceeds in the year of resale.

2. Then the calculator/computer discounts each year's cash flow to solve for a rate that will discount all the future cash flows to a present value that equals the amount of the cash invested. Once the discount rate is located, this is the Internal Rate of Return— the amount each dollar is earning while in the investment. The IRR evolved from the field of corporate finance and is a generally accepted standard measurement of performance among more sophisticated real estate investors and brokers.

Financial Management Rate of Return (FMRR)

There are several shortcomings in the calculation process to find the Internal Rate of Return. A major problem is the IRR reinvestment assumption. The IRR assumes that as an investor receives each cash flow each year from the investment, these cash flows are immediately reinvested and they continue to earn a yield equal to the IRR until the investment terminates. This can be unrealistic if the annual cash flows are modest and the IRR is higher than normal market rates. Under these circumstances, the IRR is an overstated rate.

The *Financial Management Rate of Return (FMRR)* attempts to overcome this problem by readjusting each year's cash flows in light of a "safe" rate and a reinvestment rate that is a reflection of the real world. Once the adjustments are made, a new discount rate is computed, and this is known as the Financial Management Rate of Return. In today's investment world, the FMRR is generally considered a better reflection of actual performance than the IRR.

The concepts of the Internal Rate of Return and the Financial Management Rate of Return presented here have been simplified. Readers who wish a more indepth explanation of discounted cash flow analysis are encouraged to seek additional information by reading textbooks on corporate finance, or by contacting the National Association of Realtors or the Appraisal Institute for their trade publications on discounted cash flow analysis.

REVIEWING YOUR UNDERSTANDING

1. Write down the formulas for the first-year before tax cash on cash rate and the first-year after tax cash on cash rate.

2. What is the definition of the Internal Rate of Return (IRR), and how does it differ from the Financial Management Rate of Return (FMRR)?

CHAPTER SUMMARY

Investing is defined as giving up present consumption in exchange for future benefits. Some people invest using hunches, others use an investment analysis procedure. When selecting an investment the five economic characteristics to check are: return, management, taxability, liquidity, and risk.

Real estate cash flow analysis is the process of estimating the amount of money an investor might receive each year of ownership, including the year of resale. When the cash flow process is completed, the Before Tax Cash Flow, taxes saved or paid, and the Net Spendable Income for each year of ownership is forecasted. Then the resale price of the property at the end of the investor's holding period is estimated and from this the Net Sale Proceeds is forecasted. Offering prices and rate of return estimates can be computed based upon these cash flow numbers.

Offering prices are frequently made based on the Gross Rent Multiplier approach, the Capitalization Rate approach, and double-checked by the price per square foot approach. Rates of return can be computed for the first year only, or can be based on a multi-year analysis of the investor's entire holding period.

The most common first-year rates are the before tax cash on cash rate and the after tax cash on cash rate. Multi-year rates of return should take into consideration the time value of money and use a discounted cash flow approach. The two most common multi-year rates are the Internal Rate of Return (IRR) and the Financial Management Rate of Return (FMRR). The Financial Management Rate of Return attempts to overcome the shortcomings, especially the reinvestment assumption, of the Internal Rate of Return.

IMPORTANT TERMS AND CONCEPTS

After Tax Cash Flow	Liquidity
Before Tax Cash Flow	Multi- vs. single-year analysis
Capitalization Rate	
Cash flow analysis	Net Sale proceeds
FMRR	Net Spendable Income
Gross Rent Multiplier	Time value of money
IRR	Types of rates of return
Investing	Types of risks

REVIEWING YOUR UNDERSTANDING

1. The ability to quickly convert an asset to cash is called:
   a. management
   b. risk
   c. yield
   d. liquidity

2. The risk of loss due to an increase in inflation is:
   a. financial risk
   b. interest rate risk
   c. purchasing power risk
   d. social change risk

3. Which of the following uses discounted cash flow analysis taking into consideration the time value of money?
   a. equity rate
   b. first year before tax cash on cash rate
   c. first year after cash on cash rate
   d. Internal Rate of Return

Questions 4–10 will be based on the following case study. A Cash Flow form for your use is attached.

Case Study — Older 10-unit Apartment

Asking price for an older 10-unit apartment property is $600,000. *Income and Expense Data:* Each unit rents for $700 per month, vacancy is 5%, vending machines net $800 per year. Annual operating expenses (property taxes, insurance, repairs, management) are $28,200 per year.

Financing Data: Applied for $420,000 loan @ 10% fixed monthly payments of $3,690. Down payment is $180,000 (30% of sale price).

Income Tax Information: Interest deduction for year is $41,900, depreciation is $17,400.

Potential investor's tax bracket is 32%. All passive losses are usable this year.

WHAT IS THE FIRST YEAR BOTTOM LINE CASH FLOW?

First Year Cash Flow Analysis

1.	Gross Schedule Income	$
2.	+ Other Income	+
3.	Total Gross Income	$
4.	− Vacancy/Credit Loss	−
5.	Gross Operating Income	$
6.	− Annual Operating Expenses	−
7.	Net Operating Income	$
8.	− Annual Debt Service	−
9.	Before Tax Cash Flow	$

Tax Benefit Analysis

10.	Net Operating Income	$
11.	− Interest (Loan 1)	−
12.	− Interest (Loan 2)	−
13.	− Cost Recovery (Depreciation)	−
14.	Real Estate Taxable Income	$
15.	Estimated Allowable Loss (If Loss)	$
16.	× Tax Bracket (× Line 14 or 15)	
17.	Taxes Saved or Paid	$

Net Spendable Income

18. Before Tax Cash Flow (Line 9) $
19. +/− Taxes Saved or Paid (Line 17)
20. Net Spendable Income (After Tax Cash Flow) $

4. What is the Before Tax Cash Flow? $
5. What is the taxes saved/paid? $
6. What is Net Spendable Income? $
7. What is the Gross Rent Multiplier?
8. What is the Capitalization Rate?   %
9. What is the before tax rate?   %
10. What is the after tax rate?   %

Chapter 17

Income Tax Aspects
of Investment Real Estate

Preview

This chapter discusses the impact of the basic principles of federal income taxes on income-producing real estate. Some income tax aspects for homeowners are summarized as a special interest topic and are not stressed in this chapter. Section 17.1 of this chapter outlines the major income tax advantages of owning investment real estate. Section 17.2 discusses basis and depreciation rules. Section 17.3 briefly describes the passive loss rules. Section 17.4 illustrates how gain upon disposition is calculated and how gain and taxes can be deferred by installment sales and 1031 real estate exchanges.

The material in this chapter is basic and limited to federal, not state, income tax rules. This chapter is intended to illustrate how income taxes affect real estate investment decisions. Readers must recognize that income tax rules are subject to changes after the printing of this textbook. This textbook is not intended to be an aid for tax planning, for which all readers are encouraged to seek tax counsel. When you have finished this chapter you should be able to:

1. List the major income tax advantages of owning investment real estate.

2. Describe how basis is established and why basis is important to real estate investors.

3. Outline how operating expenses, interest, depreciation, and the passive loss rules affect a property's cash flow.

4. Discuss how gain or loss is measured upon resale and how installment sale reporting and 1031 exchanges can spread or defer gain and taxes into future years.

17.1   MAJOR INCOME TAX ADVANTAGES

There are six major income tax advantages for owning income-producing real estate.

1. Interest on loans used to purchase or improve rental real estate is fully deductible against the rental income produced by the property. In some cases any leftover interest, per the passive loss rules, might also be deductible against an investor's other income. However, interest paid on other types of loans, such as consumer loans, certain raw land loans, and even some aspects of home loans, may not be fully deductible for income tax purposes.

2. For income property owners, repairs, maintenance, management, property taxes, insurance, and other operating expenses are deductible. In contrast, homeowners can currently deduct only property taxes.

3. Income property owners can take depreciation (cost recovery) deductions to shelter rental income. Depreciation is a non-cash outlay that has the same deduction impact as interest and operating expenses, which do require a cash outlay. Homeowners are not allowed to take depreciation.

4. Upon resale, if a property was held by an investor for the statutory time, it may qualify for favorable capital gain treatment if allowed at that time.

5. A real estate investor is allowed installment sale reporting when the property is sold and the seller carries financing (paper). This may save the seller income taxes by pushing a part of the taxable gain into a lower tax bracket in future years.

6. If the investor follows the rules of Internal Revenue Code Section 1031, a real estate exchange can be used to defer all gain and taxes into another like-kind property.

INVESTOR VERSUS DEALER

An investor is a person who holds property for a personal investment portfolio. A dealer is a person who acquires real estate as inventory to be resold to customers in the course of business. Why the distinction? The federal tax code treats investors and dealers differently. For example, real estate investors get all of the six major tax advantages listed in the preceding paragraph. On the other hand, real estate dealers are not allowed depreciation, capital gains, installment sales, and 1031 exchanges.

Obviously, when analyzing a particular property it will make a significant difference in terms of cash flow analysis, yield, and disposition strategy, whether a person is a dealer or an investor. There are no absolute, clear guidelines as to what behavior makes one a dealer or an investor. There are many gray areas that require the advice of tax experts based on the individual circumstances. Things to consider include number of sales, length of holding period, sales after subdividing, and so on. For the remainder of this chapter it will be assumed that an investor position applies.

REVIEWING YOUR UNDERSTANDING

1. List six major income tax advantages of owning income real estate.
2. In terms of cash outlay, how do depreciation deductions differ from operating expenses and mortgage interest?
3. Compare the income tax differences between a real estate investor and a real estate dealer.

17.2   BASIS AND DEPRECIATION

In addition to deductions for out-of-pocket operating expenses and interest paid on mortgages, an income tax deduction is allowed for depreciation, formally known as cost recovery. Depreciation is an annual bookkeeping deduction allowed by the tax code as a cost recovery for the theoretical loss in value of the property over time. In reality, the property could be appreciating in real value, but an investor is still allowed to take a depreciation loss deduction for income tax purposes. This has the impact of sheltering rental income without experiencing a cash expense or actual loss in value. The depreciation deduction is allowed only on the improvements, not on the land.

HOW MUCH IS DEDUCTIBLE?

The dollar amount of depreciation allowed each year is a function of the taxpayer's basis in the real estate, the allocation between improvements and land, and the straight-line write-off period. Basis

SPECIAL INTEREST TOPIC

Initial Basis of Real Estate

Following are various methods of acquiring title to real estate and how basis is initially determined.

1. If real property is acquired by purchase, the initial basis is the purchase price plus capitalized buyer's closing cost.

2. If real property is acquired by gift, the initial basis is the donor's adjusted cost basis, or market value at the date of gift, whichever is less.

3. If real property is acquired by inheritance, the initial basis is market value at the date of death of the decedent.

4. If real property is acquired by exchange, the initial basis is the market value of the new property, less the deferred gain from the old property.

5. The basis of a principal residence converted to a rental is the adjusted basis of the home or the home's market value on date of conversion, whichever is less.

---

refers to the property owner's cost for income tax purposes. The allocation between improvements and land is determined by an appraisal or a set of guidelines. The straight-line write-off period is established by Congress.

HOW DOES IT WORK?

First the property owner's basis must be determined. Basis is important for two reasons: (1) basis is the starting point for computing depreciation while the property is owned, and (2) basis helps to determine the gain or loss for income tax purposes when the property is disposed of in the future.

The owner's initial basis in a property is determined by method of acquisition, not by the value of the property. A $2 million property can be acquired one way and have a basis of $2 million. But the same property could be acquired another way and have a basis that is considerably lower. An investor must depreciate using basis, not value! The most common method to acquire title is to purchase the real estate. Basis upon purchase is usually the purchase price, plus a certain portion of the buyer's closing cost, called capitalized cost. During the investor's ownership, the basis will go up by capital improvements added, and will go down by allowed depreciation deductions.

Once the purchase price and capitalized closing cost have been determined, the next step is to allocate the basis between the nondepreciable land and the depreciable improvements. This allocation process is done using an appraisal, comparable sales data, or sometimes the ratio established by the county tax assessor on the property tax bill. This allocation process is tricky and is subject to IRS challenge if the allocation does not reflect current market reality. Once the improvements have been allocated, they are frequently further subdivided between real property and personal property, such as carpets, draperies, appliances, and so on, due to the different write-off rules for each.

The time periods for depreciating investments are set by law and have been subject to a lot of change. Currently, the depreciation periods for real estate are 27½ years for residential rental property and 31½ years for nonresidential rental property. Real estate must use straight-line depreciation. However, the first and last year straight-line system must be modified by what is called mid-month convention. Accelerated systems that allowed more than straight-line depreciation were abolished for all real estate acquired after December 31, 1986. Personal property depreciation has various time periods, with five to seven years being the most common. Personal property is allowed accelerated write-off using the 200 percent declining balance system. This 200 percent system must be modified using mid-year convention. Both mid-month and mid-year convention require slight modifications to the straight line and 200% declining balance systems when calculating the precise dollar amount of depreciation. The details are beyond the scope of this text. For specific information readers are encouraged to consult a tax professional.

Example:

An investor purchased an apartment property for $1 million, plus $5,000 in capitalized buyer closing costs. Per an appraisal, the allocation is 20 percent to land and 80 percent to building; no personal property items. The first 12 months' depreciation could be estimated as follows:

$$
\begin{array}{rl}
\$1,000,000 & \text{purchase price} \\
+ \quad 5,000 & \text{capitalized buyer closing costs} \\
\hline
\$1,005,000 & \text{initial basis} \\
\times \quad\quad 80 & \text{percent building ratio} \\
\hline
\$ \quad 804,000 & \text{depreciable building}
\end{array}
$$

$$
\frac{\$804,000 \text{ depreciable building}}{27\frac{1}{2} \text{ years residential rental}} = \$29{,}236 \text{ estimated}
$$

depreciation (actual amount will be slightly less due to mid-month convention . . . i.e., first year only 11½ months)

REVIEWING YOUR UNDERSTANDING

1. Discuss how initial basis is determined for real estate owners.

2. How is basis allocated between land and improvements? What is the length of depreciation allowed for residential and non-residential rental real estate?

3. Purchase price for a small commercial property is $500,000, plus $3,000 capitalized buyer's closing cost. Land is 20 percent, Building 80 percent, no personal property. What is the approximate depreciation for the first 12 months?

17.3 PASSIVE LOSS RULES

The Tax Reform Act of 1986 was a major overhaul of the federal income tax system. One of the act's many features was an attack on real estate tax shelters. The main purpose of a real estate tax shelter was to produce a paper tax loss (as opposed to an out-of-pocket loss) that can be applied against the investor's personal income. In short, paper tax losses offset real income, resulting in an increase in after-tax spendable dollars. In the meantime, the investment may appreciate resulting in a capital gain upon resale. The purpose of the passive loss section of the Tax Reform Act of 1986 was to reduce the practice of using paper real estate losses to reduce otherwise taxable personal income.

Prior to the Tax Reform Act of 1986 any annual loss (rents, less operating expenses, mortgage interest, and depreciation) could be used in the current year to offset any other current income of the investor. However, the general passive loss rules now state that real estate losses can only offset what is known as passive income. To understand the passive loss rules and their impact on real estate cash flow analysis, an explanation of income classifications follows.

According to the Tax Reform Act of 1986, income is broken into three classifications:

Active Income: Income generated when the taxpayer materially participates in an activity that produces income. Examples include wages, commissions, profits from owner-managed business, and other similar activities.

Portfolio Income: Income from paper types of investments, such as interest on savings, dividends on stocks, and coupons on bonds.

Passive Income: Income generated when the taxpayer does not materially participate in an activity that produces income. Examples include limited partnership income, business ventures where the taxpayer has no active role, and rents from rental real estate. The Tax Reform Act of 1986 states that rental real estate is considered a passive activity, even if the property owner actively manages the rental real estate. This provision was a deliberate attempt to keep rental real estate in the passive income category.

PASSIVE INCOME/LOSS OFFSET RULES

The general rule is that a passive loss can offset only passive income. Passive losses cannot normally be used to offset active or portfolio income. If passive real estate losses cannot be used in the current year due to a lack of passive income, then the passive loss must be carried forward to offset passive income that might arise in a future tax year. If future tax years do not produce suitable passive income, the carry-forward passive loss can be used to offset gain when the subject property is sold.

This change was a dramatic shift from the earlier position that a real estate tax loss could be used to offset any current income. By restricting the offset of annual real estate losses to passive income, if a real estate investor does not have passive income, the normal tax savings will not be realized in the current year. This reduces the investor's current cash flow. This in turn will reduce the investor's current rate of return and lower the interest in and willingness to invest in rental real estate.

$25,000 EXCEPTION TO THE PASSIVE LOSS RULES

The passive loss rules provide one exception to the general rule that passive losses can offset only passive income. This exception, known as the $25,000 real estate exception to the passive loss rules, will allow a qualified rental property owner to use up to $25,000 of passive real estate rental losses to offset active or portfolio income each year, after first offsetting passive income. To qualify for this $25,000 exception, a taxpayer must meet the following tests:

1. He or she must own 10 percent or more direct interest in rental real estate and not hold title as a corporation or a tax-reporting limited partnership which must file Internal Revenue Service Form 1065.

2. The owner must be active in the management of the rental real estate. "Active in management" means that the owner must deal directly with the tenants and make all management decisions, or hire a property manager to deal with the tenants. If the owner hires a property manager, they should confer periodically and the management contract should specify that the owner is the decision maker regarding the operations of the property. If a property owner leaves all management decisions to a property manager and merely receives a check and accounting statements, the property owner will probably fail the active in management test and lose the use of the $25,000 rule.

3. For the tax year in question, the rental real estate owner's modified adjusted gross income must be $100,000 or less. If the owner's modified adjusted gross income for the year is more

than $100,000, then the otherwise usable $25,000 is reduced $1 for every $2 the modified adjusted gross income exceeds $100,000. Thus, the $25,000 rule will not apply when a rental real estate owner's modified adjusted gross income reaches $150,000. Keeping with the spirit of the Tax Reform Act of 1986, this effectively reserves the $25,000 rule for moderate income real estate investors.

For the real estate investors who meet this series of tests, up to $25,000 of passive losses, that would otherwise not be usable, can be used in the current tax year to offset active and portfolio income. This in turn will increase the after-tax spendable income for the year and raise the current year's rate of return.

There are several other rules from the Tax Reform Act of 1986 which have an impact on real estate investments. These are beyond the scope of this chapter. Once again, readers are encouraged to seek competent tax counsel before entering into a real estate transaction.

REVIEWING YOUR UNDERSTANDING

1. What is a tax shelter?
2. What is the general passive loss rule?
3. What are the three tests to determine if the $25,000 exception to the general passive loss rule can be used?

17.4   CALCULATING AND DEFERRING GAIN

Once owners decide to market their properties, a series of choices arise as to how to handle the gain upon sale. A real estate investor has three basic choices: (1) sell for cash and pay the tax on the gain, (2) sell and carry some equity in a note and deed of trust and report some gain as an installment sale, or (3) do not sell, and instead do a like-kind Internal Revenue Code 1031 exchange and defer the gain and tax into the new property. This section outlines the basic principles of each choice.

CALCULATING GAIN AND TAXES OWED

Step 1: Calculate Adjusted Cost Basis

> Initial (original) basis
> + buyer's capitalized closing cost
> + capital improvements, if any
> − depreciation for term of ownership
> equals: adjusted cost basis on date of resale

Step 2: Calculate Gain

resale price
− seller closing cost
− adjusted cost basis
<u>− carry forward passive losses, if any</u>
equals: gain on sale

Step 3: Apply Capital Gain Treatment Using Current Rules

gain on sale + capital gain rules = tax owned on gain

USE OF AN INSTALLMENT SALE TO SPREAD OUT TAXABLE GAIN

Section 453 of the Internal Revenue Code provides a way to spread the gain and tax on the profit from a sale of an asset over a number of years. This avoids the paying of the entire tax on the entire gain in the year of sale.

To qualify as an installment sale, the seller must carry back financing on behalf of the buyer. The financing can be in the form of a note and deed of trust, a mortgage, a contract of sale, or other similar instruments. The seller carry loan must call for a due date in some year other than the same year as the sale. The seller carry loan can be either a senior or junior loan. Whenever the seller carries back paper, the installment method for reporting gain is automatic, unless the seller formally elects to take the entire tax in the year of sale. Installment sale reporting is allowed for real estate investors and homeowners. Real estate dealers are normally denied the use of installment sales.

Some advantages and disadvantages of an installment sale are:

Advantages

1. A way to sell a property in a tight real estate market.
2. Can lower the tax owned on the sale by throwing all or part of the gain into a more favorable, low tax bracket year in the future.
3. Can earn interest from the buyer on gain not yet reported.
4. Can pay the tax in the future with inflated (cheaper) dollars.

Disadvantages

1. Seller does not receive all of his or her equity in up front cash, thereby incurring opportunity costs on reinvestment possibilities.
2. Seller may be in a higher tax bracket when money is collected from the buyer in a future year, and thereby may actually pay more in taxes than would have been the case in the year of sale.

3. Buyer could default on the loan and the seller could be forced to proceed with a foreclosure.

There are many other aspects to installment sales not covered in this brief summary. The installment sale technique for spreading out gain may or may not be a good tax move for a real estate seller. A real estate licensee should not give tax advice; however, a licensee should recognize that an installment sale is one of several choices a seller should discuss with a tax adviser.

USE OF A LIKE-KIND 1031 EXCHANGE TO DEFER GAIN

Section 1031 of the Internal Revenue Code provides a way to move from one income or investment property to another and not recognize taxable gain. Although the rules are complicated, the basic concept states that real estate held for income or investment can be exchanged tax deferred for any other real estate to be held for income or investment. Section 1031 real estate exchanges can only be used by investors. Real estate dealers are not allowed to do tax deferred exchanges. Homeowners cannot do 1031 exchanges, but rather must use the 24-month tradeup rule under Internal Revenue Code Section 1034 (see Special Interest Topic in this chapter for details).

SPECIAL INTEREST TOPIC

Deferring Gain Upon Sale of a Principal Residence

If your principal residence is sold at a gain, the tax may be deferred (postponed):

1. If within 24 months before or after the sale of your old home, you buy another home that is equal to or greater than the adjusted selling price of your old home (Section 1034 of the Internal Revenue Code). If a homeowner trades down to a less expensive home, there may be a partial tax liability.

2. If the seller is 55 years or older and meets other ownership and occupancy provisions, up to $125,000 of homeowner gain is exempt from taxes. This exemption can only be used once in a homeowner's lifetime.

Homeowners who sell and carry financing on behalf of the buyer are allowed to use installment sale reporting to spread out gain per Section 453 of the Internal Revenue Code.

What if a home is sold for a loss? What are the income tax rules? Answer: The loss on the sale of a principal residence is NONDEDUCTIBLE! Only the loss on the sale of income and investment real estate is deductible.

Under a properly structured 1031 real estate exchange, no tax is paid upon the realized gain at the time of the transfer. Rather, the gain is carried over to the new property to be taxed when the new property is sold. Often the process is repeated, property after property, deferring gain until ultimately the owner dies. Under current rules, the decedent's heirs would receive the final property at a basis equal to market value at the date of death, and all previous deferred gains would be excused. Thus a tax-deferred exchange can become a tax-free exchange upon death.

When structuring a 1031 exchange, the different properties may have unequal equities. To balance the difference in equities, one party must give some additional items to the other. If the difference in equities is balanced using items other than qualified like-kind real estate, the party who receives the unlike property is said to have received "boot." Boot is defined as any unlike property received in the exchange. Receipt of boot can trigger some tax in a real estate exchange. Thus, to have a completely tax deferred exchange a person must avoid receiving boot.

Computation of boot and other details of 1031 tax-deferred exchanges are beyond the scope of this textbook. Readers are invited to discuss this subject with tax experts and knowledgeable real estate investment agents. The purpose here is to offer 1031 like-kind exchanges as another alternative to a regular real estate sale and payment of tax on the resulting gain.

REVIEWING YOUR UNDERSTANDING

1. List the three steps needed to compute gain upon sale of real estate.
2. What are the advantages and disadvantages of an installment sale?
3. Who can and who cannot do a 1031 tax-deferred real estate exchange?

CHAPTER SUMMARY

The major income tax advantages for owning income real estate are the deductibility of mortgage interest, operating expenses, and depreciation; capital gain treatment; use of installment sale reporting; and the ability to use a 1031 tax-deferred exchange. These advantages are available to real estate investors. Real estate dealers cannot take depreciation and capital gains, and are usually not allowed installment sale and 1031 exchange treatment.

Cost for income tax purposes is called basis. The amount of

basis is determined by how title is acquired. Basis is used to determine the amount of depreciation allowed each year and it is used to measure gain or loss upon resale. Once basis is established, it is allocated between land and improvements. Then the real estate improvements are depreciated for the time period allowed by law. Current rules are 27½ years for residential rental and 31½ years for nonresidential, using the straight-line method.

The Tax Reform Act of 1986 created the passive loss rules which state that rental real estate is a passive activity and any passive real estate loss can offset only passive income. Passive losses can no longer offset active or portfolio income unless the $25,000 exception can be applied. The passive loss rules have had the impact of discouraging some people from investing in rental real estate.

Once real estate owners decide to market their income properties, they have basically three choices of how to handle taxable gain. They could sell for cash, declare the gain and pay the tax. They could carry some financing on behalf of the buyer and treat the gain in the seller carry note as an installment sale. Finally, the owners could decide to structure a like-kind 1031 tax-deferred exchange and transfer the gain into another income or investment property.

IMPORTANT TERMS AND CONCEPTS

Basis	Passive loss rules
Boot	Straight line 27½ and 31½
Depreciation	Tax-deferred exchange (1031)
Installment sale	
Investor vs. dealer	Tax shelter
	$25,000 exception

REVIEWING YOUR UNDERSTANDING

1. Which of the following is a noncash income tax deduction?
   a. mortgage interest
   b. property taxes
   c. repairs
   d. depreciation

2. Which tax treatment does an investor receive that a dealer does not?
   a. mortgage interest deduction
   b. property tax deduction
   c. repair deduction
   d. depreciation

3. The initial basis to an owner who acquired title to real estate by gift is:

   a. donor's adjusted basis or market value, whichever is less
   b. market value at the date of gift
   c. purchase price, plus capitalized closing costs
   d. market value of new property less gained deferred from old property

4. The depreciation write-off period for residential rental property is:

   a. 31½ years
   b. 27½ years
   c. 7 years
   d. 5 years

5. For rental real estate owners, all of the following are depreciable *except:*

   a. carpets
   b. buildings
   c. land
   d. carport

6. Income or losses from rental real estate are considered to be:

   a. active
   b. portfolio
   c. passive
   d. tax sheltered

7. To use the full $25,000 exception to the passive loss rules, the rental property owner's modified adjusted gross income must not exceed:

   a. $125,000
   b. $100,000
   c. $75,000
   d. $25,000

8. When the seller of an income property carries financing for the buyer, the income tax reporting of the sale is known as:

   a. an installment sale
   b. a tax-deferred exchange (1031)
   c. a 24-month trade-up (1034)
   d. a once-in-a-lifetime exemption

9. To qualify for a 1031 tax-deferred exchange, a person must exchange:

   a. income or investment real estate for income or investment real estate
   b. real property for personal property
   c. a principal residence for a principal residence
   d. foreign rental property for U.S. rental property

10. The receipt of unlike taxable property in a 1031 exchange is called:

   a. leverage
   b. equity balance
   c. boot
   d. basis

Chapter 18

Applied Real Estate Economics

Preview

A complete investigation of a real estate investment includes a study of general economic trends in the real estate market, coupled with a detailed economic study of the value and investment return potential of the individual parcel. This chapter brings together these two elements to outline the real estate decision-making process. Section 18.1 deals with the variables that a real estate investor should consider before making an investment decision. Section 18.2 uses flowcharts to illustrate the steps in making a real estate investment decision. When you have completed this chapter you will be able to:

1. Describe why real estate investing involves multiple choices.

2. List the five steps in the scientific method of analysis.

3. Summarize the steps in analyzing a parcel of improved real estate.

4. Summarize the steps in analyzing the alternatives for developing an unimproved parcel of land.

18.1 REAL ESTATE INVESTMENT VARIABLES

As mentioned earlier, real estate is an expensive asset that is locked into a fixed location. The large initial investment frequently takes years to recoup. Because of these factors, real estate investments are heavily influenced by future changes. Real estate prices today are based on an investor's expectations of earnings tomorrow and beyond.

EXPECTATIONS

The investor could simply assume that future earnings will be similar to today's. But this is not a reasonable assumption. In fact, the key element of the investment process is the *study of how possible changes may affect future earnings.*

What are the future changes that will influence real estate values? They are economic, social, and political cycles and trends. Future real estate values will be influenced by economic events, by changes in social activities, and by the political actions of government.

Cycles and Trends

When investors seek to forecast changes in earnings, they must remember that *all* change involves either cycles—changes that recur regularly—or trends—long-term shifts in the same direction. To forecast earnings means to forecast the economic, social, and political changes that could influence earnings. This forecast must try to predict the movement of past cycles and trends into the future. Much of the material in Parts I and II of this book is intended to discuss the major influences upon such movements, so that investors can understand them and better forecast their future.

"What If"

Investors should not be concerned with every general change; only those that influence the real estate market need be of interest. To locate these changes, analysts must play a game called "sensitivity analysis." This means asking what would be the effect, if any, of each perceived change. A sample group of questions might be:

What if:

the tenant went bankrupt?

the seller could not make good on a promise of better than 90 percent occupancy?

the largest industry in town closed its doors?

the country went into a recession?

the cost of gas and electricity doubled?

zoning were changed to a land use of lower value?

a number of lenders had problems with bad loans at the same time?

auto gasoline were tightly rationed?

depreciation deductions were eliminated?

Congress removed all real estate tax advantages?

the city ordered a mandatory building code inspection?

there were a major natural disaster?

the most liberal or the most conservative local political group received a smashing majority vote at the next election?

The purpose of asking "what if" questions is not based on any particular expectation of their coming true. Rather, it is to explore how sensitive an investment is to change. No investment is completely protected; what an investor wants is an idea of what risks exist so that he or she can more accurately judge a property's profit potential.

MULTIPLE CHOICES

Real estate investment analysis involves more than assessing the likelihood of future benefits. It is also a process of selecting among alternative investments. One reason for this was noted earlier: different investors need different investment characteristics. A salaried person with a high income may need some tax shelter. An elderly person with a limited pension and no other investments needs to avoid risk of loss. A young person investing for retirement may seek a hedge against inflation.

Another reason why real estate investments involve multiple choices is that the best investment is not necessarily the one with the best characteristics; rather it is the one with the best characteristics *for the price.* If a real estate analyst had the information needed to make a foolproof forecast of future investment returns, the analyst would conclude that a particular property should be purchased. Should the investor rush out and immediately buy this property? Not

"When the tide comes in, I'm going to give you an object lesson in ill-advised, unsound and badly-researched real estate investment."

FIGURE 18.1   *Source:* Reprinted with permission from *The Saturday Evening Post,* Copyright 1973, The Curtis Publishing Co., John A. Ruge, cartoon.

necessarily, because the market may have already bid this property up to an unreasonably high level relative to its expected future returns.

If this should occur, an investor must then choose another property that will do almost as well. In fact, one should search for a property that will do well relative to its current price!

Investing Involves Outthinking the Market

At any given moment, any number of investment properties may be for sale. Every potential buyer makes some sort of analysis, either consciously or unconsciously, regarding risks, returns, and the price he or she would be willing to pay. Years later, some of the investments will turn out to have provided much more in returns than their original purchase price predicted, while others will have become investment disasters. The purpose of investment analysis, and of choosing, is to select investments that contain opportunities for future profits that the market is missing or to avoid future problems that the market is ignoring. The goal of the average investor should be to do as well as or better than the market in general. This requires enough awareness to buy or sell before prices have completely changed. Obviously, the earlier the awareness, the better off the investor.

The investor must recognize that he or she is in competition with all other investors to obtain profitable returns, be they investment dollars or amenities of home ownership. The competitive market gives greater returns to those who see advantages or problems and act on them.

DETERMINING INVESTMENT CHARACTERISTICS

Individual investments differ in location, type, size, rights, and financing. They also differ in how these characteristics affect the investment's future returns. Real estate investment textbooks contain many excellent discussions of investment types such as apartments, retail stores, and commercial office buildings.

Instead of describing the *current* investment characteristics for each type of real estate, this book has tried to focus attention on the future. Indeed, with the current revolutionary changes in the areas of energy, pollution, and public transportation, it is certain that there will be changes in investment characteristics as well.

Limits on Choice

The major limit on the investor's choice of properties is that in certain markets, not many properties are for sale at any time. Since some of these may be very unsatisfactory, only a few properties may be left from which to choose.

Investment needs also limit choice, since different types of property differ in tax shelter, risk, and management. The investor's limited funds may restrict investments further and may require borrowing and pooling funds with other investors.

FANCY FOOTWORK

Most real estate investment seems complicated enough. From time to time, however, experts discover investment techniques that appear to greatly increase investors' returns. These usually involve income tax deductions to increase the tax shelter that the property offers. Past examples include rapid depreciation write-offs, prepaid interest, depreciation of separate building components, shortened economic life, vineyard and orchard development cost deductions, and so on.

Some of the ideas suggested from time to time are perfectly legal, others are not. There is a danger that the investor will allow these special tax benefits to override a careful study of the property itself. Every gimmick or new techniques carries new risks (of legal error, an adverse court decision, a change of law, etc.), until the idea is widely used and politically accepted. This risk should be understood by the buyer and evaluated in the purchase decision.

This overview leads into Section 18.2, which concentrates on the steps in arriving at a real estate investment decision. But before you proceed, answer the questions below.

18.2   STEPS IN REAL ESTATE DECISION MAKING[1]

Real estate decision making can be viewed as a series of steps that gather real estate information, analyze the information, and then arrive at a decision based on the analysis. The formal procedure is called *the scientific method.* The scientific method involves the following series of steps.

1. Clearly identify and define the problem or purpose of the investigation. *This step is not as simple as it may sound. Unless a real estate investor knows exactly what he or she is attempting to decide, the investor will not acquire the information needed to make a sound decision. One clearly defined purpose might be to decide if now is the time to purchase a particular real estate property, which we shall call Property X.*

2. Collect relevant data. *With the problem or purpose clearly defined, the investor then gathers information that will be useful in arriving at a decision. It is equally important to avoid material that is extraneous and irrelevant to the problem at hand. An investor would attempt to gather as much economic, social, physical, and political data relevant to Property X as time and money allow.*

3. Analyze the data collected. *With the problem clearly defined and the relevant data collected, an investor must then correlate, classify, and analyze the data and arrive at a preliminary decision—often called a hypothesis. After analyzing the information, an investor may tentatively decide that Property X is the right property and that now is the time to buy.*

4. Formulate and test the tentative decision (hypothesis). *At this point in most scientific investigations, experiments are conducted to see if the tentative decision or hypothesis is correct. For real estate, it is difficult to experiment without having to*

[1] Dennis J. McKenzie, *Instructor's Guide for Real Estate Economics*, Sacramento: California Community Colleges, 1990, pp. 369–87.

make a firm commitment in advance. In other words, few sellers let an investor try the property before buying to see if the property produces the desired results. Although computer simulation is possible, frequently the only testing available is to determine how other similar parcels with similar owners are doing in the marketplace.

5. Arrive at a final decision or conclusion. *Taking into consideration steps 1, 2, 3, and 4, an investor now makes a final decision by either accepting or rejecting the tentative decision (hypothesis). If an investor decides to accept the tentative decision (to buy Property X now), it should be recognized that there is a possibility that the investor is making a mistake. In other words, there is a chance that this is not the time to buy. So an investor should then estimate the probability of being wrong and decide if he or she is willing to take the risk. If it is decided that the property is an acceptable risk, the purchase takes place.*

The scientific method is the rational way to approach real estate decisions. Unfortunately, too many people make real estate decisions based on emotions. The role of the real estate specialist is to bring rational behavior to a very emotional business. Figure 18.2 illustrates the steps in the scientific method.

STEPS IN ANALYZING AN IMPROVED PROPERTY

Using the scientific method as a basic foundation, an outline of the steps in analyzing an improved parcel of real estate follows.

Because of the high purchase price, the first step for a real estate investor is to determine if adequate financing is available. In some cases investors pay all cash, but usually financing is needed. As good as a real estate investment might be, an investor may have to abandon the project if financing is not available.

After determining whether financing is available, the next step is to analyze *national* cycles and trends. Questions that should be

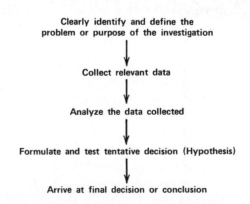

FIGURE 18.2   Steps in the scientific method.

asked include: What is the state of the economy? What is government doing with fiscal and monetary policy? How will this influence national real estate activity? How will these national changes affect the property being anlyzed?

Once national cycles and trends have been studied, an investor should look at *regional* economic changes. Important questions here include: Does the region follow national changes? Is the region insulated against national changes? Is it growing? Declining? Why? What influence will this have on the property being studied?

After regional cycles and trends have been studied, the next step is to look at *local* changes in the city or county where the property is located. Is the city following regional changes? To what degree? Does the city appear to be growing economically? Why? What are the directions of growth? How will these factors influence the subject property?

Following the study of city or county changes, an investor should analyze the *neighborhood* where the property is located. Is it a growing, stagnant, or declining neighborhood? Why? What are the urban renewal plans? Changes in transportation routes? What influence does this have on the subject property?

Once national, regional, local community, and neighborhood changes have been studied, an investor is in a position to analyze the individual subject property. This step has two phases: appraisal and investment analysis. An appraisal determines the market value of the property under consideration, while an investment analysis determines if the property is "right" for the investor's purposes. The final step is to make a decision either to purchase or not. Figure 18.3 illustrates the steps in analyzing an improved property.

STEPS IN ANALYZING ALTERNATIVES FOR UNIMPROVED REAL ESTATE PARCELS

An in-depth analysis of the various alternative uses for a parcel of land is frequently referred to as a *feasibility study.* The purpose of a feasibility study is to determine if a proposed real estate project is economically sound—in other words, will it produce an acceptable profit? Although a complete feasibility study contains numerous other substeps, Figure 18.4 summarizes the steps in determining whether a particular real estate parcel has an economically feasible use.

From Figure 18.4 it can be seen that when analyzing the alternatives for unimproved parcels, one of the first things to check for is government-approved uses and/or the prospect of obtaining a rezoning to achieve a higher and better use.

After government-approved uses have been established, an investor then checks the availability of short-term construction financing and long-term take-out financing.

After being assured of adequate financing, the next step is to determine the alternative land uses, such as residential, commercial, industrial, or rural-recreational. In some cases, there may be more than one land use, and the site must be studied for each possible

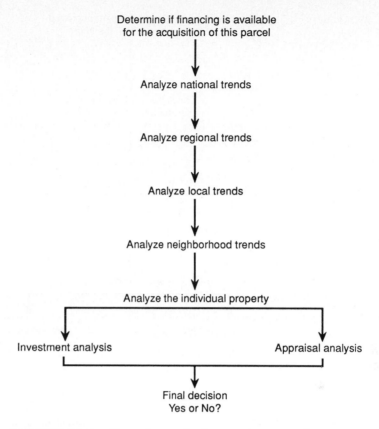

Determine if financing is available
for the acquisition of this parcel

Analyze national trends

Analyze regional trends

Analyze local trends

Analyze neighborhood trends

Analyze the individual property

Investment analysis

Appraisal analysis

Final decision
Yes or No?

FIGURE 18.3   Steps in analyzing an improved property.

use. When this is completed, a market potential study is conducted to determine if a market exists for the proposed improvements and what the strength of the market is. At the root of all market potential studies are the fundamental principles of supply and demand. What is the current and future supply of improvements of this type? What is the current and future demand for improvements of this type? These two questions form the heart of a market potential study. If the study reveals no market potential, then the analysis terminates. On the other hand, if the study reveals a good market potential, the real estate economist moves to the next major phase—financial analysis.

The purpose of financial analysis is to determine whether the project is economically sound. Having a market potential is one thing, but being able to produce a real estate improvement that will capitalize on the market potential profitability is another matter.

The financial analysis phases require the preparation of a detailed development plan, outlining what is to be constructed and the timetable for construction. Then the development costs are estimated. Once development costs are estimated, gross income, operating expenses, and net operating income are projected.

After development cost and net operating income have been estimated, the analyst selects the best available financing package. The real estate analyst then projects the cash flow generated by the project. In addition, a full appraisal is conducted to determine an estimate of the market value of the project when completed.

The last step is to make the final decision. The project is con-

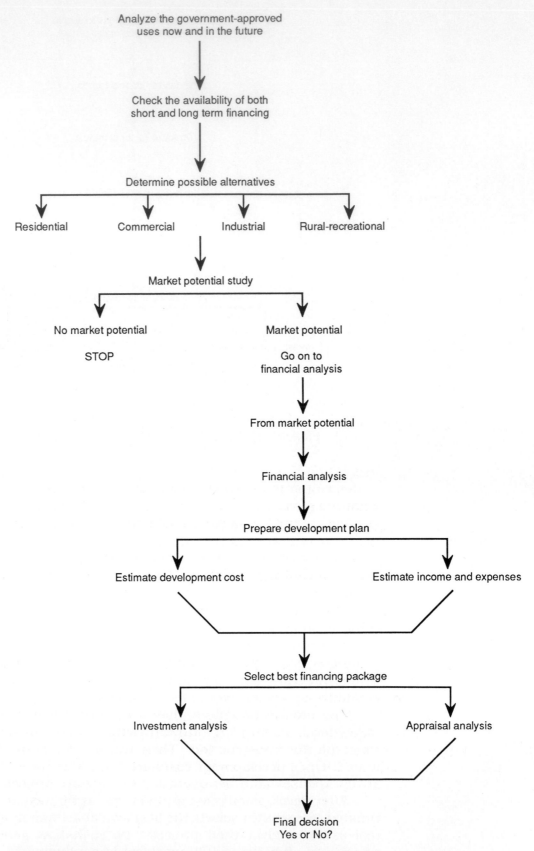

FIGURE 18.4 Steps in analyzing an unimproved property.

sidered economically feasible if all costs are covered and earnings provide a recapture of invested capital and an adequate rate of return on the investment. It must be stressed that economic feasibility is based on a forecast of future earnings, which in turn is based on projected income and expenses. Thus the entire forecast depends on *realistic projections* of future income and expenses.

REVIEWING YOUR UNDERSTANDING

Steps in Real Estate Decision Making

1. What are the five steps in the scientific method?
2. In analyzing an improved property, does the analyst study regional changes? Why?
3. Why does the analysis include both an appraisal and an investment analysis?
4. How does the analysis of an improved property differ from a feasibility study?

CHAPTER SUMMARY

Future earnings are the key element in investment profits, and forecasting these earnings is the focus of investment analysis. The forces that will cause present earnings to change are the factors in the forecast.

The analyst seeks to understand past and present social, political, and economic cycles and trends in order to anticipate future changes. Since not every future change will be important to the property being analyzed, the investor must consider the effect upon the property of each possible change.

Investment analysis involves not only forecasting future benefits but also selecting among alternative investments. The investor must choose an investment that meets the desired investment characteristics (yield, tax aspects, risk, and so on). In addition, the investor must seek to find the investment that offers the best future returns for the price. In practice, because a limited number of properties are for sale at any one time, the analyst is trying to outthink the market.

Real estate decision making should involve careful study. The five steps of the scientific method provide an outline for such study. In analyzing improved property, key factors include financing availability, the impact of possible national, regional, local, and neighborhood changes, appraisal of market values, and analysis of investment characteristics and investment value.

For unimproved properties, added steps are the review of allowable uses, determination of possible uses, estimation of market potentials, and preparation of a development plan.

IMPORTANT TERMS AND CONCEPTS

Change—cycles and trends   Profit potential
Feasibility study   Scientific method
Investment choices   Sensitivity analysis

REVIEWING YOUR UNDERSTANDING

1. The city council's unanticipated rezoning to a lower density reduces the value of a property. This is an example of a:

   a. social force

   b. political force

   c. economic force

   d. physical force

2. A game that anticipates the impact of various changes on an investment is:

   a. sensitivity analysis

   b. cash flow analysis

   c. economic analysis

   d. fail-safe analysis

3. The first step in the scientific method is:

   a. collect the data

   b. form the hypothesis

   c. analyze the data

   d. define the problem

4. A formal study of the various alternative uses for a vacant parcel of land is called:

   a. what if analysis

   b. sensitivity analysis

   c. feasibility study

   d. critical path study

5. A real estate project is considered to be economically favorable when:

   a. all costs are covered

   b. invested capital can be recovered

   c. an adequate return on investment is anticipated

   d. all of the above are possible

Chapter 19

Anticipating Change

Preview

It has been stressed how important future changes will be to the success of real estate investments and to the evaluation of any economic choice or decision. This chapter points out areas of possible future change that should be watched. In the process, it is hoped that readers will think about other possible changes. Section 19.1 studies the areas most directly connected to real estate. Section 19.2 discusses national issues, while Section 19.3 considers the most uncertain changes. Since this is not a book *about* the future, the coverage of these possible changes is quite brief. When you have finished this chapter you should be able to:

1. List at least 10 potential areas of future change.
2. Describe the nature of possible changes.
3. Show how each potential change can be monitored.

19.1   REAL ESTATE ISSUES

There are four areas of change that will have the most immediate impact on real estate in the years to come. These issues—land-use controls, the housing shortage and affordability, consumerism, and changes within the real estate industry itself—are more limited in scope than some of the larger-scale questions raised in the subsequent portions of this chapter.

LAND-USE CONTROLS

Land-use controls change as society's perception of ideal land use evolves. The most important land-use issue of the moment appears to be the environment, especially pollution. Pollution control regulations by local, state, and federal government are likely to have the most influence on public and private land use in the next decade. Serious air pollution in the Los Angeles Basin will have a direct impact on industrial, commercial, and residential real estate land uses. This in turn will have an impact on the market value of each individual property. Regulation of land use due to environmental pollution is a pattern that is expected to be repeated throughout the rest of California and the nation.

HOUSING SHORTAGES AND AFFORDABILITY

Commentators have discussed the problems of the housing industry for decades, and many cures have been tried. The four problems now concerning specialists are:

1. Pollution-related shortages of land and materials;
2. The strong cyclical variation in the cost and supply of credit;
3. Difficulty of keeping older units maintained;
4. How to provide housing that elderly and low-income people can afford.

Shortages of Land and Materials

Some cities and counties have stopped issuing building permits until new sources of water can be obtained or sewage treatment could be improved. Strict requirements for environmental impact reports have delayed many larger developments. Citizens have complained of the traffic and noise generated by new development and have forced building moratoriums, rezonings, and other actions, which have also delayed development. Problems with air pollution and expansion of necessary water and sewer supplies are having lasting effects upon the shortage of building sites.

Material shortages in the past have included cement, lumber, and bathtubs. Many shortages arose because manufacturers had to correct years of abuse in water and air pollution. Some products, such as asbestos and other hazardous materials, have pollution problems that are difficult to resolve. Correcting these problems has been costly for manufacturers, which raises prices to builders.

The "Credit-Crunch" Cycle

Credit cost and availability are monetary policy tools the Federal Reserve Board uses to help stabilize the U.S. economy. A problem is created when shifts in Federal Reserve policies create cyclical trends in interest rates. These ups and downs in interest rates have a major impact on the real estate market. Mortgage market reforms such as adjustable rate loans, more liquid secondary mortgage markets, and the influx of international capital have helped to stabilize the U.S. mortgage market, but fluctuation in interest rates will still occur to some degree in the future.

Maintaining Older Homes

Many ideas are being tried across the country, and the Office of Housing and Urban Development and other federal agencies are expanding their grants for research. Suggested concepts include rezoning, special rehabilitation funds, and formation of neighborhood groups, as discussed in Chapter 9.

Housing the Elderly and the Poor

Finally, changes to improve housing for elderly and low-income people have included:

1. Federally subsidized elderly housing projects;
2. Property tax credits for elderly people;
3. Still-unsuccessful experiments with publicly owned or subsidized housing for poverty-level households;

4. Increased emphasis on maintenance of older housing, including grants or low-interest loans to elderly or low-income families.

The housing needs of the elderly have been better handled in recent years, but the typical poverty-level household (especially if very large or very poor) is probably housed little better than it was ten years ago. Further changes in poverty housing programs seem likely.

CONSUMERISM

Newspaper headlines feature consumer rebellions, boycotts, class-action lawsuits, and mass appearances at regulatory or congressional hearings. People now tend to express their objections to the goods and services they buy. So far, this has not been as noticeable with real estate as with cars, for example. Such a lag is to be expected, since people do not buy and sell real estate very often and find it complex and hard to understand. As they become more confident at expressing objections, however, their activity probably will include real estate complaints, too.

Visible signs of this change include more lawsuits against builders or sellers over structural and soil problems. Another is the use of broker errors and omissions insurance and the use of insurance to cover house and equipment repairs in the year after sale. The increase in landlord-tenant conflict and changes in landlord-tenant law are added evidence of growing consumerism.

THE REAL ESTATE INDUSTRY

As the product changes, the people who handle it must change. The most obvious changes throughout the industry are increased knowledge (via education or training), increased specialization or a narrowing of the area of activity, and an increase in the size of business firm or organization. The size of real estate brokerage has been expanded by growth and merger, and by joining franchise chains, a growing factor in the industry. Increased cooperation between brokers seems to be a trend.

Future changes include a need for greater specialized knowledge on the part of individual brokers. One specialization, already evident, separates brokerage for a commission from consulting for a fee. Further specialization could go so far as to produce separate broker's licenses for home sales, investment property, and so forth, or to separate those who list property from those who sell it. Computers will play increasingly important roles.

REVIEWING YOUR UNDERSTANDING

Real Estate Issues

1. What appear to be the two major land-use problems? Give examples of each from your community.

2. How many examples can you give of connections between pollution and land use?

3. What four problems of housing are listed? How does each apply to your community?

4. What changes in consumer attitudes toward real estate have you noticed? List those that are favorable and those that are unfavorable.

19.2   NATIONAL CHANGES

National changes are those that involve many areas of the U.S. economy besides real estate. People outside of real estate might not even consider these changes as affecting real estate. The issues mentioned here include demography, poverty, lifestyles, inflation, and finance and trade.

DEMOGRAPHY

Demography is the study of influences on population, such as birth and death rates and migration. The most important demographic statistic for real estate is the rate of net population increase, or births in excess of deaths. World trends, as well as trends in California or in a particular country, are important because of immigration (in-migration), the effect upon demand for agricultural and other exports, and competition for world resources.

Increasing population means greater demand for food and all other resources. To the degree that real estate is fixed in quantity, an increase in population means an increase in demand and in land prices. Large immigrations are also important, as demonstrated by the past and continuing growth of the Los Angeles area. Emigration (out-migration) also affects real estate, as when job seekers left Seattle during a local recession in the late 1960s, leaving many vacant buildings behind them (see Figure 19.1). In the early 1990s, Seattle was one of the nation's most economically active cities. The Seattle real estate market has recently experienced some of the nation's most rapid price increases. What better place to note that the only certainties are taxes, death, and change!

FIGURE 19.1   Ghost Town? *UPI/Bettmann Newsphotos.*

Population Composition

Demographers also study how many people there are in each category of age, sex, race, education, and occupation. Demographers study the composition of the population because of the obvious changes that occur as people get older. The population of any area can be studied by starting with the age, sex, and household characteristics of the current population, adding the expected births, subtracting the anticipated deaths, and forecasting the net migration. Analysis of *current* populations is commonly done by all levels of government.

The population of every city, state, and nation is changing because of changes in composition and number as the people age. These changes in composition can be projected in detail. Such projections would draw conclusions about the projected mix of household sizes, incomes, occupations, and ages, which would be very relevant to real estate. Housing markets, for example, clearly go through cycles of larger versus small housing units, and this cycle is related to swings in the proportion of younger households to middle-aged ones. It is clear, therefore, that a number of future changes in housing demand are already set in motion by these current and projected changes in population composition. The 1990 Census data will provide much of the needed information.

POVERTY

The U.S. economy is able to provide a minimum standard of living. Yet we still have real poverty—too little money for safe and sanitary housing and a nutritious diet. The problem cannot simply be cured by increasing the incomes of the poor because custom, behavior, attitudes, and failure in education can block effective use of money. There is an obvious frustration created by living in poverty and seeing televised and advertised luxuries. Avenues of advancement for the talented and motivated are needed as much as ever.

The problems call for continued poverty programs, but it is *not* clear what type. Current housing programs, for example, have been criticized as much as earlier ones. New proposals range from direct rent supplements to guaranteed minimum incomes. The real estate economist should consider the effects of current programs, the impact of any curtailment, and the various major proposals for change.

LIFESTYLES

How people choose to live, within the limits set by their incomes, determines how they allocate their resources and the demand for goods and services that they present to the economy. In the past, people had to work hard to survive. In modern America, our society could provide an adequate *minimum* standard of living with far less time spent on "work" than was true in the past.

To date, however, few people have reduced their workday. Instead, many work relatively long hours and use the added income to buy a standard of living that, in this country, goes well above the minimum. The effects upon real estate are substantial. Examples include second homes, recreation resorts, expensive restaurants, acreage homesites, and new luxury hotels.

There is now open discussion of alternatives to traditional full-time employment, and one sees increasing desire for time for non-income-producing pursuits, despite possible lower incomes. It is too early to tell how widespread this movement toward nontraditional work patterns is, or whether these lifestyle changes will continue as people get older. Their effect upon real estate demand could be substantial.

TRANSPORTATION

Transportation is a major source of pollution, as well as a major user of the nation's total energy. The major methods of transportation differ in their impact upon city shape and density, as discussed in Chapter 7.

The automobile dominates American transportation, but it is clearly a major source of petroleum consumption as well as pollution. The problems of automobile pollution, petroleum price increases, and possible shortages suggest that the present auto will be altered, or its part in our society will be changed. The impact on real estate will be significant because of the impact the automobile has had in developing suburban areas.

INFLATION

Very few books about the future written during the 1960s listed inflation as a serious problem in the United States. By the 1970s, inflation was considered a major U.S. problem. Then in the 1980s the rate of inflation in the United States was drastically reduced. Where inflation will head in the 1990s is uncertain. If it remains moderate, price levels will be determined by basic supply and demand. But if rapid inflation once again occurs, the dislocations of the 1970s will once again hit the U.S. economy and this will have a destabilizing impact on the real estate market.

FINANCE AND INTERNATIONAL TRADE

Because of the size, wealth in raw materials, and location of the United States, the role of foreign trade in the economy of this country has historically been rather small when compared to the economies of other industrialized countries. The American economy has in the past been able to resist the international economic fluctuations that have rocked other nations, but the 1980s have seen an end to this protected position.

The eroding position of America's balance of payments—our historic surplus of exports over imports has been reversed and lack of confidence in the strength of the dollar abroad have caused the value of the dollar to drop. The post-World War II agreements regulating international monetary exchange have been replaced by more flexible understandings that allow currencies to float in value. And the massive changes in petroleum prices have added another dimension of insecurity to an already shaken international financial picture.

Each of these crises had effects upon real estate. Interest rates, capital availability, import costs, and export jobs are closely tied to international finance and trade issues. Each is also important to real estate values. Investors have a real concern for effective and prompt solutions of the international financial strains that occasionally emerge.

These international conflicts can lead to wars, and wars have massive repercussions on international resources and finances. Every current international economic issue—trade balances, resources, or energy—has the danger of becoming entangled with past bitter rivalries to such a degree that war can erupt. The issues themselves have effects on real estate; wars multiply these effects.

1. What is meant by population composition, and how does it affect real estate? Give an example from your community.

2. Show how attitudes toward the importance of work or leisure influence real estate use and value.

3. Can you give four reasons why poverty affects real estate?

4. How does transportation change affect the value of real estate? Why is future transportation change likely? What is the most recent transportation change in your community, and what were its real estate effects?

5. How do international issues affect real estate? Give four examples from your community.

19.3   THE UNCERTAIN FUTURE

The potential problems noted in this section are worldwide phenomena that penetrate to the core of culture and society. Although these issues may seem only remotely connected to real estate, they have a great long-range impact on land use and values. These will be among the major issues of the next generation. Here are some topics that are both uncertain and controversial.

TELEMOBILITY

The medium, or process, of our time—electric technology—is reshaping and restructuring patterns of social interdependence and every aspect of our personal life. . . . Everything is changing—you, your family, your neighborhood, your education, your job, your government, your relation to "the others." And they're changing dramatically.[1]

We don't really know whether the world will ultimately become a global village—McLuhan's thesis—or whether the impact of electronic media will make us a world of atomized individuals held together by a surface network of communications, but it is clear that the impact of electronics on communications has changed the fundamental nature of our lives. According to John Diebold, "It would be

[1] Marshall McLuhan and Quentin Fiore, *The Medium Is the Message.* New York, Bantam Books, 1967, p. 8.

difficult to overstate the magnitude of change that will take place in the lives of all of us, in human history, as a result of the information revolution that has so unobtrusively taken place in our day."[2] Alvin Toffler, who created the expression "future shock" in 1965, describes the change that confronts the last quarter of our century as a fire storm: "Change sweeps through the highly industrialized countries with waves of ever accelerating speed and unprecedented impact. It spawns in its wake all sorts of curious social flora—from psychedelic churches and 'free universities' to science cities in the Arctic and wife-swap clubs in California."[3]

Twenty years ago futurologists predicted for us a world of video telephones and copy-transmitting machines in the home. Executives working from desks in their homes, perhaps meeting with colleagues once a week or so. People shopping by catalog and television, paying bills by telephone, participate politically by cable TV, and entertain themselves by video-recorders. Such a world—a world without office buildings, without massive customer facilities, without face-to-face contact—would have great impact on real estate. Many of the futurologists' predictions have come true. What will the next century bring?

GROWTH

Population growth, although uneven among individual nations, has already been recognized as one of the world's most pressing current and future problems. Nearly always, this growth is "exponential," which means that population is growing at 2 percent each year, rather than by a constant number like, say, 2 million people each year. The problem with exponential growth is that it compounds, so that the increase in numbers grows larger each year. If it compounds long enough, the growth clearly becomes unsupportably large, as the following quotation indicates.

At the present time, starting someplace about 1946, the average annual rate of increase in the world's population is about 2 percent. Using the 1962 population as a base, and applying this rate of growth to it, shows that in 650 years—somewhat less than the time backwards to the Renaissance—there would be, in our world, one person standing on each square foot of land.[4]

Table 19.1 demonstrates the power of compounding. There are many examples in nature of exponential growth, but they all end with the collapse of growth and a sharp drop in total numbers. The world cannot hold enough people to accept 2 percent yearly growth in

[2] John Diebold, *Beyond Automation*. New York, McGraw-Hill, 1964.

[3] Alvin Toffler, *Future Shock*. New York, Bantam Books, 1971, p. 9.

[4] Don Fabun, *The Dynamics of Change*. Englewood Cliffs, N.J., Prentice Hall, 1967, pp. 1–10.

TABLE 19.1   A Familiar Form of Compound Growth

If we place $1,000 in a savings certificate at 8 percent, with instructions to reinvest the interest, it will grow to:

1 year	$ 1,080
10 years	$ 2,159
50 years	$ 46,902
100 years	$2,199,761

population for 650 years, so some form of natural breakdown will reduce it. It seems clear that there is an upper limit to population growth.

Some argue that this time is much closer than 650 years; that the world faces growing food shortages that can only be postponed at great expense and cannot be eliminated. Others point to the congestion of modern cities, and other problems. They ask if human population may have other types of limits than just food, such as the chaos that may result from excessive social pressures. The growth problem raises some fundamental questions about our future.

Population Control

For religious and social reasons, population control is quite controversial. Yet more people appear involved with personal, social, or legal population control than ever before. It is obvious that this issue will be examined even more intensely in the future. The changes that could occur, whether legal or social, would undoubtedly affect general economic conditions, trends in particular industries, the economic base of cities, and real estate values, as well as the fundamental question of future world population levels.

Resources

Exponential population growth increases the need for agricultural products, petroleum, ores, timber, and every other commodity used by people. In fact, our *per-person* use of many commodities is also increasing exponentially. This means that production must increase even faster than population. An additional complication is that the better ores, fields, and wells are usually already in production. Thus the increased production must come from new, more marginal areas, at higher costs. Accordingly, costs of production tend to go up even faster than production.

It is believed that there are limits to future increases of resource production. The limits arise from increased costs rather than from actually running out of the resources. As prices rise, it becomes more feasible to recapture or recycle the used resource than to hunt for new resources. Gold and platinum have long been in this category, more recently joined by silver and, increasingly, by aluminum and water. However, maximum recycling only *postpones* the inevitable

result of exponential growth because some resources are lost in ways that cannot be recovered by recycling.

Pollution

All human activities produce some air, water, and noise pollution. As population doubles and production per person doubles again, pollution grows. Often the growth of pollutants is hidden, because the natural system can partly purify the water and the air and muffle sounds. Sometimes, quite suddenly, a pollution problem can appear when the natural cleansing system is overcome. Society is now more aware of this, and has begun to clean up the polluting by-products of production.

The cost of correcting pollution adds to the cost of operating plants and cities and affects the demand for the plant's products or for locations in the cities. Correcting pollution shifts the cost characteristics of nearly all products, and nearly all locations, but not by the same amount for each. This causes a great sorting-out, or readjustment, between competing locations and products. In this process, some locations and products will gain and some will lose.

The Los Angeles air basin was one of the first areas in the country to become troubled by automobile-created air pollution. The research and experience of Los Angeles has produced a wealth of information. Unfortunately, that region seems to be in a race. As long as the exponential growth in the number of automobiles continues, sharper and sharper cuts in the rate of pollution per automobile are necessary just to stay even. Since pollution control gets harder and more expensive the further you go, it must be concluded that either pollution will go up or the number of autos must not grow so fast. Every other polluting human activity is a similar problem, as long as the numbers continue to grow.

Energy

The United States is increasingly an energy-driven society, substituting other energy sources for human labor. As a result, energy use per person has its own exponential growth, on top of the growth of population and the growth of industrial products.

Unfortunately, the exponential increases in energy consume fuels, such as oil and coal, that cannot be renewed or recycled. The original solution pioneered in the 1950s and '60s was nuclear energy. However, due to serious disasters worldwide, the development of nuclear plants in the U.S. has come to a halt. Other alternatives—breeder reactors, fusion, geothermal energy, tides, winds, solar energy—require immense effort to be significant energy sources during our lifetimes. It is clear that energy demands of the next decade or so will continue to be borne mostly by oil and coal.

Every aspect of production, resource allocation, and land-use determination is heavily influenced by energy availability and cost. The oil shortages that emerged with conflicts in the Mideast have

had major effects upon real estate, as have increases in oil and natural gas prices.

Most of the world uses much less energy per person than the U.S. does, but the growth rate of their use of energy per person is rising much faster. This means that worldwide competition for oil, gas, and coal is increasing rapidly. The result will be continued price increases, as well as pressure to develop new energy sources and reduce energy use.

From these changes in energy price and use will come changes in real estate. Examples include additional emphasis on insulation and other aspects of energy conservation. Energy change will affect many industries; local economies will then feel the effects, and, of course, real estate will be touched by these changes.

REVIEWING YOUR UNDERSTANDING

The Uncertain Future

1. Define the concept of *telemobility*. What is its significance to real estate? Can you give an actual example from your community?

2. Explain why the rate of net population increase is so important.

3. What is *exponential growth?*

CHAPTER SUMMARY

There cannot be a real summary of this chapter because no one can write a summary of the future! Others might see very different potential strengths and weaknesses. What is yours?

IMPORTANT TERMS AND CONCEPTS

Consumerism	Inflation
Exponential growth of:	Land-use controls
Energy	Lifestyles
Pollution	Limits to growth
Population	Telemobility
Resource use	Transportation

Answers to Reviewing Your Understanding Questions

Chapter 2

1.	b	6.	a
2.	d	7.	c
3.	b	8.	a
4.	c	9.	d
5.	a	10.	b

Chapter 3

1.	b	6.	a
2.	d	7.	b
3.	a	8.	c
4.	c	9.	d
5.	d	10.	d

Chapter 4

1.	d	6.	b
2.	a	7.	a
3.	c	8.	b
4.	c	9.	c
5.	c	10.	a

Chapter 5

1.	d	6.	c
2.	c	7.	a
3.	a	8.	c
4.	c	9.	a
5.	c	10.	d

Chapter 6

1.	b	6.	c
2.	c	7.	d
3.	a	8.	a
4.	d	9.	d
5.	a	10.	d

Chapter 7

1.	b	6.	b
2.	d	7.	d
3.	a	8.	d
4.	c	9.	a
5.	b	10.	d

Chapter 8

1.	a	6.	c
2.	d	7.	b
3.	c	8.	c
4.	d	9.	c
5.	d	10.	d

Chapter 9

1.	b	6.	c
2.	c	7.	d
3.	a	8.	d
4.	d	9.	d
5.	a	10.	a

Chapter 10

1.	b	6.	a
2.	c	7.	d
3.	d	8.	c
4.	b	9.	b
5.	a	10.	c

Chapter 11

1.	b	6.	b
2.	c	7.	c
3.	d	8.	c
4.	d	9.	a
5.	a	10.	b

Chapter 12

1.	d	6.	b
2.	c	7.	d
3.	a	8.	b
4.	a	9.	d
5.	b	10.	c

Chapter 13

1. a		6. c
2. b		7. d
3. a		8. c
4. c		9. a
5. d		10. d

Chapter 14

1. c		6. d
2. a		7. b
3. d		8. a
4. c		9. d
5. b		10. a

Chapter 15

1. a		6. b
2. c		7. a
3. d		8. d
4. a		9. d
5. c		10. a

Chapter 16

1. d		6. $10,301
2. c		7. 7.14 GRM
3. d		8. 8.7% Cap Rate
4. $8,080		9. 4.5%
5. $2,221 saved		10. 5.7%

Chapter 17

1. d		6. c
2. d		7. b
3. a		8. a
4. b		9. a
5. c		10. c

Chapter 18

1. b		4. c
2. a		5. d
3. d		

INDEX